SUPERB FEATURES OF THIS GUIDE:

—Specific ways to get started writing without wasting time in paralyzed pondering

—Actual examples of how bits and pieces of information are put together to form a riveting whole

—The seven sure-fire keys to readability

—How to make sure you are writing with your own natural voice

—Picking the words with the most "punch"

—Avoiding fatal fuzziness of meaning

—Making certain of your grammar and spelling

—An index designed to let you swiftly find the solution to special problems

—Wonderful passages from great writers to demonstrate the different kinds of good writing

All of the above are just part of the total approach that makes A NEW GUIDE TO BETTER WRITING the best book on the subject today.

MEET THE AUTHORS

RUDOLF FLESCH, author, teacher, editorial consultant and member of the guiding faculty of the Famous Writers School, was born in Vienna, Austria. He received his Doctor of Laws degree from the University of Vienna. In 1938, Dr. Flesch came to the United States, became an American citizen and, in 1943, received a degree of Doctor of Philosophy from Columbia University.

Dr. Flesch is the author of ten books, including the notable WHY JOHNNY CAN'T READ and, most recently, HOW TO BE BRIEF.

A. H. LASS, noted lecturer, teacher, editor and educator, has numerous books to his credit as editor, author, or co-author. His writing activities have included his being a columnist for such newspapers as the New York *Post*, *Herald Tribune*, and the Boston *Traveler*.

Mr. Lass has published many articles in prominent magazines and has appeared on various radio and television shows as a discussion panelist on topics related to education for students of all ages. Since 1950 he has been the Principal of the Abraham Lincoln High School in New York City.

A NEW GUIDE TO BETTER WRITING

(Original title: The Way to Write)

By RUDOLF FLESCH and A. H. LASS

WARNER BOOKS

A Warner Communications Company

WARNER BOOKS EDITION

Original title: *The Way to Write*

This Warner Books Edition is published by arrangement with
Harper & Row, Publishers.

Warner Books, Inc.
75 Rockefeller Plaza
New York, N.Y. 10019

Ⓦ A Warner Communications Company

Printed in the United States of America

First Warner Books Printing: December, 1982

Reissued: August, 1984

10   9   8   7   6

CONTENTS

PART II WHILE YOU WRITE

TO BETTY AND ELIZABETH

ACKNOWLEDGMENTS

The authors wish to express their sincere thanks—

To Arnold Horowitz and Murray Rockowitz for their invaluable assistance in constructing the exercises and test materials and for their many constructive suggestions.

To Norma Tasman and Benjamin Levine for their penetrating criticisms.

To Earle McGill who opened his door to us and gave us a "local habitation."

To Dorothy Shapiro Arnof who hovered maternally over the manuscript from beginning to end. We are grateful for her patience and understanding, her unerring good taste, and her sound editorial judgment.

PREFACE

America is full of people who *want* and *need* to write better. They have forgotten what they learned—or should have learned—in school or college. The writing skills they once possessed have grown rusty. They aren't sure about what is grammatically correct. Faced with a typewriter or a blank sheet of paper, their minds go blank. They don't know where or how to get ideas, or what to do with them when they get them. They can't get started writing. And once started, they don't know where or how to stop.

The Way to Write is meant for those who want to do something about improving their writing, but have found other books either too academic or too specialized. Here is what this book will do for you:

First, it deals with the thinking and planning that go into the daily writing chores of adult life. The explanations in the text itself and the exercises at the end of each chapter are aimed at increasing your ability to get your thoughts down on paper in a simple, orderly, intelligible fashion.

Second, we have tried to give you an understanding of the tools of writing—sentences, paragraphs, words. Through carefully directed practice and exercises, you'll learn how to make the English language behave and say what you want to say, in the way you want to say it.

Finally, you'll gain a sensible and thorough working knowledge of the basic rules of grammar, usage, spelling, punctuation, etc. We have stripped these rules down to essentials and presented them in an easily intelligible form. They are all you will need to help you avoid common errors. The handy test-yourself quizzes will give you a check on your progress.

Learning to write isn't at all the grim and dull business people imagine it to be. On the contrary, you can get real fun and excitement out of it. We have tried the methods and materials of this book with thousands of students in the classroom. We know that they work. And we know, too, that students enjoy learning to write this way.

Of course, you don't have to be told that you won't learn to write merely by hoping or wishing—or by just reading this book. You'll have to *work* at the job. That means doing

9

the exercises in each chapter. That's why we've filled this book to the brim with exercises—so that you'll have ample practice actually doing the things that will improve your writing. There just is no substitute for doing the work yourself.

This book won't make you into another Shakespeare. Nor will it help you earn extra money selling stories or articles to popular magazines. But it will, we hope, teach you to write simply, clearly, correctly—and in a grown-up way.

R. F.
A. H. L.

1 HOW TO START

The trouble with writing starts right at the beginning. There you sit, pencil in hand, a blank sheet of paper before you, and you don't know how to start. Maybe you have some ideas you want to express, some words and sentences you want to use, but what you have in mind just isn't ready to be put on paper. Somehow you have to change it from a vague thing in your head to something you can take and write down; and you don't know how.

There's Nothing the Matter with You

Don't think there is anything unusual the matter with you. That kind of trouble is common among people who haven't done much writing—it doesn't matter whether they are 15 or 50. Naturally, if you are a born writer, that's different. Then you will have an urge to write. You will have no trouble getting started. Words and sentences will come to you by themselves. But born writers are few, and the chances are that you're not one of them. Like most people, you will probably have to learn how to write step by step. And, like most people, you will think the first step the hardest.

Don't Just Start

Well, how does one start to write? It will take us a little while to tell you about it, but the most important thing is this: *Don't just start!* Don't think the main thing is to get going, and, once you have got something on paper, you will run along nicely. If you do that and put down words and sentences that come to mind at the moment, you have simply postponed the time when you will look down at your paper and not know how to go ahead. Sooner or later—probably sooner—that moment will come; only this time, instead of a blank page, you will have a beginning that isn't any beginning and doesn't lead you anywhere.

11

Make a Plan

So *don't just start.* Don't let that blank white page frighten you into action. Take your time. Slowly work out in your mind what you are going to say. In other words, *make a plan.* A piece of writing, like everything else you do, has to be planned. Think of a week-end trip, for instance; you can't just blindly go ahead on Saturday morning, not knowing what's going to happen. Instead, during the week, you make plans. You make up your mind when you want to start and when you want to be back; you decide where you want to spend Saturday night and what you want to do on Sunday morning; you get yourself a map and find out which route to take; you spot a place to eat lunch and another to eat dinner; and you work out a different route to go back on Sunday afternoon and evening. When you are through, you have a plan: You know *where to start, where to go first, second,* and *third,* and *where to end.*

Don't Get Lost—Plan Ahead

Writing works the same way. The thing to do is to plan ahead, to map out beforehand that word-trip you are going to take. Know your starting point, your next way-station, and the next, and the next, and be quite sure you know where you are going to land at the end. And since you are planning for something that is made of words, make sure your plan is *in words*—not just vague, unclear notions in your mind which you'll have trouble pinning down when you get around to them. It's very easy to believe you have words and sentences in your mind, when actually you have only a string of form-less or half-formed ideas. For instance, if you want to explain to a friend how to get to your house, you may *think* you know the way so well that the words you need will be right on tap. But when it comes to telling your friend, you may find that in reminding yourself you thought of the bus stop as "the one before you pass that good bakery," and of the corner where you turn as "the one with the house that stood empty all last year." So you'll have to start all over again really planning your explanation in words and sentences that will make sense to your friend.

Write It Out

There is a simple way to avoid this trouble: *Write your plan out.* Put down on paper the start, the main in-between stops, and the end. Only in this way can you be quite sure that you *have* a plan. Then, with your sketch in hand, you can go ahead and work out your piece of writing, step by step and without any danger of losing your way. That's the way all speakers, lecturers, and writers work. It's the way we wrote this book, the book you're reading now. We spent a long time in working out a plan before we started to write.

Let's see how it works. Let's go back to the friend who doesn't know how to get to your house. You sit down to write him (or her). Before you start your letter, you take another piece of paper and put down your plan. You think of the start, the main points on the way, and the end. So you write something like this:

> Take E2 bus at station
> Get off corner Pine St.
> Walk 2 blocks Hill Avenue
> Turn right into Chestnut St.
> House is No. 823

Now that's a good, practical plan for you to use. Mind you, it wouldn't do your friend much good. He would probably still get lost. But it helps *you* to tell *him*. As long as you stick to it, you will write directions that your friend can use—for example, like this:

> When you get off the train at the station, walk to the other side of the square. There is a bus stop in front of the bank building. Take the E2, "Pleasant Hts." bus. If you have to wait awhile, don't get impatient; the bus runs every 20 minutes.
>
> Get off the bus at the third stop after the bridge, corner Hill Avenue and Pine Street. You will see an A & P store and a gas station at this corner. Watch out for them after you cross the bridge.
>
> From Pine Street walk two blocks ahead on Hill Avenue, that is, in the direction where the bus is going. The next corner is Maple Street and the second is Chestnut, where we live . . .

You see how easy it is to work it out, once you have a good plan to go by.

Giving directions is, of course, only one example. The same applies if you want to tell a story—let's say about a week end you spent at your cousin's. Again, be sure to put the events one after the other, *in order*.

How to Tell a Joke

Or let's take another example where you can see the point even more clearly. Everybody knows that some people are good and some clumsy at telling jokes. What makes the difference? Simply this: If you are good at telling a joke it's because you always know *beforehand* exactly how you are going to tell it. You know the things you must mention right away, you know what to tell next, and you know, *word for word*, the "punchline"—the point of the story. If all this is not clear in your mind before you tell the joke, you'd better not try to tell it at all. Nobody will laugh and you'll be terribly embarrassed.

How would you tell this joke?

> A boy answers his father that he doesn't think much of getting up early in the morning, walking before breakfast, and so on. His father has told him that he did all this when he was a boy and thought nothing of it.

This does not seem very funny. But if you think about it for a minute, you'll see that the joke lies in the father's saying that he "thought nothing of it" and the boy's answer, "I don't think much of it either." So you'll have to plan on telling the story like this:

> Father says: "When I was a boy, etc."
> Father ends: ". . . thought nothing of it."
> Boys answers: ". . . don't think much of it either."

Filling in the details, you say:

> Father was lecturing Junior, who liked to sleep late: "When I was your age, I got up at six every morning, walked ten miles with my dog, and thought nothing of it."
> "Well, Dad," Junior answered, "I don't think much of it either."

There Are Other Ways, Too

In other words, you cannot write or even tell anything without a plan. But let us add this: We don't mean to say that the parts of your plan must always follow in the same order. As a rule, it's the safest thing to start at the beginning, go on to the middle, and wind up with the end. But sometimes you may want to tell things in a different way. For instance, here are directions for a week-end guest that start at the end:

> You know that we live at 823 Chestnut Street, Pleasant Heights. But since you want to come by train, let me tell you first that we never use the Pleasant Heights stop, but always get off at Greenville, which is much nearer to our house.
>
> So when you take the train, be sure to ask for a ticket to Greenville. . . .

Or suppose you want to tell about that week end with your cousin. Suppose nothing much happened on Saturday, but you had a wonderful time at a party Sunday night. So, for a change, you might first tell all about the party and then a little about what happened before.

Even in telling a joke you have a little leeway in the way you tell it, as long as you stick to some plan that will not spoil the story. For instance, you could tell the little story about Father and Junior this way (although we think the first way was better):

> Junior was quick with an answer the other day.
>
> "When I was your age," Father had said, "I thought nothing of getting up at six, walking ten miles, and being back for breakfast."
>
> "You thought nothing of it?" Junior replied. "Well, I don't think much of it myself."

Before you start to write:
1. Take your time and think about what you are going to say.
2. Put your main ideas into words.
3. Work out what order your ideas should be in.
4. Put this plan on paper.
5. Never start to write without a plan.

Exercise 1. Work out a writing plan for each of the topics below. Each section deals with different types of materials: describing an experience or event, telling a story, presenting an argument, etc.

Describing an experience or event:

1. A friend has written to you asking for a description of the place you work in. List all the information you would include in your description.
2. Choose a familiar haunt of your own or your friends'. It may be your men's club, the meeting room of your fraternal order, your sorority headquarters, your favorite summer resort, or a place where you go on outings or picnics. List the things that you would tell someone about these places.
3. Here's one for the men. Your (sister, girl friend or wife) is all set to go to a party on Saturday night. You think that some of the things she is wearing—the hat, for instance—are slightly odd. Plan a description of her get-up. (Be honest and accurate —but be gentle, too!)
4. Revenge is sweet. Here's a chance for the girls to get even. Your (brother, boy friend, husband) is highly unconcerned about his appearance. (Just like a man! Color scheme? Style? Never heard of it!) Plan a description of him, listing all the characteristics of his dress. (Don't be too harsh with him. He's a man after all!)
5. You know what the family living room looks like on a Sunday morning with the papers strewn about, or the dinner table on a Sunday or a holiday. List the details that you would include in a description of these scenes.

Telling a story:

1. You have just heard a radio presentation of the Theatre Guild or some other dramatic program. Make a plan for retelling the story to a friend. Leave out the unnecessary details.
2. You have just seen an exciting baseball, football, or basketball game. Make a plan for an article you are going to write for your club, company, union newspaper on the game. Remember to include all important events.
3. Write to a friend about your brother's (husband's, boy friend's, sister's) role in World War II. List the highlights of his (or her) career in the armed services, stressing his (or her) personal accomplishments.

Presenting an argument:

1. List the arguments you would use to persuade someone to join your organization (political club, union, social club, etc.).
2. You have been designated as spokesman for your group to present grievances about working conditions to your employer. List the conditions that need improvement. What arguments would you use to convince your employer that changes should be made?

3. Jot down all the arguments you would present to your employer to convince him that you deserve promotion to a higher position and an increase in salary.
4. List all the evidence you know to support some theory (scientific or otherwise); superiority of the male (or female) sex, causes of depressions, war, the atomic hypothesis, etc.
5. Take sides on some important social or political issue of our time and list your arguments for or against. "How to solve the problem of juvenile delinquency," "How can we settle our labor problems?" These are only examples of the kind of problems we mean.

Hobbies and sports:

1. Plan a talk on your favorite sport in which you will tell how to develop skill in some phase of it. Some examples: "How to lay down a bunt"; "How the T-formation works"; "How to make a set shot"; "How to make a 'chop' in tennis or ping-pong."
2. Choosing your favorite recipe, explain to a friend how to prepare it: what materials are necessary, how to prepare them, pitfalls to avoid.
3. List the benefits of your hobby. Show the kind of pleasure you derive from it and the information, materials, and time necessary to be successful at it.
4. If you play a musical instrument, tell how you mastered it, the steps you went through until you learned to play it. Be careful to explain all technical terms.
5. A friend of yours is planning to spend a week end in your city or town. Write him, telling him of the high spots he ought to see.

BEFORE WE GO ON

Before you read on, let's explain something. The chapter you have just read deals with any kind of writing—a letter to a friend, a short joke, anything. The next three chapters deal only with longer pieces of writing. They contain much the same material as the first chapter, explained in more detail.

Naturally, if you just want to write a letter or make a brief speech, you won't want to go through all the steps we are going to describe—collecting information, making a plan with numbered items, building up each idea.

But that doesn't mean that you may skip these three chapters. *They are the most important ones in the book.* If you write a long paper, you will want to use everything in these chapters. And if you write something shorter, most of it will be helpful. Even if you write a postal card, the principles will apply.

So read on and don't worry. We are just trying to make writing easier for you.

2 HOW TO GET IDEAS

We told you that before sitting down to write you must have a plan. If you think of the examples we gave you (giving directions, describing a week end, telling a joke), that may seem simple to you: you just take the main points of what you want to say, line them up in order—and there you are. But if you have to write or tell something a little longer, you'll find that the preparations take a little longer too. What are the main points? Maybe you don't have enough; maybe you have too many. What are you going to say about these points? You don't know: you have to work out a plan for each of these points. What order are you going to use? There seem to be several possible arrangements. Which is best?

The longer the piece of writing (or speaking), the longer and fuller the plan-making must be. In fact, the more time and thought you put into your planning, the easier you will find it to write. Professional writers often spend a month or more in the preparation of an article they write in a day. The authors of the famous play, *Life with Father,* spent two years in working out a plan—and then wrote the play in 17 days.

Therefore, in learning how to write, what's most important is learning how to plan *before* writing. You may have thought that grammar and usage and punctuation are most important, but that isn't so. If you don't know any grammar, you will have much trouble with your writing; but if you don't know how to plan, *you simply can't write*.

List Your Ideas

Your plan is a list of the ideas you are going to use. For a longer job of writing, you have to write them down; otherwise you'll forget half of your ideas before you get around to the actual writing. Your ideas have to be in order; otherwise the list won't help you. (Think of a speaker and his notes. If the notes are in a mess, the speech is ruined.) To put your ideas in order, you have to sort them out first. To hitch up a train, you have to know which is the engine, which are the pullman cars and the coaches, which is the diner, and which is the observation car. And to sort out your ideas, of course, you have to have enough of them in the first place. You can't make a train out of just the diner and one coach.

So the making of your plan consists of three things:

1. Getting ideas.   3. Putting them in order.
2. Sorting them out.

Where Do Ideas Come From?

How does one get ideas? Well, let's see. How do you get ideas for telling a friend how to reach your house? You get these from things you know and have seen—that is, from *using your own experience.* How do you get ideas for telling a joke? Most often from someone who told it to you—from *listening.* And how do you get ideas for a longer piece of writing? Most often from *reading.* So there are three ways of getting ideas: *your own experience, listening to others,* and *reading.* Let's look at each one.

Let's say there has been a discussion in your family about radio commercials. Nobody seemed to mind them particularly, but you just hate them; and you haven't been able to tell your family why. You are annoyed. You know the subject will come up again, and next time you want to have all the answers ready. Or you may even have an itch to write down, once and for all, why you think those radio commercials are so bad. To do that, you need a plan and you need some ideas.

Your Own Experience

To get ideas, you first use your own experience. You have heard hundreds or even thousands of commercials; you know what they are like; you know what's wrong with them. Or do you? In trying to pin down your experience, you find that it's hard to remember exactly or to describe what you remember. You wish now you had disliked those commercials less and paid more attention to them. In short, you haven't been as good an observer as you thought you were. As you put down what you know from observation, you find it doesn't amount to much. It won't convince anyone else of your point of view.

You see now that if you want to write from your own experience, you have to work at it all the time. You have to go through the world with your eyes and ears wide open and soak up experiences like a sponge. Day and night, you have to be a reporter on the job, and your mind has to take down in shorthand whatever happens around you.

Impossible? No, not quite. There are people like that, men and women who seem to be natural journalists or novelists, born writers whose minds automatically store up what they see and hear. But most of us don't have such minds. If we want to write from our own experience, we piece together whatever scraps of memory we can find. Usually we see that we don't know enough about our subject and decide to find out more. Next time our observation will be much sharper because we know what we are looking for.

So to find out more about radio commercials, you sit down for days to listen to them. You force yourself to pay close attention to them; you take notes; you fix them in your memory by any means you can think of. After a few days, you really know something about them. You know how long they usually are, how often they come on, how many are spoken and how many sung, and which you dislike especially and why. Maybe you have also heard a few you don't dislike so much, and one or two you actually like. By observing your subject closely for a set purpose, you have learned much about it; you have gained many new ideas; and even your point of view may have changed. Your experience has helped you to find something to write about.

But while you were gathering that experience, you realized that it wasn't enough for your purpose. You couldn't spend more than a few days on it, and most of each day you were busy with other things; and even when you did listen, you studied the commercials on only one station. There is a limit to what you can do by yourself. Also, when it comes to collecting information, you can't rely on yourself alone, because your likes and dislikes get in the way. No matter how sincerely you tried to give the same attention to all commercials, the fact remains that you probably found out more about those you liked than about the others.

Other People's Experience

Therefore you turn to your next source of information: other people's experience. You try to remember what other people have said about commercials, which ones they liked or disliked and why, and which ones they remembered or didn't remember. Again, you won't get many ideas this way if you just try to remember what people said at various occasions in the past. If you really want to find out what other people think about radio commercials, you go and ask them.

You don't have to be formal about it, but as far as you are concerned, you conduct a series of interviews, your own private public-opinion poll. One of your friends says ordinary commercials are all right, but singing commercials he can't stand; another one says he never listens to the radio anyway; your cousin says he knows of a station where there aren't any commercials; and your aunt says she likes commercials because she wants to know who pays for the program.

You take notes of all this and of what other people tell you. Then you see where it fits in with your own ideas. You find that some of it is useless because it has nothing to do with your subject (like the opinion of the friend who never listens to the radio); some is valuable because the point of view is different from your own (like that of your aunt); and some of it may be useful if you could be sure of it (like the station your cousin told you about).

In other words, information that comes directly from other people is worth getting—if you can rely on it. If you know your cousin would never tell you anything he isn't sure of, then you don't need to hesitate before using the argument. But if you are not quite sure—and you can't be because everybody makes mistakes—then you can't use the information until *you* know how *he* knows. He has to tell you more about it: what station it is, where you can find it on the dial, and whether it has regular entertainment programs like other stations. Then you can see for yourself. You can go through the same steps of observation he went through and check the truth of what he said. Or again, if you know your cousin isn't the kind of person to make things up, you can let the matter go at that and use the information—maybe adding where it came from.

You're Getting Somewhere

Now you have a few ideas: your own notes and what a dozen other people told you. You are getting somewhere. You look over your notes and you find that you have some good ammunition:

> 1. Exact quotes from some 20 commercials you have listened to.
> 2. Views of seven people who dislike them and four people who like them.
> 3. Half a dozen reasons for disliking or liking them.

4. A few commercials everybody seems to hate and one or two most people seem to like.

5. A long list of odds and ends of information that don't seem to fit in anywhere—like announcers' voices, commercials in the middle of the program, false claims for drugs and cereals, comedians who "kid" their sponsors, and so on.

But all that isn't good enough for your purpose. After all, neither you nor any of the people you talk to have any special knowledge of radio. What you have is just a collection of miscellaneous facts and opinions; it doesn't even begin to cover the ground. To convince other people of your point of view, you have to be sure why commercials are the way they are, what can be done about them, and what has been done about them, and what are the ideas of some of the experts on the subject.

Ideas From Books

This is the point where you need books. You can't travel around the country and interview half a dozen experts on radio, but nowadays you don't have to. You can go to your neighborhood public library, or any other library, and within half an hour get the opinions of the leading experts on practically any question in the world. Here is how you do it:

Before you go to the library, make a list of the most important things you want to find out. Don't go there just "to look up radio commercials," but get some definite questions down on paper. Do most people like them or dislike them? How long have we had them? What is being done about them? Are there any laws or rules about them? With such a list you will get twice as far in a library.

Don't think your subject is so odd that there couldn't possibly be anything written about it. There is no such subject. There are specialists for everything. You can find printed information about the best method of collecting junk and about how to write a fan letter.

How do you find the information? The first rule is: Don't get sidetracked. Your library has thousands of books; some big libraries have millions. Except for a few, they are of no use to you now because they don't deal with radio commercials, and that's what you're after. So don't browse. Some other day, yes; but not this time. Go straight to your subject and stick to it.

How to Find a Book

To find books on your subject, use the card catalog. See whether your subject is listed, maybe under the name you use for it ("Radio commercials"), maybe under some other name like "Radio advertising." Not everybody uses the same name for the same thing, so you may have to think of various names. Sometimes the names in library catalogs are turned around like "Advertising, Radio," and you will find what you want not under R but under A. Be sure not to look for a bigger subject than the one you are after; don't look for Radio but for "Radio commercials." If you look for Radio, you will at once get sidetracked into books on radio engineering, radio sets, and whatnot.

When you have found your subject in the catalog, look at the cards filed under that subject. Each card stands for a book on the shelves. Write down the name of the author, the title, and the "call number" of each book. Now you can find it yourself or the librarian can find it for you.

How to Read a Book

Suppose you find two books that look useful to you: *This Fascinating Radio Business* by Robert J. Landry, and *The People Look at Radio* by Paul F. Lazarsfeld and Harry Field. Now you are up against the question: How do you read a book? Of course, you know how to read a book, but that isn't quite what we mean. How do you read a book if you are looking for information on a special topic? Again, the first rule is: *Don't browse.* You can browse not only through a library but also through a book, picking up interesting bits here and there. That's fun, but not when you are after something you want to find out. Does a book have something like a library catalog that you can use to start you off? Certainly: It's the index in the back. When you are collecting information, you should start every book at the end by looking for your subject in the index. So take your two books on radio, look up "Commercials" in the index, and start directly with the pages given under that subject.

Some books, of course, don't have an index. The next best thing to use is the *table of contents* in front. Usually the chapter headings listed there will tell you where to start reading. If there is no table of contents either, or if the table of contents doesn't tell anything about what's in the chapters, then you'd better not use that particular book at all. Remember, don't waste your time browsing.

Often the best way to get information out of books is not to read books but to use a short cut. Simply go to the shelf of encyclopedias and look for your subject in every encyclopedia the library has. You will find that the encyclopedia writers have done most of your work for you: in each subject they have studied the best books and boiled them down. And to help you still more, they have usually listed the books they used at the end of the article, so that you know where to go for more information. (There are all sorts of encyclopedias, and each one is a little different from the rest. Learn how to use them. Pick half a dozen subjects, like oriental rugs, or penicillin, or Buffalo Bill, or Bali, and see what you can find out about them.)

Try the Magazines

But suppose you don't get anywhere this way with your radio commercials. Your library doesn't have the two books we mentioned on page 24, nor any other books that would help you; and there isn't anything on radio commercials in the encyclopedias either. That may easily happen. After all, radio commercials have been written about only in the last few years and it takes some time for any subject to get into books and encyclopedias.

Don't give up. If you can't find information in books, you can always find it in magazine articles. For your purpose, magazines articles are even handier than books because they are shorter and more to the point.

Articles are not listed in the library card catalog because that's unnecessary: there are ready-made printed catalogs for almost all magazines. So, if you want to find out what articles have been written on your subject, look through the volumes of these catalogs, or indexes, and take down the names of the authors, titles, dates, and so on. Always use the *Readers' Guide to Periodical Literature* first. This index lists articles in most of the popular magazines. Every library has it. Usually that will be all you need. Start with the latest volume of the *Readers' Guide* and work your way back as far as seems necessary. (Be sure to learn how to use the *Readers' Guide*. Look for many subjects in it until you are fully familiar with the setup and the abbreviations.)

Suppose you have picked from the *Readers' Guide* the following articles on radio commercials:

> "Radio's Plug Uglies" by Robert Littell, in the **Reader's Digest** of August 1942, pages 1 to 4, volume 41;
>
> "Report on Plug Shrinkers: Summary of Feelings of 15,000 Readers Against Offensive Commercials" in the **Reader's Digest** of October 1942, pages 58 to 61, volume 41;
>
> "Feeling Tired?" by Lewis Gannett, in the **Atlantic Monthly** of August 1945, pages 115ff., volume 176;
>
> "Yes, I'm Tired: Reply to Lewis Gannett" by Paul Hollister, in the **Atlantic Monthly** of January 1946, pages 133 to 135, volume 177;
>
> "Radio Advertising, a National Headache" by C. E. Warne, in **Current History** of April 1946, pages 308 to 314, volume 10 (new series);
>
> "What Can Be Done to Improve Radio? Fight Begun on Excessive Commercialism" by L. Free, in the **New York Times Magazine** of August 25, 1946, pages 9ff.

How to Take Notes

With all this—and possibly some encyclopedia articles and books, you have much more than you can possibly use on the subject of radio commercials. The next question is: When you sit down in the library to read all these articles and books, what kind of notes should you take? We could answer this by telling you whether you should use cards or sheets and what arrangement you should follow; but we don't think that's very important. Just keep three things in mind:

1. Don't take notes you won't be able to use.
2. Take enough notes so that you don't have to go back to the same article or book.
3. Make sure you'll find your source again if it becomes necessary.

Let's start with our *first rule:* Don't take notes you won't be able to use. Of course, you can't be quite sure of what you need until you sit down to write; but you have your plan. If you have brought a list of questions to the library, be sure to use it while you are reading. Don't waste your time taking notes on something that doesn't answer any of your questions.

Second rule: If you do find answers to your questions, be sure to take enough notes. Remember, when you read over your notes, you will have forgotten most of what you have read. Your notes will have to tell the story.

Third rule: Never forget to put down the author, title, and call number of a book, or the author, title, magazine title, date, and page number of an article. You'll save yourself time and trouble.

Don't just take down what you have found and where you found it. Remember, you can use only information you can rely on. When you ask other people about your subject, it is important to know who they were and how *they* knew. The same is true of people who tell you about your subject in print. You probably have a feeling, like most people, that anything that's printed is more reliable than something you just heard being *said*. Don't depend on that. There are just as many mistakes, errors, and foolish ideas in print as in talk.

About the Author

So, whenever you read for information, try to find out two things about the author: (1) Who is he? and (2) How does he know?

Of course, you know the author's name. Try to find out a little more. Is he really an expert on your subject? What kind of expert? What would be his natural point of view? You can find out much about these things by simply looking at the title page of a book or the note about the author of a magazine article. For your little study of radio commercials, it's very important for you to know that Mr. Landry, the author of *This Fascinating Radio Business*, works for a broadcasting company, that Mr. Lazarsfeld, the author of *The People Look at Radio*, is a university professor, and that most of the authors of the magazine articles you listed are well-known professional journalists.

Next, ask yourself, how does the author know? This one isn't quite so easy, but there are two tips we can give you. In the first place, most authors of books tell "how they know" in the preface. (Now we have told you about the four things you should look for in every book: the index, the table of contents, the title page, and the preface.) In the second place, if an author repeats something he has read somewhere else, he usually gives the source in a footnote or in a note at the end of the chapter or book. In other words, you don't have to *read* footnotes. They simply mean, "You can check this if you want to."

For most of your reading, these simple rules will do. Either you get the writer's own ideas and opinions, which you can check by what you know about his work and his experience; or you get information the writer has read, which you can check by going back to the source.

To get ideas:
1. Use your own experience. Observe your subject as closely as you can.
2. Ask other people about your subject. Be sure you know how they know.
3. Use the library. Find books on your subject through the catalog, and articles through the *Readers' Guide*. Use encyclopedias also. In a book, use the index and read the title page, table of contents, and preface. In an article, look for a note on the author. Find out who the author is and how he knows. Don't overrate printed information.

Take enough notes. Always note the source.

Exercise 1. Drawing on your own experiences and those of your friends and relatives, list your ideas on three of the following:

1. Improving your city or community.
2. The joys of living in the city or in the country.
3. Types of employers you have had.
4. Types of teachers you have had.
5. Your ideal teacher, doctor, lawyer, motion picture actor or actress.
6. The kind of books you like best and why.
7. The benefits of camping.
8. Why you like or don't like the comics.
9. Your favorite subject when you were in school.
10. How you feel about television.
11. Radio programs you like or don't like and why.
12. What parents should know about their children.
13. The kinds of movies that should be made more often.
14. The benefits that come from taking part in sports.
15. Arguments for or against co-education.

Exercise 2. Consult books or magazines in your library to add to your ideas on one of the following subjects:

1. The future of the United Nations.
2. Who shall control atomic energy?
3. How can labor and capital solve their problems?
4. How can radio be improved?
5. The problems facing modern youth.

6. Shall we have compulsory military training?
7. Has American education failed?
8. The place of the newspaper in modern life.
9. The future of America.
10. The problem of racial and religious discrimination in America.

Exercise 3. In a brief paragraph for each, tell what sort of information can be found in the following reference books. How is this information arranged?

1. *World Almanac*
2. *Encyclopaedia Britannica*
3. *Who's Who in America*
4. *Dictionary of American Biography*
5. *Readers' Guide to Periodical Literature*

Exercise 4. Consult the card catalog of your library to see whether the library has copies of any of the following books. Write the call numbers of any books listed.

1. *From Many Lands,* by Louis Adamic
2. *Radio Drama in Action,* by Eric Barnouw
3. *TVA,* by David Lilienthal
4. *The Education of T. C. Mits,* by Lillian R. Lieber
5. *The Good Earth,* by Pearl Buck
6. *A Treasury of Laughter,* by Louis Untermeyer
7. *The Natural History of Nonsense,* by Bergen Evans
8. *13 Against the Odds,* by Edwin R. Embree
9. *The Roosevelt I Knew,* by Frances Perkins
10. *Some of My Best Friends Are Soldiers,* by Margaret Halsey
11. *Trail to Light,* by R. P. Parsons
12. *Walden,* by Henry David Thoreau

Exercise 5. The following questions test your ability to use your public library intelligently:

1. What is meant by the call number of a book? Why do books have call numbers?
2. What is the difference between an author card, a subject card, and a title card?
3. What is the call number of all books on the technique of journalism?
4. Give the author, title, and call number of one book on journalism that may be found in your library.
5. Give the title and call number of one book by each of the following authors who is listed in the card catalog of your library: (1) H. L. Mencken, (2) Cecil Roth, (3) Agnes Repplier, (4) Mary Antin, (5) Wallace Stegner.
6. Distinguish between the table of contents of a book and its index.

7. Where in a book can you usually find out in what year it was first published? Why is it sometimes important to have this information?
8. Where can you usually find the date of publication of the particular copy of a book which you own?
9. How are biographies arranged on the shelves of your library?

Exercise 6. Which of the following magazines does your library keep on file?

McCall's	Coronet
Atlantic Monthly	New Yorker
National Geographic	Survey Graphic
Reader's Digest	Esquire
Popular Science Monthly	Harper's Magazine
New York Times Magazine	

Exercise 7. Consult the *Readers' Guide to Periodical Literature.* Tell in which issue of which magazine you could find articles on each of the following:

1. Streptomycin	7. Railroads	13. The FBI
2. Juvenile delinquency	8. China	14. Baseball
3. The United Nations	9. Russia	15. Football
4. Labor unions	10. Vampires	16. Movies
5. Education	11. D.D.T.	17. College
6. Food	12. Malaria	18. Women

3 HOW TO PUT YOUR IDEAS IN ORDER

Now you have all the ideas you need for your piece of writing. But you can't write yet. You have to *sort out your ideas* and *put them in order* before you can start. When you bring home a bag of groceries, you can't use them right away. You have to sort them out and put them in order before you can prepare a meal.

Let's first take a look at what's in the bag. What ideas do you have now on radio commercials? Here they are:

1. Notes on 21 commercials you listened to. (You disliked 18 and liked three.)
2. Singing commercials you listened to.
3. Notes on how long the commercials were and how often they came on.
4. Your friend dislikes singing commercials especially.
5. Your other friend never listens to the radio but hates commercials anyway.
6. Your aunt likes them because she likes to know who pays.
7. Your cousin found a station without commercials.
8. Some announcers' voices are particularly annoying.
9. Commercials in the middle of the program are often irritating.
10. Some commercials about drugs and cereals are misleading.
11. Some comedians "kid" their sponsors. They are fun to listen to.
12. Out of 100 people asked by the **Reader's Digest,** 85 were against commercials; the other 15 didn't care.
13. Broadcasters have a rule that limits commercials to 15 per cent of the program time.
14. Commercials compared with ads in newspapers and magazines.
15. Soldiers abroad missed commercials.
16. There are now 900 radio stations in the United States.

Altogether, this looks like an excellent collection of ideas on radio commercials. Now sort them out in groups and see what you get.

Sorting Out

First of all, find those ideas that don't belong at all. (In the grocery bag there are a couple of light bulbs you picked up downtown—they don't belong with the food.) Look at each item on the list and see whether it fits your topic. There are three that clearly don't fit: 5, 7, and 16. Cross them out. Now your list looks like this:

1. Notes on 21 commercials you listened to. (You disliked 18 and liked three.)

2. Singing commercials you listened to.

3. Notes on how long the commercials were and how often they came on.

4. Your friend dislikes singing commercials especially.

~~5. Your other friend never listens to the radio but hates commercials anyway.~~

6. Your aunt likes them because she likes to know who pays.

~~7. Your cousin found a station without commercials.~~

8. Some announcers' voices are particularly annoying.

9. Commercials in the middle of the program are often irritating.

10. Some commercials about drugs and cereals are misleading.

11. Some comedians "kid" their sponsors. They are fun to listen to.

12. Out of 100 people asked by the Reader's Digest, 85 were against commercials; the other 15 didn't care.

13. Broadcasters have a rule that limits commercials to 15 per cent of the program time.

14. Commercials compared with ads in newspapers and magazines.

15. Soldiers abroad missed commercials.

~~16. There are now 900 radio stations in the United States.~~

Now sort out the 13 ideas you have left. To do this, go through your list and look for items that belong together. Some of your ideas are only different ways of saying the same thing; some are big ideas for which other, smaller ideas are only examples or illustrations; some groups of two or three ideas are of the same kind. To sort out your ideas, you need one main idea for each group; the others, if there are more, will be your examples, illustrations, or details. In other words, shuffle your ideas around for a while and see how they arrange themselves. If you are patient, they will. Here is how it might work out with your radio commercials:

1. Disliked commercials.
   a. Those you disliked (18).
   b. Annoying announcers' voices.
   c. Commercials in the middle of the program.
2. Liked commercials.
   a. Those you liked (3).
   b. Comedians who "kid" their sponsors.
3. Singing commercials.
   a. Those you listened to.
   b. Especially disliked by your friend.
4. How long are commercials and how often do they come on?
   a. Your notes.
   b. Broadcasters' rule that limits commercials to 15 per cent of program time.
5. Do people like commercials?
   a. Your aunt likes them because she wants to know who pays.
   b. 85 out of 100 people asked by Reader's Digest disliked them.
   c. Soldiers abroad missed them.
6. Misleading commercials about drugs and cereals.
7. Commercials compared with ads in newspapers and magazines.

Look how you went about sorting out your ideas. You now have *seven groups* instead of *13 single ideas*. Five of these seven groups are divided into smaller units; to show that on paper, you indented them and put letters rather than figures in front. One of your original ideas (the notes on the commercials you listened to yourself) you divided into two; it just happened naturally.

Putting in Order

And now that your ideas are sorted out, you can put them in order. That sounds simple; but it's the most important part of this whole business of writing. We told you right from the start that planning is the main part of writing, and that it consists of getting ideas, sorting them out, and putting them in order. But it's the putting-in-order where you really do your planning and, in fact, where you form in your mind the thing you're going to write. It's the putting-in-order that makes people laugh at a joke, or cry at a movie, or cheer after a speech. What a reader reads, or a listener hears, is simply ideas put in order.

Your seven groups of ideas on radio commercials are *not* in order. If you followed that list in your writing, your reader would never understand what you were driving at. He needs your help. He will never get where you want him to go unless you lead him there step by step.

We cannot give you any general rules for putting your ideas in order. There are hundreds of different ways of preparing a meal, and all of them will work well if you are a gifted cook. But there are traditional ways and widely known recipes which are "safe" even for poor cooks. If you want a "safe" method for putting your ideas in order, here it is:

A Good Order for Ideas

First of all, be sure of your *point of view*. You can't go into everything you know about your topic. It would take much too much time and it would be a very dull thing to do anyway. Rather, choose your point of view—the position from which you are looking at your subject. Once you have found that, you will know which parts of your subject you are going to discuss and which you are going to skip, and you will see some natural order for what you want to say. In our example, your point of view is, of course, that you want to present an argument against radio commercials. So you skip everything except a discussion of whether commercials are good or bad, and you divide what you write into two main parts: arguments *for* commercials and arguments *against* commercials. (Naturally, you have to show the other side of the case, too.) Then you decide on the order. You might present the case for commercials first and the case against them (the side you're on) afterwards. Or you might start off with your own side, then show what the arguments are on the other side, and wind up with showing why your arguments are better than theirs.

Naturally, you could write about radio commercials from many other points of view, too. You could write their history. You could discuss them as a special kind of advertising. Or you could compare what they sell and in what way. In each case, your point of view would lead you to a different side of the subject and to a different order in writing about it.

Fitting Ideas In

After you have picked your point of view and the best order, look at your list of groups of ideas and see how they fit into that order. In our example, you will find that you can make one section (*against* commercials) out of Group 1 (dislike commercials), Group 3 (singing commercials), Group 6 (misleading commercials), and Point 5b (disliked by 85 per cent). The second section (*for* commercials) will consist of Group 2 (liked commercials), Group 7 (favorable comparison with ads), and Points 5a and 5c (liked by your aunt and soldiers abroad).

Now you know the two main sections of what you are going to write. You have planned the largest part of your piece of writing and you know what's going to go into it and in what order. What next?

Next you remember that you can't expect your reader to know as much as you do about the subject. You just spent some time digging up information about it. Much of what you are going to say will be news to your reader. You can't spring your arguments against radio commercials "cold" on someone who may never have given them much thought. So before you discuss the pros and cons of commercials, you give your reader something that will help him understand what follows—the general idea, the background, the definition of what you are talking about. You define commercials and tell what they are. This is where you can use Group 4 on your list: "How long are commercials and how often do they come on?"

If you had a different kind of subject, your general section would be different, of course. If your subject is a person, you will tell about his family background and his youth. If you write about a problem, you will explain how it came about. If you describe an event, you will tell about what happened in general before you go into details.

Beginning and Ending

Now you have the main part and the section that leads up to it. There are two more things missing that have to be planned: *the beginning* and *the end*.

The more important of the two is the ending. Your ending will decide what will stay in your reader's mind after he is through with what you wrote. Therefore you will have to make your ending strong and put your main idea into it. The best thing is to make it a summary of everything you have said. Be sure of a good ending before you start to write and don't waste it on the way.

What would be a good ending for your argument against commercials? How can you repeat in a nutshell what you said? Think hard. A summary of your facts? Not bad. Statistics? Possibly. A horrible example? Maybe. Or how about a convincing comparison with something similar? How about this, for instance:

> Imagine a party at your house. Everything is full of noise, music, and fun. Everybody is having a wonderful time. But every fifteen minutes or so, through the whole evening, you have to stop the party "cold" for two minutes, while a salesman steps into the middle of the room and gives a long sales-talk on soap, or laxatives, or oil, or cigarettes, or coffee. Before long, there won't be any party, because nobody will be able to stand it.
>
> All radio entertainment is forever interrupted in the same way. And most Americans are unable to stand it any longer.

Ideas in Order

And now you have everything planned but your beginning. How should you start? The best thing is to start with something that will whet the reader's appetite and get him interested. Make him pay attention. Start with an anecdote, or a startling incident, or a vivid detail. You need a bait. In our example, a good vivid description of a commercial will probably be a good beginning. Since you will want this to ring a bell in the reader's mind, take one he is likely to recognize, from a popular program. And since you will also want this to be an example of a commercial that spoils the program—making your main point right at the start—take one that is particularly annoying. Look over your notes, pick the one that fits best, and there is your start.

Altogether, then, our "safe" order for ideas looks like this:

1. A bait for the reader (catching his interest).
2. The general idea or background of your subject.
3., 4. (5). The main body of your piece of writing, divided in two or three sections, depending on your point of view.
5. or 6. The ending (repetition in a nutshell).

Now let's see, in detail, how this would work out for our piece on radio commercials:

Radio Is Being Spoiled by Commercials

1. Vivid description of particularly annoying commercial on popular program.
2. What are commercials?
   a. Definition.
   b. Brief history.
   c. How long and how often (broadcasters' 15 per cent rule).
3. Against commercials.
   a. You and most of your friends dislike them.
   b. Many other people dislike them too (**Reader's Digest** statistics).
   c. Reasons for dislike: annoying announcers' voices, interruption in middle of program, others.
   d. Kinds especially disliked: singing commercials, misleading commercials, others.
4. For commercials.
   a. People who like commercials (your aunt, soldiers abroad, others).
   b. Reasons for liking them (gratitude to sponsor who pays, others).
   c. Comparison with ads in newspapers and magazines.
5. Summary of case against commercials. Comparison with interrupted party.

More Examples

As we said before, you can use this "safe" order for anything you write. Let's look at some other examples. Suppose you want to write about General Eisenhower. Here is a possible plan:

1. Anecdote that shows his personality (to catch the reader's interest).
2. Life up to World War II (family background and youth).
3. World War II up to D-Day (first section of your main story).
4. World War II after D-Day (second section of your main story).
5. Post-War Period (third section of your main story).
6. His place in history (what you think about him).

Or suppose you write something about skiing. You might put your ideas in this order:

1. Vivid description of your last time on skis (to catch the reader's attention).
2. How skiing became an American sport (filling in background).
3. The pleasures of skiing (your main argument—first part).
4. The dangers of skiing (main argument—the other side of the picture).
5. Why skiing is your favorite sport (repetition of your point of view).

So you see, practically every subject can be written up in this "safe" order. And remember, once you have put your ideas in order, writing is easy.

---

1. When you have collected your ideas, make a list of them.
2. Sort your ideas out in groups. Leave out those that don't belong.
3. Then put your ideas in order. A good order is this;
   a. Bait for your reader.
   b. Your subject in general.
   c., d. (e.) Main body of your piece of writing, divided according to your point of view.
   e. or f. Main idea in nutshell.

Exercise 1. Each of the following groups contains *one* main idea and several other ideas that are merely examples, illustrations, explanations of the main idea. Put down on a separate sheet of paper the main idea and then list under it the ideas that explain or develop it more fully.

1. Remember the Maine; Make the world safe for democracy; war slogans; Remember Pearl Harbor.
2. Open Door Policy; Truman Doctrine; American foreign policy; Monroe Doctrine.
3. League of Nations; world government; The United Nations; nationalism.
4. Unsanitary living conditions; causes of poor health; absence of medical care; inadequate diet.
5. Overemphasis on athletics; commercialization; evils of intercollegiate sports; failure to provide for the mediocre athlete.
6. Advantages of city life; wider choice of vocations; variety of human types; accessibility of places of interest.

7. The actual writing; gathering ideas; steps in writing an essay; making a plan.
8. The interview; studying the help-wanted ads; how I got the job; sending a letter of application.
9. (For the men) calling on the girl; the next day; a blind date; my friend's suggestion that I meet his cousin; going to the dance; getting dressed for the dance.
10. (For the girls) the arrival of the cousin; the next day; a blind date; my friend's suggestion that I meet her cousin; going to the dance; getting dressed for the dance.

Exercise 2. Each of the following groups of words and statements contains *two* main ideas and several other ideas that are merely examples, illustrations, explanations of the main idea. Put down the two main ideas and then list under them the ideas that explain or develop them more fully.

1. Eagles; ducks; quail; game birds; owls; birds of prey; pheasants; hawks.
2. Ice-skating; swimming; baseball; winter sports; tennis; skiing; summer sports.
3. Foul-shooting; batting; fielding; floor play; set shooting; pitching; basketball; guarding; baseball.
4. Abridgement of freedom of speech; Bill of Rights; persecution of minorities; dictator; doctrine of racial superiority; equality of opportunity; academic freedom; democracy; elected representatives; fascism.
5. Addiction to sarcasm and gossip; attractive appearance; skill in conversation; reasons for unpopularity; pleasing personality; selfishness; consideration for others; sense of humor; reasons for popularity.
6. We should send food to the starving peoples of the world. The United States should assume leadership in world affairs. We must solve our own problems first. We should support democratic nations throughout the world. A high tariff to keep the goods of other nations out of the United States is a good policy for us to follow. The United States should not be concerned with the affairs of the world.
7. Our doors should be closed to all further immigration. We have too many people to provide jobs and homes for already. Our country was made great by the immigrants who built it. Many potentially fine American citizens are suffering in DP camps. Further immigration would weaken the quality of the American people. Our country is large enough to absorb more people; therefore more immigration is desirable.

Exercise 3. Here is a list of *main* ideas. Under each one list at least three ideas (sub-ideas or sub-topics) that explain, illustrate, or are examples of the main idea.

1. Water sports.
2. Woodwind instruments.
3. Uses of the dictionary.
4. Physical properties of oxygen.
5. Qualities of a good teacher.
6. Types of dance steps popular today.
7. Equipment needed for model-airplane building.
8. Why every high school pupil should learn to typewrite.
9. Why golf is a more valuable sport to master than baseball.
10. How seeds are scattered.

Exercise 4. The following groups of words are ideas (sub-ideas or sub-topics) that explain, illustrate, are examples of, or develop a main idea. For each group state a main idea that will be accurate and specific and broad enough to cover all the sub-ideas.

1. Lions; tigers; leopards.
2. Gorillas; chimpanzees; orangutans.
3. Tuba; cornet; trombone; trumpet.
4. Andrew Johnson; Calvin Coolidge; Harry Truman.
5. Bob Feller; Spud Chandler; Dizzy Trout; Tex Hughson.
6. Arturo Toscanini; Leonard Bernstein; Leopold Stokowski.
7. *Gone With the Wind; Rebecca; Two Years Before the Mast; The Razor's Edge.*
8. Robert E. Lee; Stonewall Jackson; Pierre G. Beauregard.
9. Dictionary; *World Almanac; Readers' Guide;* encyclopedia.
10. Carelessness; lack of attention to work; failure to get to work on time.

Exercise 5. The following are jottings of ideas for a theme. Choose the one that would be the title of the theme. Then list the main ideas and the ideas that develop, explain, illustrate, or give examples of the main idea.

1. Cooking over a campfire; return home; our camping trip; departure from home; experiences at camp; sleeping outdoors; driving to the camp.
2. The White House; the train ride to Washington; the Lincoln Memorial; a trip to Washington; the night-ride home; the Washington Monument; interesting sights.
3. The newspaper reader; the rush for the exit; the male flirt; a ride on the subway; the gossipers; the rush for seats; types of riders; the tired worker.
4. Crime stories in newspapers and movies; the relationship of the problem to our national welfare; guidance and psychological counseling in schools; causes of juvenile delinquency; training for parents; racial tensions; lack of recreational facilities; provision of playgrounds and other places for wholesome recreation; an instance of juvenile delinquency; punishment of delinquent

parents; steps toward a solution; parental neglect; better housing; slums; the problem of delinquent youth; bad companionship; legislation to improve social and economic conditions; definition of juvenile delinquency; recent statistics on the number of juvenile delinquents; facts about juvenile delinquency; statistics on the types of crime committed by juvenile delinquents.

Exercise 6. Prepare a plan for an essay or theme on one of the following topics:

1. The Family Next Door.
2. Houses I Have Lived In.
3. My Job.
4. Baby Sitters I Have Known.
5. A Fishing Trip.
6. Are Comic Books a Menace?
7. Around the Breakfast Table.
8. Inside a Beauty Parlor.
9. Portrait of Me Twenty Years From Now.
10. Keeping Tropical Fish as Pets.
11. Man's Best Friend.
12. The UN or a World Federation?
13. I Hate Sports.
14. Soap Operas.
15. My Career as an Actor.
16. Why Read a Newspaper?
17. Thanksgiving Dinner at My Home.
18. The Day I Played Hooky.
19. William Lloyd Garrison: Fighter for Freedom.
20. History from Novels.
21. Photography, a Fascinating Hobby.
22. If I Had Three Days to Live.
23. Employers I Have Tamed.
24. My First Trip in an Airplane.
25. Haym Salomon, a Hero of the Revolution.

Exercise 7. Write an effective, attention-attracting opening paragraph for a paper on the topic you selected from Exercise 6.

Exercise 8. Write an effective, clinching, closing paragraph for an article on the topic you selected from Exercise 6.

Exercise 9. Using the plan you have drawn up and the opening and closing paragraphs you have prepared, write a complete paper on one of the topics listed under Exercise 6.

4 HOW TO WRITE UP YOUR IDEAS

With your ideas in proper order, you have reached the point where you can write them up. If it's a simple job of writing you want to do, you have done everything up to here in your mind: you have planned what you are going to say, you have thought of ideas to use, and you have decided in what order you are going to use these ideas. If it's a longer piece of writing—like our example about radio commercials—you have gathered ideas from a number of sources, made notes about them, and drawn up a list of them—a plan from which you are going to work. Now the writing starts. You take the plan and the ideas you have in your mind, or the list of ideas and the notes you have on paper, and write them up.

Why do you have to do that? Why can't you just use your working plan as it is, or simply copy your list of ideas and your notes? Why do you have to go to the trouble of making sentences and paragraphs out of them?

The answer is, of course, that you are writing something for someone else to read. Your list of ideas and your notes are good enough for your own use; but they are too hard for anyone else to figure out. So you have to put them into proper shape for reading.

Plans Are Not for Reading

The most important difference between your plan, with your notes, and something that's fit to read is this: Your plan and your notes tell the story in too much of a hurry. They are good reminders for yourself, but they are too brief for a reader. He would read the words, but they wouldn't register in his mind. At best, he would do a "double-take" the way you have often seen it in the movies. You would tell him something and two minutes later he would suddenly say: "Hey! What? What was that you said?"

So you have to say enough about each of your ideas to make it stick in the reader's mind. The bare statement will never be enough; you have to fill the reader's mind with pictures and facts and details that will add up to what you want to say. Take your time. Use what you know about your sub-

42

ject, or the notes you took before you started to write. Your plan was something like a timetable: now take the trip. Tell the reader enough about each stop to make him feel as if you had taken him along.

Describing a House

Suppose, for instance, you have moved to another town and are writing a letter to one of your old friends. Naturally, you will want to write him about the trip, the town, the place where you work, and the house you are living in. It would never do to write about the house like this:

> We live in a two-story, six-room house.

Your friend wants to know much more. He wants you to tell him what the house is like. You have to make him see the house; you have to lead him through it in your letter and show him each room. Here is what you might write:

> We live in a house on Chestnut Street, which is about ten minutes from Main Street. The house is a typical colonial house, white, with green shutters. It sits a little back from the road, and there is a nice front yard with two big old trees. Inside, it looks like this: When you come in the front door, you are in a little hall where there is not much else but a hall closet and the stairs going up right in front of you. There are two glass doors right and left and you get glimpses of the living room to your right and the study to your left. Suppose you first go into the living room. It's shaped like an "L" that's hugging the front porch. The door to the front porch is right across the door from the hall . . . .

Describing something is simple. Think of all the things to see, and tell about them in the natural order in which you would look at them. Be sure you give the reader enough details so that he can form a picture in his mind. And be sure you line them up in some order he can easily follow. Don't make it hard for him like this:

> Our house is fine, except for the bathroom, which is much too small for our family. It's only ten minutes from Main Street. The living room is shaped like an "L," and there are two big old trees in the front yard . . . .

Stick to things the reader can see. Don't get sidetracked. Your reader will be puzzled if you get off your subject like this:

> . . . Suppose we go first into the living room. It's shaped like an "L" that's hugging the front porch. The door to the front porch is right across the door from the hall. We haven't been using the porch much, but we did have supper there one evening last week when Grandfather came down from the farm. He likes to eat outdoors. You should hear him telling about the way things were when he first settled in this part of the country some sixty years ago. He really had to start from scratch. One winter, he said, there was so much snow. . . .

Never mind Grandfather's old yarns. Tell your friend about your house.

How to Do Something

You have now learned the three main rules for writing up an idea:

1. Use enough details.
2. Follow a natural order.
3. Stick to your subject.

These rules apply not only to descriptions, but to every kind of idea. If you want to tell a story, for instance,—something that has happened—you do the same thing: You tell the reader exactly what happened, from beginning to end, and nothing else.

You probably think you would do that anyway, without our telling you. But would you really? It isn't always easy, particularly not if you want to give your reader directions and tell him how to do something. That means you have to tell your reader how something happens in such a way that he can *make* it happen himself. Let's take for example a simple, everyday process like tying a bow-tie. How would you go about explaining it? Maybe like this?

> To tie a bow-tie, knot the ends of the tie in a bow and pull them nice and even.

You can see that this won't do. Here you go again:

Take the right end and loop it over the left end. Before you do this, make sure the right end is an inch or two longer than the left end. Naturally, you should do this before a mirror . . . .

That's better, but the order is all wrong. Begin at the beginning:

Stand before a mirror. Put the bow-tie under your collar. Pull the right end so that it is an inch or two longer than the left end. Up to this point, as you see, there is no difference from tying any other tie. But after that, a bow-tie is more difficult to tie than an ordinary necktie. I suppose that's the reason why they sell far more ordinary ties than bow-ties. Maybe people would have stopped wearing them altogether if it hadn't been for Frank Sinatra. Somewhere I read that he . . . .

Now you're off your subject. Try again, remembering our three simple rules. You will still not find it easy to give good directions. But you can do it if you go through the whole process step by step in your own mind, and write it down exactly as you would do it yourself, one step after the other, like this:

Stand before a mirror. Put the bow-tie under your collar. Pull the right end so that it is an inch or two longer than the left end. Now take the right end with your right hand and loop it over the left end. Pull it up inside and then cross it, so that it hangs again on the right side. Pull tight. Now both ends should be about the same length. Next, with your right hand, make the wide part of the right end into a loop, holding the two narrow parts between your thumb and your index finger. Take the left end with your left hand, put it over the right end and push the wide part through the loop between your right hand and your neck. Pull tight. Then adjust the bows and ends to the same length.

Now you have put in all the steps in their right order, and you have stuck to bow-tying. You have explained the process so that your reader can follow your directions.

Writing Up Other Ideas

Let's see how our three rules work with other kinds of ideas. Take some general statement, like "Railroads are losing business to airlines." This is the kind of idea you might want to use, along with others, in a longer piece of writing. How do you go about writing it up?

First of all, be sure you know exactly what the idea is. There is no trouble on that score with ideas like "Description of our house" or "How to tie a bow-tie," but be careful when you are writing up more general ideas. *What is the exact meaning of each word? What exactly was it you had in mind when you included the idea in your plan?* "Railroads are losing business to airlines." Does that mean that airlines are making money? No, not necessarily; it means that what money they are making is *at the expense of railroads.* Does it mean that railroad travel is becoming old-fashioned? Not necessarily; it just means railroads are losing *business.* So keep that in mind: The idea to write up is that railroads are losing money and airlines are cashing in on that.

Building Up the Idea

Once you are quite sure what your idea means, you will also know what *kind* of details you need to write it up. To describe something, you have to tell the reader about things to see; to explain a process, you have to tell about things to do. What kinds of details do you need for other types of ideas? Naturally, only those that fit. You will have to pick your details in such a way that *together* they will give the reader exactly the idea you want to write up.

For the idea "Railroads are losing business to airlines" you will therefore need details—facts, examples, illustrations— that will show, in different ways, that this is actually so.

This is where you make use of the work you have done before you started to write. In your notes—or in your mind— you have stored up a number of such details; all you have to do is to take as many as you need, put them in order, and write.

Of course, if you have no such details ready, or not enough of them, your writing will be just an empty repetition of your idea in different words, like this:

> Railroads are losing business to airlines. More and more, planes are being used instead of trains. Passengers and freight are gradually shifting from one means of transportation to the other . . . .

That kind of thing your reader will forget as soon as he has read it.

But if you have done what we told you to do in the first three chapters, you will be in no such trouble. You will have enough details on hand from your own experience or from what you heard or read, and writing them up will simply be a matter of putting them in order and not getting off the subject.

The Most Natural Order

There is no hard-and-fast rule for putting details in order. The most natural order is this: Use your details to build *up* your idea and wind up with the biggest or strongest. For instance, suppose you have the following three details on railroads and airlines: your impressions at a visit to the local airport, something your uncle told you, and some statistics you read in a magazine article. The strongest of the three is, of course, the printed article; the weakest is your own brief observation. So the natural order would be this:

> At a visit to our city airport I saw many passengers and I thought that not so long ago most of them would have used the railroad. I remembered what my uncle had told me. Among the executives of his company, air travel is now the rule. No wonder: according to statistics I read in **Harper's Magazine** . . . .

When you write about such a general idea, it's particularly easy to get off your subject. Watch out for that. In no time you have written something like this:

> . . . . I remembered what my uncle had told me. Among the executives of his company air travel is now the rule. The company considers the saving in time worth the extra expense. But, my uncle said, they can afford it anyhow. They have had a few very good years. . . .

Now how do you get back to the statistics you found in the *Harper's Magazine* article? You can't. You're sidetracked. You should have remembered to stick to your subject.

It makes a great deal of difference, of course, *how* you use your details. You may have enough of them, in good order, and still not get your idea firmly in the reader's mind. Remember that in describing your house, or bow-tying, you had to show your reader exactly what's what. The same applies to all other ideas. You have to *show* your reader. You have to make him see—or, maybe, hear or feel. You have to tell him when and what and how and, if possible, how far and how long and how many. He will remember your main ideas better if you answer all the little questions he may raise. For instance, he will more easily remember your point about railroads and airlines if you write like this:

> The other evening I spent an interesting half hour watching hundreds of incoming and outgoing passengers at our brand-new city airport. I was struck by the thought that ten, fifteen years ago almost all these people would have made their trip by train. And I remembered a casual remark by my Uncle Bill . . . .

You see the difference? We were just a little more specific this time; but now the reader will see—and remember.

Giving Reasons

To write up a general statement of fact, like that about railroads and airlines, you will naturally use examples, illustrations, and statistics to round out the idea. But you can also go further and tell the reader why. If you give him reasons, the facts will stick even more firmly in his mind. For instance, you might say that railroads are losing business to airlines because air travel is much faster, and you might give some examples of the difference in time.

Sometimes you will have to write up ideas that are not facts at all, but only your own opinions. For such ideas you cannot use examples or statistics; you have to write them up entirely by giving reasons for them. If there are enough reasons and they are good enough, the reader will be convinced.

For example, let's take the idea "Women will always wear silly hats." That's not a fact—you can't prove it—it's simply your opinion. Let's see how you would handle this.

Again, make sure first you know exactly what the idea is. A silly hat is something that doesn't make sense as a head-covering; always means not only at present and in the past, but also in the future. Do you mean to say that? You do? All right, then that's the way to write it.

The Topic Sentence

In writing up an idea, it is often useful to state in one sentence what you have in mind. This statement of the idea is called a "topic sentence"; it's the bare idea as you have it in your plan, put directly into your piece of writing. You can start with it and add your reasons or details, or you can put it at the end after you have built up to it. It doesn't make much difference as long as your reader will know exactly what you are talking about.

So suppose you start simply:

> Women will always wear silly hats.

Don't just go on repeating the idea without giving any details or reasons:

> Women will always wear silly hats. They'll keep on covering their heads with things that don't make sense. I think it's a habit with them.

If you write like that, your reader will know that you haven't worked on this idea before you started to write. You haven't done any planning or listing of points or taking notes. You haven't shown the reader why you think so and why he should think so, too.

Adding Details

So you go back to your notes—or to the ideas on women's silly hats you have stored up in your mind—and you find two items you can use:

> Silly hats worn in Paris after the liberation.
> Silly hats worn in the Middle Ages.

Mind you, these are not illustrations of the fact that women will *always* wear silly hats—you can't give any examples for something that's going to happen in the future—they are *reasons* why you *think* it will happen.

Now comes the question: Are these two items enough? Will they convince the reader that you are right? Looking them over, you rather think they won't. So you try to think of a third reason. You remember pictures you have seen of African native women with huge "hair-do's" filled with ribbons and sticks and stones. They are not exactly hats, but the principle is the same. Together with the other two details, this might do. So you add:

> Huge hair-do's worn by African natives.

Next question: In what order are you going to use these three reasons? The natural order would be to wind up with the strongest reason—but which is the strongest? You are not sure, but you suppose it's the fact that French women took to silly hats in spite of all the misery they went through during the German occupation. So you write up your ideas in this order:

> 1. Topic sentence.
> 2. Silly hats worn in Middle Ages.
> 3. Huge hair-do's worn by African natives.
> 4. Silly hats worn in Paris after liberation.

Now you are on your way—as long as you don't make that old mistake of getting off your subject:

> Women will always wear silly hats. Throughout history they have been putting the most senseless and ridiculous things on their heads, like those two-feet-high pointed cones you see in pictures of the Middle Ages. Even in darkest Africa there are tribes where the women wear huge elaborate hair-do's, filled to the brim with ribbons, sticks, and stones. With these they wear rings through their noses and dozens of bracelets. They think that's the only proper outfit to go around in. There's a story about an explorer . . . .

But we have given you enough examples to make that point, haven't we?

Comparisons and Contrasts

There is another method you will find useful in writing up your ideas: *comparisons* and *contrasts*. For instance, if you want to describe a helicopter to someone who doesn't know what it is like, you might say: "A helicopter is like any other airplane, only instead of wings on the sides it has something like a windmill on top." In other words, you are describing a helicopter by comparison and contrast with another airplane.

Comparisons and contrasts help the reader to grasp your

idea because they tie it up with something he is already familiar with. But they will help him only if they are to the point; otherwise they will throw him off the track. For instance, you might compare the competition between railroads and airplanes to that between railroads and buses. That would be a bad comparison because there is an important difference: airplanes are faster than railroads, but buses are slower. It would be better to compare the struggle between the railroads and the airlines to that between the horse and the automobile; that would really put the reader's mind on the right track.

The same applies to contrasts. You might contrast women's hats with women's shoes. There is a difference, of course, because hats are worn on the head and shoes on the foot. But the difference is not what you want to stress; you want to show the reader that women's hats are silly. A better contrast would be with men's hats. They, too, don't keep men's ears warm in the winter, but they certainly make more sense than women's hats.

So don't forget to use comparisons and contrasts, but be sure they fit.

A Good Mixture

Of course, when you actually write up an idea, you don't think about all these things. You think of the plan you have made for your writing, and of your subject. Quite often, what you write will be a mixture of description, explanation, facts, statistics, reasons, comparisons, and contrasts—you will have used whatever seemed to fit best. There's no harm in that, of course; anything is good for writing that will make for good reading.

For instance, suppose you are writing up the idea "Large families are good to grow up in." This is an opinion for which you will have to give reasons, and naturally you will want to make your point also by descriptions, comparisons, contrasts, and other details. So you may write this:

> Most people's families are smaller than those their parents grew up in. They don't know what they are missing. I have three brothers and four sisters and I know that a large family is fun. There was always something going on at home, and instead of going out for entertainment, we played host to many other children in the neighborhood. All their families were much smaller, of course, and I am sure they envied us our happy home.

Of course, "only" children may be very happy too. But they will be lucky if they find seven really good friends such as those I have right in my own family. And they will never have all those weddings and family reunions and nephews and nieces and birthdays every month or so. I know I was lucky to grow up in a "full house."

This is such a mixture of description, reasons, comparisons, and contrasts, and so on, that it is even hard to tell which is which. But that doesn't matter. The main thing is that the idea is written up with enough details so the reader will fully understand what you were thinking and why.

After getting ideas and putting them in order, you are ready to write. Follow your plan and use the ideas you have gathered.

Remember three rules:
1. Use enough details.
2. Follow a natural order.
3. Stick to your subject.

Use any detail that will help the reader think along with you: details to see, steps in a process, facts, reasons, comparisons, and contrasts. Always be as specific as you can.

If you are in doubt about the natural order, put the strongest idea last.

Exercise 1. Using the suggestions given in this chapter, write up your ideas on any topic in each of the following groups of topics. Notice that for each group of topics you will have to write up your ideas somewhat differently. For some, all you will need will be details. Others will call for explanations with facts and statistics. Many can be written up only by giving reasons. Of course you can combine all these methods in dealing with most ideas. That is probably what you will do to put real flesh and bones on your ideas, to make them seem alive and convincing.

What does it look like?

1. Your favorite home run hitter has just crossed the plate with the winning run and the packed stands are cheering wildly. Describe the scene for a friend who wasn't able to attend the game.
2. You have just returned from a date. Describe (a) the gown you wore if it was a formal or (b) the things you did that you'd want to tell a friend.
3. Mother has just set the table for the old family get-together

for Sunday dinner. Describe the scene just as everyone sits down to table.

4. If you are lucky enough to have a car of your own, describe it and try to make the rest of us green with envy.

5. Think back to your trek to work this morning. Describe the place where you work and its surroundings.

6. Each one of us has a spot in town or country that is a particular favorite. Describe this spot to indicate why you like it so much.

7. Describe the luncheonette or restaurant where you eat at lunchtime.

8. A friend of yours is a very snappy dresser. Describe him as he sets out on a date.

9. You feel that your favorite movie actress or actor is irresistibly good-looking. Try to convince someone else of that fact.

How to do something:

1. Here are some for the men:
   a. How to lay down a sacrifice bunt in baseball.
   b. How to keep a jalopy in shape.
   c. How to hang a picture.
   d. How to splice an electric wire.

2. And for the ladies:
   a. How to dance the samba or rhumba or tango, etc.
   b. How to apply make-up.
   c. How to knit a sweater.
   d. How to shop.

3. A variety of topics:
   a. How to sail a boat.
   b. How to find an article in the *Readers' Guide to Periodical Literature.*
   c. How to conduct a meeting using parliamentary procedure.
   d. How to play the banjo, guitar, ukulele, or any other musical instrument.
   e. How to make a woodcut (or etching, or lithograph) or water color or oil painting.
   f. How to introduce people to each other.
   g. How to play ——— (the party game you like best).
   h. How to set a table.
   i. How to write a letter of invitation to a party.
   j. How to introduce a guest speaker.
   k. How to keep standing on ice skates (or make a figure eight).
   l. How to keep score at a baseball game.
   m. How to plan a well-balanced meal.
   n. How to make a Windsor knot in your tie.
   o. How to prepare a picnic lunch.

p. How to run an office.

q. How to paddle a canoe or row a boat.

r. How to do the crawl, breast, or side stroke.

Do you agree or disagree?

1. Write on any of the following general ideas taking either the affirmative or negative point of view:
   a. Big business threatens American "free enterprise."
   b. The era of gallantry in men has passed.
   c. The United Nations is the answer to the Battle of the Peace.
   d. Democracy is the most desirable form of government.
   e. There is no such thing as an amateur in sports.

2. Read the lead editorial in your favorite morning newspaper. Take issue with or defend the point of view taken by the writer. Do the same for a letter in the letters-to-the-editor column.

3. Your favorite radio commentator has just discussed a vital issue of the day. Present your views on the subject in question.

4. How do you stand on these issues?
   a. All 18-year-olds should be allowed to vote.
   b. Socialized medicine is advisable.
   c. Presidents should be elected for only two terms.
   d. There should be a single large labor organization.
   e. Proportional representation is desirable.

Give your reasons:

1. List the reasons why or why not:
   a. Double features in the movies should be eliminated.
   b. Soap operas should be eliminated from radio.
   c. Television will soon take the place of radio.
   d. Fashions in men's clothes should be radically changed.
   e. Television will change the living habits of Americans.
   f. A college education is essential for success in business.

2. You are going to ask your boss for an increase in salary. Prepare the reasons that you will present to him in order to achieve your goal.

3. You are trying to sell a famous product. Draw up a sales talk including ample reasons why the prospective customer should buy.

4. No one agrees with you but you still feel that—
   a. Sport shirts should be acceptable in business offices during the summer.
   b. The crooner should be taken off all radio programs.
   c. Children should not be allowed to listen to "horror" programs.

Try to convince some friend of one of these.

5 HOW TO TIE YOUR IDEAS TOGETHER

To get your ideas across to a reader, you have to put them in order. But that isn't quite enough. You can't rely on your reader to follow that order and to understand, without being told, how one idea leads into the next one.

In conversation, there is usually no such problem: the other person can hear you, look at you, and follow your line of thought by the tone of your voice, your little gestures, and the expression on your face. For instance, suppose you tell someone:

> My grandfather was a very rich man. Every Christmas he used to give me five dollars.

The person to whom you are talking can look at you and see whether you show pride and satisfaction in saying these sentences, or whether your face and voice show disappointment.

But a reader can't look at you. He has no way of guessing. For him you must spell things out. For instance, you can tie your ideas together this way:

> My grandfather was a very rich man. **As a matter of fact,** every Christmas he used to give me five dollars.

This will tell the reader that you are satisfied and that you think your grandfather was doing well by you.

Or you can write the sentences like this:

> My grandfather was a very rich man. **And yet,** every Christmas he used to give me five dollars.

Now you have told your reader something different. You have shown him that you feel your grandfather should have been more generous than he was.

So, with the help of **as a matter of fact** and **and yet,** you have shown your reader the connection between the ideas in your mind. These words and expressions (they are called "connectives") tell the reader exactly in what way the ideas are tied together.

Connectives

The English language has a great many of these connectives, and every writer should have a handy supply of them on tap. Some of them are used by everyone in everyday talk and will look rather informal on paper. Some others are used mostly in writing and will give your sentences and paragraphs a more formal and bookish air. There are far too many of them to list them all, but here are about two dozen that will be useful for most purposes. The first column in this table shows the informal connectives; the second column shows the more formal connectives; the third column shows how they are used; and the fourth column gives examples:

Informal connectives:	More formal connectives:	How they are used:	Examples
and		To connect two ideas of the same kind	I was out at the lake last week **and** I am going there again tomorrow.
besides, also, what's more	furthermore, in addition, again	To add another thought	Two postal cards are often more effective than one letter. **Besides,** they are cheaper.
			The French are leaders in the world of fashion. They are **also** famous cooks.
			Competitive games are good exercise. **In addition,** they teach the players teamwork.
first, next, then, finally, meanwhile, later, afterwards, since then nearby, above, below, in front, beyond, to the right, to the left	eventually	To arrange ideas in order, time, or space.	**First,** drink some fruit juice. **Next,** have a bowl of soup. **Then** eat the main dish. **Finally** have some pie and coffee.
			There was much unrest in the following years. **Eventually,** there was a series of violent incidents.
			We walked across the bridge. **To the right** was the Post Office; **to the left,** the First National Bank.

Informal connectives:	More formal connectives:	How they are used:	Examples
but, still, however, on the other hand, yet	nevertheless, rather	To connect two contrasting ideas	I like paintings. But I don't seem to understand modern art.
			He is 85 years old. And yet, he manages to keep up with world affairs.
			Nobody likes to pay taxes. Nevertheless, no nation can exist without them.
in fact, as a matter of fact	indeed	To connect an idea with another one that points it up	Last week I was ill. In fact, I had to stay in bed until Saturday.
			The original Czech system of government was much like the American. Indeed, their constitution was modeled after ours.
for example, for instance, in other words		To add an illustration or explanation	Rare things are valuable. For example, rare stamps are sold for thousands of dollars.
			Edison was a true genius. Take for instance his invention of the phonograph.
			There is no such thing as an "unlucky number." In other words, this idea is a pure superstition.
so, therefore	consequently, accordingly	To connect an idea with another one that follows from it	I ate too much lobster. So I got sick.
			The show was over. Therefore I went home.
			The President vetoed the bill. Consequently it never became a law.
of course, though	to be sure	To grant an exception or limitation	Everybody in the family went to the picnic. The baby, of course, had to stay at home.
			He said he would study all Sunday. I doubt it, though.

Informal connectives:	More formal connectives:	How they are used:	Examples
			On the average, Americans are taller than their parents. **To be sure,** there are many exceptions to this rule.
in short, in brief	**to sum up**	To sum up several ideas	Scientists say that we should eat food that has all the proteins, fats, carbohydrates, and vitamins we need. **In short,** they recommend a balanced diet.

Other Word-Bridges

But, you will say, books and magazines are full of sentences without these connectives. And still they hang together and the reader doesn't miss the connection between the ideas. Is there some other way of tying ideas to each other?

Yes, there is. But it's not as easy to see as these little word-guideposts, and it's not as easy to use either. Here's the secret: *You can tie two sentences together simply by putting into the second sentence a word that points to a word you used in the first.* You can use the same word, or you can use some other word that means the same thing. Here are a few examples:

Last week it snowed for two whole days. The paper says it was the heaviest snowfall in six years.

Each house of Congress has a number of committees. The work done in these committees is often more important than the debates on the floor.

At a recent meeting of an optical society, a one-step camera was described for the first time. This invention may bring about a revolution in photography.

The best argument against vegetarianism is the Eskimos. They seem to thrive on a diet of nothing but meat.

The San Francisco cable cars were invented in 1873. Before that time, people had to use horsecars.

Relationship in Meaning

Finally, there is a third way of tying ideas together. It's the neatest of them all, and still the reader can't miss the connection between the ideas. You do it without any connecting words whatsoever:

Most people like popular songs. A few prefer Mozart and Bach.

There is a contrast here, which the reader will feel because the ideas in the two sentences are closely related. He doesn't need to be told that:

> Most people like popular songs. But a few prefer Mozart and Bach.

He understands the *but* without having it said for him. Here is another example:

> Slowly, he walked across the hall. He took out his key and opened the door of the apartment.

Again, the sentences themselves show that one action follows the other. It would be superfluous to add *then* and write the two sentences this way:

> Slowly, he walked across the hall. Then he took out his key and opened the door of the apartment.

So you see that the connection between two sentences can be *felt* even without a connecting word.

Sometimes, however, the reader may feel such a connection when you don't expect him to. You'd better watch out for mistakes like this one:

> On December 7 the Japanese attacked Pearl Harbor. On December 8 the family celebrated my birthday.

These sentences seem to say that there is a connection between the attack on Pearl Harbor and the writer's birthday. And that doesn't make sense, does it?

Paragraphing

And now that you know how to show the connection between your ideas, you will naturally want to know how you can do the opposite thing: show the reader that there is a break between what you have just said and what is going to follow. How can you tell him that you are through with one group of ideas and want to talk about something else? You know the answer, of course: you start a new paragraph.

Suppose you write:

> Everyone should make it a habit to read the daily paper to keep abreast of current events. Through the newspaper,

he will get information that is necessary for his work and a proper background for intelligent conversation. But newspaper writing is not meant to last. Nobody is interested in "yesterday's paper." Once the next issue has been printed, the paper is changed from reading matter into rubbish. Books are different. They are meant to be preserved and to be read for years. Some of them—the "classics"—were written centuries ago and are still being read. People who read nothing but the latest books are missing a great deal.

Did you notice at what point one group of ideas ends and another one starts? Yes, you are right. It's between ". . . the paper is changed from reading matter into rubbish" and "Books are different." But as it stands, the reader has to guess that there is a shift at this point. Why not show him, so that he can be sure? Here is how:

> Everyone should make it a habit to read the daily paper to keep abreast of current events. Through the newspaper, he will get information that is necessary for his work and a proper background for intelligent conversation. But newspaper writing is not meant to last. Nobody is interested in "yesterday's paper." Once the next issue has been printed, the paper is changed from reading matter into rubbish.
> Books are different. They are meant to be preserved and to be read and reread for years. Some of them—the "classics" —were written centuries ago and are still being read. People who read nothing but the latest books are missing a great deal.

So a new paragraph simply means that the next sentence starts a different group of ideas. It's a signal to the reader that he should now turn his mind to something else. Many years ago writers used a special paragraph sign like this ¶, but now we mark a paragraph merely by starting a new line and leaving some white space in front.

Connecting Paragraphs

But though a new paragraph always marks a new line of thought, it doesn't stand by itself. The new group of ideas has *some* connection with the group of ideas dealt with in the paragraph before. Therefore, paragraphs have to be tied together just like sentences. To go from one paragraph to the next, the reader needs one of the three connecting links we have shown you: the first sentence in each of your paragraphs should either have a connective in it, or a word that refers to a word in the last paragraph, or it should be related in meaning to a sentence in the last paragraph. Look at the beginning of the second paragraph in our example, "Books are different." This ties the paragraph to the first one by the second method: the word **different** stands here for "different from newspapers" and refers to the newspapers mentioned before.

And now let's take a whole piece of writing and see how its ideas are tied together:

Yesterday I had an opportunity to see how a newspaper is made. Our friend, Mr. Rogers, the sports editor of the Record-Journal, was kind enough to show us around the building.

Record-Journal ties second sentence to **newspaper** in first.

Mr. Rogers led us first to the third floor, where the editors work. He pointed out the row of rattling teletype machines on which the wire-copy comes in. Then he showed us the horseshoe-shaped copy desk where copyreaders work on rewrites and headlines. The other part of the room was filled with shirtsleeved, smoking editors, typing busily. Next we saw the photographers' room and rows of darkrooms, which we were not allowed to enter. Finally, there was the morgue—rows and rows of file cabinets filled with clippings. Mr. Rogers let us look up the clippings about our cousin Tommy who was one of the Flying Tigers.

The second paragraph starts a new group of ideas. It starts with **Mr. Rogers**, repeated from last paragraph.
He means **Mr. Rogers** in the sentence before.

Notice **first, next, then,** and **finally** in these sentences.

The **other part of the room** at the beginning of the sentence refers to **copy desk** in the sentence before.

The same word **clippings** appears in two sentences and ties them together.

It was noisy enough on the third floor. But on the second floor the roar was deafening and

The new paragraph shows another break. It tells the reader that we are now going down from the third floor to the second. The paragraph is tied to the last one by the words **third floor,** repeated from the first sentence of that paragraph. The second sentence is tied to the first in three ways: by the con-

Mr. Rogers had to shout his explanations. The presses were running at full speed, turning out the papers that would be on the streets in a few minutes. I stopped listening to Mr. Rogers and just stood and looked. Of course I had read about printing

nective **but**, by the repetition of the word **floor**, and by the word **roar**, referring back to **noisy**. The presses were running in the next sentence explains the **roar**.

Stood and looked reads as if printing presses were something new to me; the connective **of course** in the next sentence says that this isn't quite so.

presses before. But I had never understood what the word meant. I had never seen these

The next sentence starts with the connective **but**.
The two last sentences in the paragraph are tied together in meaning. Both start the same way: **I had never . . .**

tremendous machines producing written ideas with machine-gun speed.

The words **producing written ideas** tie the end of the third paragraph to the beginning of the first, **how a newspaper is made**.

Meanwhile Mr. Rogers was pointing out the linotype machines . . . .

The new paragraph marks another break in the thought. It is tied to the earlier one by the connective **meanwhile**.

Be sure the reader knows how your ideas are tied together. To do this, use:
1. connectives;
2. words that point to words you used before;
3. sentences closely connected in meaning.

To mark a break between two groups of ideas, start a new paragraph.

Be sure to connect paragraphs in the same way as sentences.

Exercise 1. For each of the following sentences, choose the connecting word from those in parentheses that will tie the ideas together correctly.

1. Two or three times they looked in my direction. _____ I lay so quiet that they could not see me.   (But, And, For)

2. I cannot help the constant use of the word *scuttled*, _____ there is nothing else that so aptly describes the furtive, hurried, crooked progress of a crab.   (though, so, for)

3. Would you like to make spatter prints of leaves? _____ get a clean sheet of paper, a leaf, an old toothbrush, and a bottle of red ink.   (Finally, Therefore, First)

4. She has lived here in New York City for many years, _____ when Jim asked her where Grant's Tomb is, she couldn't tell him.   (and, but, in fact)

5. When you are first learning to type, the task seems hopeless, _____ you are often tempted to give up.   (For example, In fact, But)

6. When you are first learning to type, the task seems hopeless. _____ as you continue, you begin to realize that you are making steady progress.   (But, And, Therefore)

7. Jill is an incorrigible punster. The other morning, _____, when the doctor told her to use tincture of myrrh for her cold, she sighed resignedly and muttered, "Oh, well! The myrrh the merrier."   (besides, for instance, though)

8. Jill is an incorrigible punster. The other morning, _____, when the doctor told her to use tincture of myrrh for her cold, she couldn't think of a thing to say.   (besides, for instance, though)

9. We know that our opponent is always fair, just, and patient. _____ we also know, to our cost, that he never overlooks a mistake or makes the smallest allowance for ignorance.   (But, In fact, Therefore)

10. I soon rose to a position of importance in the firm, for I was energetic, popular, and conscientious. _____, my father-in-law owned the place.   (Besides, Therefore, For example)

11. When I was twelve years old, my uncle offered to give me cello lessons. I wasn't interested in music at that time, _____.   (besides, though, therefore)

12. For an embarrassed half hour I tried to make conversation with her father and mother. _____ I heard her coming down the stairs.   (Finally, Therefore, In fact)

13. Setting up an aquarium requires care and patience. _____ you must wash the gravel thoroughly, to be sure that it will not muddy the water.   (So, First, But)

14. Ivar leaped recklessly out of the moving taxi. _____ he dashed up the stairs of the old brownstone house.   (Though, Then, But)

15. She was a courageous, positive personality. _____ she had her moments of discouragement, but she never revealed them to her friends.   (And, Of course, In fact)

16. He could not find his blue tie, _____ he wore the red one.   (next, so, besides)

17. He is an outstanding student. He is _____ a versatile athlete. (also, therefore, in fact)
18. He is an outstanding student, _____ his average for the term is over 95 per cent.   (but, though, and)
19. Mix cocoa, cornstarch, and water in the upper part of a double boiler. _____ put this mixture on the fire and boil it for ten minutes.   (Next, First, So)

Exercise 2. Here is a recipe for a French omelet with certain key connecting words left out. Fill in the blanks so that the recipe makes sense. Select the proper words from those listed below. (Can you imagine what would happen to that omelet if you or your mother put those connecting words in the wrong place?)

(1) _____ break eggs into bowl. (2) _____ beat slightly to mix until they can be taken up on spoon. (3) _____ add seasonings and liquid which may be cold water, milk, or stock. In the meantime have ready a smooth, hot pan in which butter has been melted. Shake the pan so that every part is coated with butter. (4) _____ pour beaten eggs into pan. While eggs cook, shake pan lightly. With fork or spatula, gently lift egg. Tip pan, so that some of uncooked portion can run to side. When egg is puffed, creamy, and lightly browned on the bottom, take pan in left hand, tilting pan downward. With knife, loosen edge of omelet from pan. Make slight cut in middle at each side at right angles to the handle of the pan, but not entirely through the omelet. (5) _____, fold quickly, and turn on to a hot plate from which it is to be served, at once.

finally	then	next	first
and	or	before	at once

Exercise 3. In the following paragraphs, one sentence is not clearly connected with the sentence that comes before. Find that sentence and supply the appropriate connecting expression. You may have to use a word, a phrase, a clause, or even a complete sentence to make the connection clear.

1. After being stranded for three days on the ice floe and suffering intensely from hunger and exhaustion, Grenfell realized that he must have food or he would die of starvation. Though he hated to do so, he was compelled to kill one of his dogs and eat the raw meat. This food kept him satisfied until he was rescued. He established many schools and clinics which bear his name.
2. Poor Louis seemed destined by nature to become the butt of every practical joke we could devise that summer at camp. Whenever some dupe had to be chosen to go on a fruitless errand for the keys to the oarlocks, for a can of striped paint, or for a paper stretcher, Louis was inevitably the victim. We all considered it great fun. I regret our youthful thoughtlessness.

Who knows what deep psychological wounds we inflicted on him by our teasing and our ridicule?

3. I lavished almost maternal care on my four little white mice. One day, when I took time off for a baseball game, my excited brother burst in on me in the midst of a third strike, trumpeting forth the news of several additions to our mouse population at home. Under a tangle of newspaper strips, I saw six pink, hairless newborn mice. I was well enough acquainted with mouse lore to realize that any mice other than the mother would kill the babies if left within reach. I carefully moved the babies to a separate cage, furnished them with a bed of absorbent cotton, placed them in a well-heated room, periodically fed them through a medicine dropper. Within eighteen hours every one had died.

4. The real-estate agent was driving the blissful newlyweds out to look at a cozy cottage in a small suburban town. On the trip, the agent began to praise the cottage, the neighborhood, and the town. As a final inducement, he asserted that the town was so healthful that no one had ever died there. The newlyweds looked happily at each other and agreed that a town in which nobody dies is a fine place to live. On entering the place, they passed a long funeral procession. The surprised husband looked inquiringly at the agent. "Don't be alarmed," replied the latter; "that was the undertaker. He starved to death."

5. In the eighteenth century, Englishmen had a reputation throughout Europe for their love of eating. Visitors to England were often amazed at the large quantity and fine quality of the fish and meat consumed. They could not understand the English attitude toward vegetables, which were served only as trimmings to meat. English cooks seemed as unable to prepare an appetizing vegetable dish as they were to prepare anything better than "brown water" by way of coffee. Vegetables were very abundant at the time and were grown in the gardens of both rich and poor.

6 HOW TO TALK TO A READER

There are many kinds of English. What kind of English are you supposed to write? Are you supposed to write like Lincoln's Gettysburg Address, or like your favorite comic strip, or like Shakespeare, or like this book? Or can you write any way you feel like, as long as it's English?

There's no simple answer. It all depends on the circumstances. If you were the President of the United States and had to make a solemn speech, then the Gettysburg Address might be a good model to follow; but if you were just writing a letter to a friend, it certainly would not. The things to keep in mind when you write are the occasion and the audience; the right kind of English is always the one that fits the situation.

How can you tell which is the right kind? Actually, it's easier than you think. When you talk to someone, you naturally use the language that suits the occasion and the listener. No one has any trouble with that. You talk to your younger brother one way, and to your old aunt another way, and to a total stranger still another way. Without thinking about it, you look at the person before you and say either "Hi!" or "Hello!" or "How do you do?"

Let's take another example. If you want to buy an ice-cream cone, you don't say "I wish to purchase one single portable helping of this flavorsome frozen dessert." That would be like trying to pay for it with a ten dollar bill instead of a nickel. And if you want to buy a new car, you don't walk into a store and say "I guess I'll have a car"—or pay for it in nickels instead of bills. On both occasions, you use the words and the type of money that fits the situation.

The point is that both nickels and ten dollar bills are regular American money. You *can* use a ten dollar bill to pay for an ice-cream cone, and a bag of nickels to pay for a car. But you won't—it would mean nothing but trouble for everybody, including you. In the same way, if you use the wrong type of English in speaking or writing, you'll get into trouble.

66

The Right Tone

Suppose you are writing a letter to a friend. Among other things, you want to tell him that there is practically no place in your neighborhood where high-school boys and girls can meet after school. So you start like this:

> Dear Jim:
>   Doubtless you are aware of the fact that there is a close relationship between the recent rise in juvenile delinquency and the lack of adequate recreational facilities for adolescents.
>   . . .

Ridiculous, isn't it? Certainly you would never talk to Jim like that. Then why write something you would never say to him? You can make such a mistake only if you write without thinking of your reader. As soon as you forget for whom you are writing, you are in danger of using the *wrong kind* of English.

But suppose you are seriously concerned about the boys and girls in your neighborhood, and you want to do something about it. So you sit down and write a letter to your Mayor. That's every citizen's privilege, isn't it?

> The Honorable Randolph P. Simpson
> Mayor of the City of Yourtown
> City Hall
> Yourtown, California
>
> My dear Mr. Mayor:
>   Doubtless you are aware of the fact that there is a close relationship between the recent rise in juvenile delinquency and the lack of adequate recreational facilities for adolescents. The conditions in Yourtown offer a striking illustration of that relationship. In this neighborhood, for instance, recreational facilities for adolescents are totally absent . . . .

Now that would be the start of a pretty good letter. It's not perfect in its approach (we'll go into this later) but the *tone* is right. After all, if you had gone to see Mr. Simpson personally about conditions in your neighborhood, you wouldn't have walked in and said "Hey, Randy, listen here. Our boys got no place to go. . . ." Instead, you would have tried to make a good impression, to put your best foot forward and to be as polite as you could be. In the same way, when you present your case in writing, the proper language to use is the formal and impersonal kind of English.

Formal and Informal English

But just what is formal English and what is informal English? Of course, you can tell which is which when you see it or hear it, but when it comes to writing, that's a different matter. Most people find it hard to draw the line: they put on their everyday language when they should be all dressed up, or act stiff and formal when they should be relaxed and friendly. The second of these two mistakes is more common: formal English has a way of creeping into your writing in spite of all your efforts at being natural and relaxed. You may think it's the easiest thing in the world to write a little thank-you note after a party—something like "It was a wonderful party. I haven't had so much fun in a long time." But before you know it, you have written something that sounds awkward and stilted, like: "Please let me express my gratitude for having been a guest at your house last Saturday night. I enjoyed the evening enormously, more than almost any other I can remember." (You may have enjoyed it, but nobody would think so from the way you said it.)

Actually, the English language is something like a big layer cake. The bottom layer is the language you use with your family and friends in everyday conversation. The next layer is the language you use with them in more serious talk or in writing. Next comes the language you use in conversation with people outside your own circle. Then follows the language you use in more formal meetings with strangers. Finally, you reach the top of the cake, which is the kind of English that's reserved for letters to officials, and for other rare, very formal occasions. Here's how you can tell the layers of the cake from one another:

Choice of Words

In the first place, watch the words you use. Most English words belong to the whole language, but some are peculiar to certain layers only. For instance, think of expressions like wise guy or corny or it's swell. They belong to the bottom layer of the language and you would hardly use them in writing. Other words, like I guess (instead of I think) or sure (instead of surely or certainly) have a somewhat higher standing, but are still very informal and wouldn't be proper in anything written except, maybe, letters to your friends. On the other hand, take a word like **aware**. (Remember, we started that letter to the Mayor with "Doubtless you are aware.") That word belongs to the top layer of the language. It has its place in a formal letter, but it would stick out like a sore thumb in informal speaking or writing. You don't say, "I am aware I am going to miss the bus." In such an everyday sentence you would say, "I *know* I am going to miss the bus."

In fact, there are words that are even more formal than the top-layer words—words that belong to the frosting of the language, so to speak. For instance, instead of **I am aware** you can also say **I am cognizant of.** Cognizant is a perfectly good English word; it's in all the dictionaries. But it's so highly formal that it is rarely appropriate. Often you are tempted to use such a word because you have picked it up somewhere and want to show it off. There is nothing wrong with that if you are quite sure you know what the word means and how it is used; but don't try to drag it in where it doesn't belong. A very formal word that's out of place is much worse than a common, everyday word for the same thing.

Casual Expressions

The second difference between the lower and the upper layers of the cake is the *way* in which words are used. In informal English, we are casual and don't bother as long as the listener or reader gets the general idea. In formal English we try to say *exactly* what we mean. For example, in everyday conversation we exaggerate and say things like **I hate spinach** or **I am starving.** In formal English we don't use words in this fashion. We try to say what we really mean—for example, **I dislike spinach** or **I am hungry.** Also, in informal English we are often vague and say **the whole gang** when we mean **the Smiths, the Browns, the Blacks, and the Joneses.** So formal English often uses the same words as informal English, but in a more exact way.

Writing and Speaking

The third difference is the difference between writing and speaking. Informal English is more often used in speaking, formal English more often in writing. Therefore, if you want to write informally, you will try to make it look and sound like spoken language; if you want to be formal, you will show the reader that you are *writing*. There are certain ways of doing this. For instance, you can choose between I do not and I don't, it is not, and it isn't, I will not and I won't, it is and it's, that is and that's, let us and let's, you will and you'll, I am and I'm, and so on. If you use the shorter forms (with the apostrophe), you will come closer to the spoken language and what you write will look informal. On the other hand, you will avoid these shortened expressions in more formal writing.

Private and Business Letters

Suppose an applicant for a job has referred you to two former employers. One of them happens to be a friend of yours and you write him a private letter to check on the reference. The other is unknown to you and you write him a business letter. Here are the two letters:

Mr. Joseph M. Dutch President Kiddifun Co. Joeville, Ala.	Mr. Edward C. French Personnel Manager Toymakers, Inc. Edville, Ky.
Dear Joe:	Dear Mr. French:
Do me a favor, will you? A Meredith Mumm has applied for a job with us as assistant bookkeeper. Among others he gives your company as a reference. He says he has worked for you for two years and quit "because the job was monotonous." This sounds a little fishy and I'd like to know what's what before I hire the man. Otherwise he seems okay to me.	Mr. Meredith Mumm, who has applied to us for a job as assistant bookkeeper, has listed your company as one of his previous employers. According to his application, he served with you from September 1945 to July 1947 as calculating-machine operator and left on his own account because the job was "too monotonous."
Regards to Mary and the kids. How's the rest of the old gang?	I should be much obliged if you could tell me whether Mr. Mumm's statements are correct and whether you would recommend him as an assistant bookkeeper.
As ever,	Sincerely yours,

What is the difference between the two letters? Of course, some of the ideas are different, since you told your friend certain things you didn't tell Mr. French, and put some things into the letter to Mr. French that weren't in your letter to Joe. But what about the *style* of the letters? The letter to Joe is more informal than that to Mr. French. What makes it so are expressions like **the old gang** and phrases like **This sounds a little fishy**. On the other hand, in the letter to Mr. French, there are words like **previous** and phrases like **on his own account** that give the letter a more formal tone. These are the things that mark the letter to Joe "private" and that to Mr. French "business."

Business English I: Be Friendly!

However, as you see, there isn't too much difference between the tone of the letter to Joe and that to Mr. French. And that's a very important point. If you think that a business letter has to be stiff and impersonal, then you are quite wrong. That's old-fashioned. It used to be the rule that business letters had to be impersonal; people preferred the passive voice and wrote "this company" instead of "we" and "the undersigned" instead of "I." But that was long ago. Nowadays it's good form to keep a business letter friendly. If it's natural to use "I" and "you," by all means do it. Talk to the addressee of your letter just as you would if you met him in person.

Business English II: Don't Grovel!

In fact, if you want to learn Business English, we'll have to let you in on a secret: there is no such thing. Good business English is nothing but just good English, period. What used to be called Business English is utterly discredited nowadays. Hardly any modern company uses that language any more. So don't think that you'll have to master phrases like **We beg to acknowledge** and **Your favor of the 13th inst. at hand** and **Looking forward to your early reply, we beg to remain** and so on. If by any chance you have picked up that style at some time in your business career, forget it and start right here and now to write letters that are direct and straightforward. The begging and all that sort of thing just don't fit into modern American business. Maybe it's right for Japanese, where they say "your honorable slave" or for Spanish where they sign letters with "s.s.s.q.b.s.m.," which stands for, of all things, "Forever your servant who kisses your hand." But this isn't good English. Sit up straight while you write (or dictate)—and don't grovel!

Business English III: Don't Fumble!

Even when the tone is right, the approach of business letters—or memos or reports—is often wrong because they start the wrong way. Naturally, you can't expect anyone to read with proper attention and interest what you have written if you don't tell him right at the beginning what it is about and in what way it is going to concern him. But many business-letter writers need a warm-up period before they get down to business. They mumble and fumble before they get to the point—and they put all that mumbling and fumbling right into the letter! They would start the letter to Mr. French like this:

> Dear Mr. French:
> The object of this letter is to ask the kind co-operation of your company with regard to one of your former employees who has recently filed an application for employment with this company. We should be greatly obliged if, after due consultation of your files, you should be kind enough to answer the series of specific questions set forth below:
> a. From September 1945 until July 1947, did you have in your employ. . . . .

Such a beginning would have made Mr. French very impatient. He would have had to read seventy-two words before finding out what the letter was about—namely, Mr. Meredith Mumm.

In the same way, the letter to the Mayor on page 67 could have been improved. It starts with a long, abstract sentence about juvenile delinquency and recreational facilities without telling the Mayor what the letter is about. It *should* have started with a statement about recreational facilities in your neighborhood, and that impressive long sentence should have been saved for the end.

A statement of your purpose is usually the best way to start a business or formal letter. For other types of writing there are several good ways to start, but whatever you do, you must catch the reader's interest and give him an idea of what is going to follow. The first sentence or paragraph should be like a show window that makes people stop and walk into the store.

Suppose, for instance, you write an essay about movie double-features. How can you get your reader interested in what you have to say? The simplest way is to plunge right into your subject:

> Many American movie houses offer their customers two full-length pictures on one program. The pros and cons of these so-called double-features have been discussed for years.

In this first paragraph you have defined your subject, told that there is a difference of opinion about it, and invited the reader to go on and read more about it. That's a good, direct beginning. It's far better than any roundabout approach to your subject—like this, for instance:

> The American economic system is based on the principle of free enterprise. This means that business in this country is being run for profit. The price the customer pays for any piece of merchandise includes not only the cost but also a fair return for the seller. It is therefore unusual and an apparent exception to the rule when two items are offered for the price of one.

Starting with Incident or Anecdote

But plunging directly into the subject is not the only way of catching the reader's interest. You may also start with an incident, an anecdote, or some personal experience—something that will appeal to the reader's curiosity or feelings. Here's an example:

> The other evening I went down to our neighborhood movie. The marquee read: "THE GENERAL AND THE LADY with Gary Cooper and Ingrid Bergman, plus GORILLA HUNTERS with Humphrey Bogart and Bette Davis." That looked like an entertaining program and so I walked in.

Sometimes it may spoil the effect if you take too long getting around to your subject. This opening, for instance, would be too slow:

> The other evening I went downtown. I had first thought of just going for a walk, but after a while it began to rain. I could have gone to see my friend Stephen, but somehow I wasn't in the mood. I just walked along, not paying much attention to the weather, until it began to rain harder. By that

time I had reached the corner of Main Street and Walnut and I could read the program on the marquee of the Strand . . . .

Starting with a Bang

There's also a third method of starting, but it's a little tricky. You can get your reader interested by saying something about your subject that is startling, striking, or unexpected. This means that you have to make a special effort to find something of that kind; but if you do, it's an excellent way to start. For your essay on double-features, you might use this opening paragraph, for example:

> If your grocery store started to wrap a piece of blue cheese with every loaf of bread, you would be surprised. But if your neighborhood movie puts on an hour's worth of Hollywood by-products with every featured picture, you take it for granted.

Or you might surprise the reader with the following:

> Anyone who goes once a week to a double-feature show is willingly throwing away one per cent of his life time.

In other words, use any device to catch your reader's interest in your subject. Don't let him get away once he has started to read.

Use formal or informal English, whichever is appropriate to your reader and your topic.

Whether your writing will look formal or informal depends on the words you use, the way in which you use them, and whether you make them sound more or less like spoken English.

Catch your reader's interest in the beginning. Start by plunging directly into your subject, or by an interesting illustration or incident, or by a striking statement about your subject.

Exercise 1. Rephrase each of the following into more formal English. Do not attempt a word-for-word translation; simply restate the idea in more formal language. Avoid absurdly stiff or flowery constructions.

1. If you want to get along with your fellow-workers, you've got to meet them halfway and remember that they're human, too.
2. Practically everyone likes to go to the movies. They help you

lose yourself in another world for a few hours, and they take your mind off your troubles.

3. The surest way to get ahead in your work is to stick to the job and do it the best way you know how.

4. The climate here is terrible! One day it's freezing cold and it rains cats and dogs; the next day it's dry and dusty and as hot as blazes.

5. You'll be able to write better if you take time off first to jot down your ideas and make a sort of plan of what you're going to say.

6. He's strong as an ox, but not as smart.

Exercise 2. Rephrase each of the following into informal English. Do not attempt a word-for-word translation; simply restate the idea in less formal language. Avoid unnecessarily crude or slangy constructions.

1. The first step we must take, it appears to me, is to confront the reality.

2. Two basic questions are involved in this issue. Each question must be and can be answered affirmatively.

3. Equality of opportunity is the kernel of the American creed. Every American youth is entitled to the democratic right to choose his own lifework and to pursue it on the sole basis of his fitness and ability, in fair competition with all others.

4. The extent to which it contributes to the public welfare should be the primary criterion for evaluating any proposed legislation.

5. I am aware that many object to the severity of my language, but is there no cause for severity? I will be as harsh as truth and as uncompromising as justice. On this subject I do not wish to think or speak or write with moderation.

6. Our continent, our hemisphere has been populated by people who wanted a life better than they had previously known. They were willing to undergo all conceivable hardships to achieve this better life. They were animated, just as we are animated today, by this compelling force. It is what makes us Americans.

Exercise 3. Which topics in the following list lend themselves to a formal style? Which topics should be handled informally? Which can be treated either formally or informally, depending on the reader for whom they are intended?

1. My Enemy, the Dentist.

2. Window Shopping.

3. Job Opportunities in Aviation (or some other field).

4. On Being a Redhead.

5. What Can Citizens Do to Lessen Racial and Religious Tensions?

6. Some Useful Plastics.
7. Bells.
8. Characters in Fiction Whom I Dislike.
9. A Prejudice I Got Rid Of.
10. Penicillin: Saver of Lives.
11. Antarctica and the Future.
12. Astrology, a Pseudoscience.
13. Psychoanalysis and the Movies.
14. Raising Pigeons for Fun and Profit.
15. The Growing Interest in Good Music.

Exercise 4. Select one of the topics in Exercise 3 which you feel lends itself readily to formal treatment. After working out a carefully organized plan, write a theme of about 300 words on this topic.

Exercise 5. Repeat Exercise 4, this time selecting a topic suitable for informal treatment. Try to maintain a conversational tone in your theme.

Exercise 6. Write an effective beginning for *each* of the following. Use any of these devices: a statement of your purpose in writing; a direct plunge into your subject; an incident, an anecdote, or a personal experience.

1. A letter of application for a job.
2. An essay about the various types of people one may observe on a bus, trolley or subway car.
3. A letter to a friend written while you are on a trip in another part of the country.
4. A plea to the members of your organization to contribute clothing to needy Europeans.
5. A letter to a newspaper or an issue of current interest.
6. An article describing how public-opinion polls are conducted.
7. An essay on hitch-hiking.
8. A letter to your U. S. Congressman favoring (or opposing) federal aid to housing, compulsory health insurance, etc.
9. An essay on juke boxes.

7 HOW TO SAY IT ON PAPER

Did you ever stop to think how odd it is that you have to learn how to write your own language? In a foreign language, of course, there is nothing odd about it: when you learn French, you have to learn not only how to speak and read, but also how to write. It's all part of learning the language. But why should you learn how to write English? You have spoken it all your life, and you know how to read and write. Now here you are still at it, still learning how to write English. Why? What else is there to learn?

The answer is that written English is not the same language as spoken English. People don't write the way they talk. If you took shorthand notes of their conversations and put them all down word for word, they would never look like written English. They would be a shapeless, rambling mass of words that would baffle any reader. Important ideas would be missing because in conversation many things are understood without being said; others would appear over and over again because in conversation people keep repeating themselves.

So writing isn't just putting talk on paper. It's much more than that: It's a short-cut method of expressing ideas without the rambling vagueness of ordinary talk. It's putting your ideas in such a way that they will be immediately clear to someone who reads them.

How do you go about it? How can you pack your ideas so tightly that the reader understands your meaning right away as his eyes follow the lines? What language short-cuts can you use in English?

Childish Talk

Let's begin at the beginning. Have you ever paid any attention to the way a small child talks? Have you ever heard your little brother say this kind of thing?

A man came and Mummy went downstairs and Mummy told the man Daddy wasn't home and so the man went away

77

and so Mummy went back upstairs and Mummy said the man
wanted to talk to Daddy . . . .

Of course, you would never write like that. You wouldn't
even talk like that. But just what's wrong with it? What is it
that makes it so different from written English?

The first thing you notice is that it never stops. It goes on
and on and on without a break. That's something you can't
do in writing. You have to show the reader where one idea
ends and the next one starts; you have to give him a little
time to catch his breath between ideas. Actually, you do that
in talking too, but you do it automatically by pausing for a
moment and drawing a fresh breath. What your little brother
really said was this:

> A man came (breath) and Mummy went downstairs (breath)
> and Mummy told the man Daddy wasn't home (breath) and
> so the man went away (breath) and so Mummy went back
> upstairs (breath) and Mummy said the man wanted to talk
> to Daddy (breath) . . . .

In writing, you mark the place of each little pause-for-
breath with a period. Each period is a stop sign that means:
"Here I would pause for a split second in talking. Do the
same in reading."

So let's put periods into our example and see what we get:

> A man came. And Mummy went downstairs. And Mummy
> told the man Daddy wasn't home. And so the man went away.
> And so Mummy went back upstairs. And Mummy said the
> man wanted to talk to Daddy . . . .

Now it certainly looks awkward. As soon as we put in the
periods we see that all the and's and so's are unnecessary.
They are nothing but wasted words that clutter up talk. Let's
try again without a single and or so:

> A man came. Mummy went downstairs. Mummy told the
> man Daddy wasn't home. The man went away. Mummy went
> back upstairs. Mummy said the man wanted to talk to
> Daddy . . . .

That's better, but it's still far from good. For one thing,
there are now *too many* periods in it. The reader has to stop

too often; he would like to read on without all these jerks. In the second place, there are too many repetitions of Mummy and the man. Some of them are unnecessary and we can get rid of them by using the personal pronouns he and she. (If you want to know more about pronouns and how they work, look up PRONOUNS on pages 215-19.) So, leaving out a few periods and repetitions, we get:

> A man came. Mummy went downstairs and told him Daddy wasn't home. He went away. She went back upstairs and said he wanted to talk to Daddy . . . .

If you compare this with the way your little brother said it, you will see that we have translated a piece of spoken English into written English. Did you notice how we did it? The main trick was *to make one sentence do the work of two*. At first it was ". . . and Mummy went downstairs and Mummy told the man Daddy wasn't home . . ."—two sentences, tied together with and. Then, when we wrote "Mummy went downstairs. Mummy told the man Daddy wasn't home," we had two sentences, with a period in between. But when we made it into "Mummy went downstairs and told him Daddy wasn't home," we had only one sentence —a sentence with one "subject" (Mummy) and two "predicates" (went and told). In this way we managed to give the reader two ideas without an unnecessary in-between stop or an unnecessary pronoun. (There is more about this in the chapter on VERB AND SUBJECT on pages 210-15.)

Now let's see how this time-saving trick works with a few other examples:

Two Sentences with Period in Between	*Sentence with One Subject and Two Predicates*
I live very far from town. I have to take a long bus ride.	I live very far from town and have to take a long bus ride.
Abraham Lincoln freed the slaves. He furthered the cause of democracy.	Abraham Lincoln freed the slaves and furthered the cause of democracy.

Two Sentences Tied Together with and or but	
Everybody in the family likes good food but everybody hates doing the dishes.	Everybody in the family likes good food but hates doing the dishes.

Television has made great progress, and it will soon be in many homes.	Television has made great progress and will soon be in many homes.

So far, so good. Sentences with a double predicate are really so easy that they are hardly worth talking about. But it's important to know that they are the first step in changing spoken English into written English.

Relative Clauses

The next step is just as easy. Instead of using a double predicate in a sentence, we can also use either who or which. Who and which are called *relative pronouns* and introduce *relative clauses* (more about all that on page 194). For instance, instead of "Many young people would like to go to college and cannot afford it," you can say "Many young people *who would like to go to college* (relative clause), cannot afford it." Or instead of "A college degree is expensive and does not always pay," you can say "A college degree, *which is expensive* (relative clause), does not always pay."

The point is that by using who or which you have made an independent clause into a relative or dependent clause—a group of words that can't stand by itself. If you say ". . . which is expensive . . ." and nothing else, it doesn't make sense. A dependent clause always needs an independent clause to lean on. You can't use it without the main part it belongs to. It's only an attachment. (See page 194 on THE SENTENCE and CLAUSES.) In other words, written English is built like furniture or machinery that comes in unassembled parts and has to be assembled before it can be used. To write English that is easy to read, you have to know how to assemble the parts.

Tool Words

For this you need tools, of course. For instance, if you want to put together two sentences that deal with the same person or thing, you use who or which—the "relative pronouns." You make one of the sentences into a clause with who or which in front and hang it onto the other. If you want to show that two sentences are related in some other way, there are other tool-words you can use. All of them are words you know well and have used a million times. The trick is to be sure how they work and to put them where they fit.

Let's say, for instance, you want to put the following two ideas into one written sentence: "Harry lives in the city" and "Harry earns much money." First of all, you notice that both sentences deal with Harry. So you can put them together with who, either as: "Harry, *who* lives in the city, earns much money," or as "Harry, *who* earns much money, lives in the city." But you would like to show some other connection between the two ideas. How about connecting them in space? Let's see. The tool word that deals with place is where. This gives us "Harry lives in the city, *where* he earns much money." By using where we have stressed the place.

Now let's look for tool-words that deal with time. There are four of them: when, while, before, and after. Let's see what we get:

Harry lives in the city when he earns much money.
Harry lives in the city while he earns much money.
Harry lived in the city before he earned much money.
Harry lived in the city after he earned much money.

These four words stress time. Notice that they mean different things. When says simply that two things are happening at the same time; while says they happen during the same period; and before and after show which comes first and which comes second—either Harry earned much money in the country and then moved to the city, or he earned his money in the city and then moved to the country.

Other Tool-Words

Next, let's use words that show that one thing is the *reason* for another. There are two such words: because and since. They give us: "Harry lives in the city *because* (or *since*) he earns much money." In other words, Harry is the sort of person who would move to the city to earn much money.

Now let's turn it around and say that Harry's income is *not the reason* for his living in the city. We want to hint that he is the sort of person who likes country life. Again, we have two tool-words for that purpose: although and though. We say: "Harry lives in the city *although* (or *though*) he earns much money."

Finally, let's try to put the two ideas together in such a way that one depends on the other. For that we use the word *if* and write: "Harry lives in the city *if* he earns much money." To the reader this means: If you meet Harry on Fifth Avenue, you can be sure his finances are in good shape.

Of course, this is an artificial example. But it illustrates how tool-words work. Here's a better example (still using Harry): "If the rumors are true, Harry is now living in the city." (Let's leave him there.)

There are many more of these tool-words (they are called SUBORDINATE CONJUNCTIONS, see page 194), but those we have mentioned are the most important for you. Once you know how to deal with **who, which, where, when, while, before, after, because, since, although, though, and if,** and have them ready whenever you need them, you will be able to make your ideas much clearer. With these subordinating conjuctions and the connectives we talked about in Chapter 5 you will be able to show the reader exactly how your ideas are related to each other.

Which Clause First?

Now let's go one step further. To understand you fully, your reader has to know not only how one idea is connected with the other, but also which of the two is more important. If you write "Hitler has often been compared with Napoleon, although there are many differences between them," which looks more important: the similarities between the two men or the differences? To the reader, it will seem that you wanted to stress their differences. But if you write "Although there are many differences between Hitler and Napoleon, the two men have often been compared," the stress is on the word **compared** and the reader will expect you to go on and show *why* they have been compared with each other. In other words, *the idea that stands at the end* is usually the more important one and the reader will take it for granted that it contains the main thought.

How can you apply this to those two-part sentences joined with a tool-word? That's simple. Nine times out of ten the first part of such sentences is the important one and the second part—the one that starts with the subordinating conjunction—is less important. So the thing to do is to turn most of these sentences around. Make it a habit to think one step ahead: if the next idea is one of those added, minor thoughts, write it first, at the beginning of the sentence. Here are some examples:

Before I say "yes" or "no," I would like to get some more information.

While I am on the subject, let me give you a few statistics.

Though I like to listen to the radio, I can think of better ways to spend an evening.

When you read this letter, I'll be in Los Angeles.

You see how all these sentences are built? The less important thought is expressed in a clause with if, while, though and so on, and is tucked in *before* the main clause. This isn't *always* the best way to write a sentence, but most often it is. Putting the main point last—the one that ought to be stressed —will improve almost all sentences.

And now that we know about double-predicate sentences, subordinate clauses, and where to put them, let's translate a whole piece of spoken English into written English. Study the two passages on this page. The one on the left side shows a series of ideas the way you might talk or think about them; the one on the right side shows the same ideas, rewritten for better reading. Study these two passages closely. Look at the rambling, awkward sentences in the left-hand passage and what was done with them in the "rewrite." Note the two double-predicate sentences in the right-hand passage, beginning with Since we can and We take it. Study the use of the subordinating conjunctions when, if, since, and though, and see how easy it is to read and understand the sentences because all the subordinating clauses have been put in *front*. And be sure to look at all those ideas that were buried between other thoughts and have been put into the "show window" at the end of the sentence.

The telephone is part of our world today but it was invented by Alexander Graham Bell and he couldn't have known about that. In fact, we don't look at it as a miracle. Most of the time we don't think about it at all. It is commonplace to us. We can go into any drugstore and we can make a call for a nickel and so we take the telephone for granted. We don't give it a second thought. Businesses wouldn't be so efficient if they

When Alexander Graham Bell invented the telephone, he couldn't have known how much it would be part of our world today. If we think about it at all, we certainly don't look at it as a miracle. Since we can go into any drugstore and make a call for a nickel, the telephone is commonplace to us. We take it for granted and don't give it a second thought. But if there were no telephones, businesses would be less efficient. If there had no telephones and people would spend hours and hours writing letters and notes if they had no phones and all over the country families and people would have different lives if they had no telephones. Most of us are using the telephone all the time, quite naturally, the way we use knives and forks, but some people don't. They have never learned to like the telephone.

were no telephones, people would spend hours and hours writing letters and notes. If there were no telephones, American family and social life would be different. In short, we are a telephoning people. Though there are still some people who have never learned to like it, most of us use the telephone as naturally as we use knives and forks.

Don't ramble. Tighten up your sentences with
1. double predicates;
2. relative pronouns;
3. subordinating conjunctions.
As a rule, put the subordinate clause first.

Exercise 1. The following sentences are fairly clear in meaning. But they all need tightening up. Some are childish in their construction. Some can be combined into one sentence. In others it may be necessary to make one part of the sentence a relative clause or a subordinate clause.

Rewrite these sentences and make them say what they should say more directly, more accurately. Make them sound more "grown-up."

1. The new governor enacted many repressive laws. He also levied heavy taxes.
2. Tubby was a goldfish and he lived in a round fishbowl and everyone used to watch him and he had no privacy, so he decided to do something about it.
3. Ruth has a large collection of phonograph records. Barbara has a large collection also.
4. Trigger was a frisky little dog, and he knew many tricks.
5. Richard opened the door. He asked the stranger to come in.
6. The manager walked into the office, and we all became very quiet.
7. She started to speak, and Joe's book fell to the floor with a loud crash.
8. The French Club is going to present a play at an assembly this term. The Spanish Club is going to present one, too.
9. Harry is an excellent dancer. So is Irene.
10. She had braised the meat. She also had boiled the potatoes.

11. Charlie bought two pairs of slacks yesterday. He bought a sleeveless sweater, too.
12. In this movie Dorothy Lamour is a Hawaiian princess and she falls in love with an American sea captain, but the chief says that white men are taboo and she has to be thrown into the ocean as a sacrifice, and so Bing Crosby and Bob Hope decide to rescue her.
13. Franklin D. Roosevelt had an excellent radio voice, and he delivered many important speeches over the radio.
14. His "fireside chats" were informal talks, and they commanded an audience of millions.
15. The house had been built nearly a century ago, and it was very shabby and weatherbeaten.
16. Golf is a sport that keeps growing in popularity. Tennis, too, is getting more and more popular.
17. The male fish is more brightly colored than the female. He also has a long swordtail.
18. She used to keep her money in an old shoe. She also kept some under a loose board in the floor.
19. The clock struck just as I rang the bell, and I knew I had arrived too late.
20. The witch wanted to torment the philosopher, so she married him, but he was very kind to her and he didn't mind her wickedness at all, so she became angrier and angrier and she tried out all her magic spells on him, and so he was able to learn them all and so he became even wiser than before.
21. We reached the camp, and storm clouds began to gather in the sky.
22. We drove to Albany in Fred's car. We returned by boat.
23. Harry's favorite pastime is building model airplanes. He also likes to collect stamps.
24. Sidney Carton was in love with Lucy, but she married Charles Darnay instead, but Carton was still devoted to her, and later Darnay was going to be executed, so Carton changed places with him, and thus Carton gave his life to save Lucy's husband.
25. Susan lives across the street, and she often walks to work with me.
26. I went swimming every day last summer. I also played lots of tennis.
27. You'll have to bring a pen and a pencil with you. You'll also have to bring a notebook.
28. Henry David Thoreau lived near Walden Pond for many months, and he wrote a book about his experiences there, and it has become an American classic.
29. We had started a fire going, and we gathered around it to warm our drenched, shivering bodies.

Exercise 2. In the next five sentences you have a summary of one of the most famous modern radio plays. It is now being made into a motion picture. Rewrite this summary so that it sounds as exciting as it really is. The sentences will need considerable overhauling. Try your hand at this repair job making use of all the suggestions given in this chapter for improving sentences.

1. This play is about a woman and she is an invalid and she can't get out of bed.
2. She is all alone and she keeps wondering why her husband doesn't come home, so she tries to telephone him at his office.
3. The line is busy, so she tries again, and she overhears a conversation and two men are talking and they are planning to murder someone.
4. She telephones the police station and tells a policeman what she had heard and she asks him to do something to prevent the murder, but he thinks she's just an hysterical woman and besides he says he doesn't know where the murder's supposed to take place or who the plotters are and so there's nothing he can do.
5. Time passes and the woman becomes more and more nervous and she keeps recalling what the two men were saying and gradually it dawns on her that she herself is the person they were planning to murder, and she can't get out of bed and no one's at home with her and she keeps trying to call for help on the telephone, but no one will believe her story, and so all she can do is lie there and wait until they come to kill her.

Exercise 3. In the blank space in the following, insert the correct tool word (subordinating conjunction) that deals with time.

1. I had finished two years of high school _____ I went into the Army.
2. _____ Betty Smith finished *A Tree Grows in Brooklyn*, she started on her second novel.
3. Many cheerful persons sing _____ they are working.
4. _____ I drive my car, I make every effort to obey traffic signs.
5. It is always best to think a problem over carefully _____ making a decision.
6. Most people engage in vigorous outdoor sports _____ they go on vacation.
7. The boy cried _____ he heard that he could not go to the circus.
8. _____ the baseball season is over, the World Series is played.

Exercise 4. In the blank space in the following sentences, insert the correct tool word (subordinating conjunction) that shows the reason or its opposite or that says something will happen provided certain other things happen at the same time.

1. _____ he knew he would get into trouble, he went.
2. _____ we were only content with what we had, the world would be a better place to live in.
3. He was discharged _____ he neglected his work.
4. There will be a baseball game at Forbes Field tomorrow _____ it does not rain.
5. He continued to try _____ he knew that he was doomed to failure.
6. Children like western movies _____ there is much action in them.
7. _____ Roy Rogers is very popular, he is frequently asked for his autograph.
8. We are hoping that the United Nations will be a success _____ the League of Nations was a failure.

8 HOW TO SAVE WORDS

In the last chapter, we told you to use double-predicate sentences and subordinate clauses in your writing; this would make it look like written rather than spoken English. But what's the actual difference to your reader? Why would he want to have your thoughts served up in double-predicate sentences and subordinate clauses rather than in a string of simple sentences? Naturally because this will save words. To understand what you are driving at, he has to follow with his eyes so and so many lines on paper. If you push your thoughts together into fewer words, he can read faster.

But you can save your reader many more words. Cutting down on the number of sentences is just the first step. There are many other ways of saving words.

Weeding Out Words

How do you go about saving words? One way, of course, is to throw out all the words you don't need. If you write something about a tiny little kitchen, look at it again and strike out the word little—a tiny kitchen *must* be little. If you write about a long-distance telephone call, strike out telephone—long-distance call will do. That kind of thing is easy. All you need to do is watch out for all those words that don't add any meaning to what you are saying. They crop up in everybody's writing and it's a simple chore to weed them out. Here are a few more examples:

> They were discussing about the next steps to take.
> He was leafing through the pages of the book.
> There was a question as to whether there was enough time.
> Why don't you come and visit us some time?

Clauses Into Phrases

But there are more important ways of saving words. We have told you about turning sentences into subordinate clauses. You can go on from there and turn subordinate clauses into phrases—groups of words that do *not* start with relative pronouns or subordinating conjunctions. (See pages 195-98 on THE PHRASE.)

Often you can make a phrase out of a relative clause simply by striking out such words as *who was* or *which is*. For instance:

> Our neighbor, ~~who was~~ the mayor of the town, was always very friendly to us.
> Corn, ~~which is~~ a North American plant, is now grown in many parts of Europe.
> Mozart, ~~who was~~ a child prodigy, became one of the most famous composers of all times.

At other times, you have to do a little more than leave out the relative pronoun:

Automobiles, which used to be a symbol of wealth, are now very common.	Automobiles, once a symbol of wealth, are now very common.
Any man who is an American by birth can become President.	Any native American man can become President.

Prepositional Phrases

The most common word-saving phrases, however, are those that start with a preposition. In some way or other, almost all subordinate clauses can be turned into prepositional phrases. This is something you do all the time in your speaking and writing:

As soon as spring arrives, we'll go out to the lake every Sunday.	In the spring we'll go out to the lake every Sunday.
While we were having dinner, he started an argument that lasted all evening.	During dinner he started an argument that lasted all evening.
When you come to the third traffic light, turn left.	At the third traffic light turn left.
If you are lucky, you'll get there before everybody else.	With luck you'll get there before everybody else.

As you see, prepositional phrases are excellent word-savers. Again, the trick is to put them at the beginning of your sentences wherever possible, so that the main thought is saved for the end.

Infinitive Phrases

Still another handy word-saver is the infinitive phrase. It is used most often instead of a clause beginning with *that* or *so that:*

Open the window so that you get some fresh air.	Open the window to get some fresh air.
I want to try this on so that I am sure it fits.	I want to try this on to make sure it fits.

Word-Saving Syllables

But the English language has a much more interesting word-saving trick than all these. Aside from clauses, phrases, and words, it has a dozen or two little syllables each of which can take the place of several words.

Here is a simple example: Suppose you walk along Main Street with a friend of yours. Suddenly you turn to him (or her) and say: "Let's go over to the side of the street that is in the shade."

Does that strike you as the way you would actually say it? Of course not. You don't talk in such roundabout fashion. You would naturally say: "Let's go over to the *shady* side of the street."

Now what exactly have you done with that sentence? You have left out a relative clause—that is in the shade—and used instead a single word that expressed the same idea—shady. In this way, you have saved yourself and your listener four words—that is in the. The remaining word shade you kept; but—to make it say the same thing as the whole clause, you put a y at the end so that it became shady. In other words, you saved four words by simply adding y to the word shade.

But you have also done something else. By adding y, you have changed the word shade into a different *type* of word. Shade is a noun; shady is an adjective.

Grammar Saves Words

Well, what does that matter? Why do you have to know about these differences in grammar? Will that help you to do a better job of writing?

Yes, it will. Here's how. As soon as you can tell the different types of words, you can also tell what type of word can take the place of those you want to get rid of. Actually, what you do to shorten "Let's go over to the side of the street that is in the shade" is this: You look at the clause you want to get rid of—that is in the shade—and see that it belongs to (or "modifies") the noun side. So the word you need to put in front of that noun is an adjective. You take the most important word in the clause—shade—add an adjective-ending y, and there you are: "Let's go over to the shady side of the street."

That sounds quite difficult, but actually you do that sort of thing all the time without giving it a second thought:

Instead of this:	*You say this:*
Last time we met it was on a day when it rained.	Last time we met it was on a rainy day.
The cake had a flavor that reminded me of nuts.	The cake had a nutty flavor.
There was nothing left but a few nails that had rust on them.	There was nothing left but a few rusty nails.

Of course, y is not the only syllable you can use to turn clauses into adjectives. Here are a couple with like:

She put on her best behavior, which was like that of a lady.	She put on her best ladylike behavior.
He got about in a contraption that was somewhat like a jeep.	He got about in a somewhat jeeplike contraption.

How about using ful?

We were greeted with a smile that was full of joy.	We were greeted with a joyful smile.
He was a driver who took great care.	He was a very careful driver.

How about less?

A little hall that has no windows makes a good darkroom.	A little windowless hall makes a good darkroom.
This strikes me as a joke that has no point.	This strikes me as a pointless joke.

Each of these four little syllables can replace a clause of four or five or six words. To show that something is *like* something else, you use y or like; to show that it is *full* of something else, you use the syllable *ful*; and to show that it is *without* something else, you use **less**.

Using Adverbs

Now let's turn to other types of words. How can you shorten this sentence: "The crowd cheered in a way that was wild?" Of course you know how. You simply say: "The crowd cheered wildly." You add **ly** to **wild** and save five words. Again, this means that you have changed the types of words: **wild** is an adjective, **wildly** is an adverb. The adjective **wild** belongs to (modifies) the noun in the sentence (**way**), the adverb **wildly** belongs to (modifies) the verb (**cheered**). So to save a clause that belongs to a verb, you look for an adjective in that clause, add **ly** to make it an adverb, and throw out all the other words in that clause. For example:

I was waiting for that letter until I became impatient.	I was waiting impatiently for that letter.
I was thinking of staying home all Sunday and studying and I was serious about it.	I was thinking seriously of staying home all Sunday and studying.

Using Other Parts of Speech

Once you are quite sure of your types of words—or "parts of speech"—you can shorten your sentences easily. Just pick the proper syllable and switch from one type of word to the other. Do you want to make verbs into adjectives? Here's how:

He covered the two miles with a speed that amazed everybody.	He covered the two miles with amazing speed.
They gave us a welcome that warmed our hearts.	They gave us a heart-warming welcome.
The furniture was full of decorations that had been painted by hand.	The furniture was full of hand-painted decorations.
He came to the party in a tuxedo which he had rented.	He came to the party in a rented tuxedo.
I must apologize for my behavior which was to be regretted.	I must apologize for my regrettable behavior.
That was a show you could really enjoy.	That was a really enjoyable show.

So you see that with **able, ed,** and **ing,** you can turn verbs into adjectives and save many unnecessary words.

You can also use **ed** and **ing** to form participles from verbs and make clauses into participial phrases:

When I remembered that the gift was meant as a surprise, I stopped in the middle of my sentence.	Remembering that the gift was meant as a surprise, I stopped in the middle of my sentence.
As it was parked right in front of our house, the trailer was a great nuisance.	Parked right in front of our house, the trailer was a great nuisance.
Since I had already eaten three pieces of pie, I politely refused to take another one.	Having already eaten three pieces of pie, I politely refused to take another one.

Now how about turning verbs into nouns? You can use **ing** for that too. (A verb-noun ending in **ing** is called a *gerund.*)

Not everybody likes it when he has to dance on a crowded floor.	Not everybody likes dancing on a crowded floor.
Often the beauty of a dress lies in the way it is worn.	Often the beauty of a dress lies in the wearing.

How about turning adjectives into nouns? Let's try **ness** for this:

I didn't quite realize that the idea was so foolish.	I didn't quite realize the foolishness of the idea.
What impressed me most was the fact that he was completely bald.	What impressed me most was his complete baldness.

Other Word-Saving Syllables

Now we have mentioned altogether nine word-saving syllables: y, like, full, less, ly, able, ed, ing, and ness. But these are only examples. There are many more. There is **ment** (as in astonishment, amazement, and embarrassment); **ion** (as in expression, creation, or embarkation); **ize** (as in modernize or emphasize); **fy** (as in fortify or amplify); and so on and so on. There are combinations of these, like **izement** (as in aggrandizement) or **fication** (as in fortification). Then there are syllables you put in front of words, like **un, re,** or **mis.** Here are a few examples of what you can do with these:

He left his work before he could finish it.	He left his work unfinished.
I handed in a report that I had written over again.	I handed in a rewritten report.
I looked at my name, which was spelled wrongly.	I looked at my misspelled name.

In short, there are many ways of saving words. Many unnecessary words you can simply leave out. Some sentences you can shorten by using prepositions, some others by using an infinitive or participle. And if you know how to make good use of all the word-saving *syllables* of the English language, you can sometimes boil down your thoughts into surprisingly few words.

Let's try *all* these methods for once and see what happens. Below are two passages that contain exactly the same ideas. But in the left-hand column no words have been saved. There are two-hundred and eighty-seven words. The right-hand column has been boiled down. It has one hundred and eight words. Study the two passages and see how this was done. Look at the superfluous words—crossed out at left and simply left out at right. Then look at the various word-savers we have used in the right-hand column; they are black print.

Washington comes as a surprise to anyone who arrives there from another American city. Most people who visit Washington are used to other places where they step from the station onto a downtown square full of a ~~large~~ crowd ~~of people, taxis, trucks, and other vehicles~~. But when these people emerge from Union Station ~~in Washington~~, they find themselves in ~~an entirely~~ different situation. Right in front ~~of them~~, across from ~~the~~ Union Station, is the ~~National~~ Capitol. They usually gaze at it ~~steadily for a while~~. It looks very ~~calm and~~ serene ~~to anybody who sees it for the first time. In the city,~~ Washington has no skyscrapers ~~at all~~. But it

After other American cities Washington comes as a surprise.

Emerging from Union Station, the visitor, used to stepping from the station onto a crowded downtown square, finds himself gazing at the serenity of the Capitol.

Instead of skyscrapers, Washington offers him wide avenues

has wide avenues with lower buildings ~~lined up to the right and left~~. Practically all of these buildings are made of gleaming white marble ~~stone~~. They look as if they would never change ~~in the course of time~~ and so Washington does not seem as restless as other fast-growing American cities.

lined with white marble buildings.

Washington is not like New York or Chicago. These cities grew up in a haphazard way and almost by accident. But in Washington those who founded it had a plan ~~for building it~~. They hired ~~a man named~~ L'Enfant who was an architect from France. So Washington looks a little ~~bit~~ like Paris or other cities in Europe. It is beautiful because there is real harmony among its monuments and buildings. Naturally, some ~~of them~~ are exceptions ~~to this~~, but ~~they~~ do not really matter. Some ~~of them~~ have been added only recently, for example the National Gallery or the Jefferson Memorial ~~and so forth~~. These buildings and monuments also follow the single pattern that has been worked out for the city.

In-stead of restlessness, it has timelessness.

Unlike New York or Chicago, Washington is not the result of haphazard and accidental growth but of planning.

Designed by the French architect L'Enfant, it has a European, Parisian air; with few exceptions, its monuments and buildings harmonize beautifully.

Even recent additions like the National Gallery or the Jefferson Monument follow the unified pattern.

Be brief.
Save words by
   1. leaving out unnecessary words;
   2. turning clauses into prepositional, infinitive, and other phrases;
   3. using word-saving syllables like *ly, able, ful, less, ing,* and *ness.*

Exercise 1. Each of the following sentences contains one or more unnecessary words or expressions. Rewrite each sentence, cutting out all repetition.

1. Though he is a recent immigrant from a foreign country, he talks English without a trace of an accent.
2. I have a friend of mine who owns a set of the *Encyclopaedia Britannica*.
3. When the storm broke, the golfers hurriedly dashed for shelter.
4. Meowing on the porch was a scared, frightened tiny little kitten.
5. I had a bad attack of insomnia last night, and I was unable to sleep.
6. The boy landed on his two feet.
7. After he settled in New Jersey, Walton became a stingy miser and lived alone in solitude all by himself.
8. If your handwriting isn't legible, you will have to rewrite your memorandum over again.
9. The medal was awarded to him posthumously, after his death.
10. Later in his life Beethoven became completely deaf and could not hear at all.
11. America has been built by the co-operative effort of many different kinds of people, working together.
12. I can remember back to the days when I liked nothing but jazz music exclusively.
13. The desire for admiration is a universal craving, possessed by all people.
14. You know that Tim has been falsely slandered; he is really a brave, courageous man.
15. She turned her sad, unhappy face to me and spoke in a tired, weary voice.
16. The consensus of opinion is that we should have a daily rehearsal every day for the next two weeks.
17. It is clearly evident that we must operate immediately, without delay.
18. I witnessed a very unique demonstration of mental telepathy last night.
19. Where are you going to?
20. The first broadcast of this play on the air was its premiere on December 16 at 10 P.M. in the evening.

Exercise 2. Using any of the word-saving devices discussed in this chapter, rewrite each of the following sentences. In some, a clause may be shaved down to a phrase; in others a phrase or a clause may be reduced to a single word; in still others an appositive may do the trick.

1. Unfortunately, we arrived during the season when it rains much of the time.
2. The moon, which was the color of silver, shone down upon the lake.

3. Mr. Stern was my supervisor during my first year. He encouraged me to prepare myself for a higher position.
4. Tony is a pianist who is very talented.
5. The girl who is wearing the red hat is my cousin.
6. The child followed her everywhere with devotion such as a dog displays.
7. Bill entered the room. He looked about him suspiciously.
8. Your conduct at the dance was such that it shocked everybody.
9. It was a warm, romantic evening, full of moonlight.
10. If it could talk, that house which is located on Ninety-second Street might reveal many secrets.
11. Without making any noise, we entered the house, which was darkened.
12. You have been wrongly informed about my intentions.
13. I've just received a letter from Mr. Jenkins. He's the personnel manager at the Bethlehem Electric Company.
14. Your decision is one that is not just.
15. He opened the door with a smile that seemed to welcome us.
16. He always has a manner that is very cheerful.
17. The old woman, who didn't have a penny, refused to accept my gift.
18. He seemed to take pleasure in making us feel mystified.
19. This is a tool that has many uses.
20. I spent the night in a warehouse that was infested with rats.
21. The news, which startled us, made us change our plans in a way that was abrupt.
22. He likes his coffee without any sweetening in it.
23. We shall have to make our drive to raise funds more intense.
24. I was taken aback at the insolent way he was talking. I did not expect it.
25. Ethel was worn out by the ordeal. She looked old and haggard.
26. The women of America spend millions of dollars annually in an effort to make themselves beautiful.
27. One of the marks of the wise man is the fact that he is patient with the stupid way in which others behave.
28. My Aunt Tillie sent me a tie that had been painted by hand. It was a Christmas gift.
29. It is an atrocity of many hues that dazzles the beholder. I would not dare to wear it.
30. Some person without any sense of responsibility must have designed it for the sole purpose of making the wearer feel embarrassed.

Exercise 3. In each of the following sentences, the italicized portions can be expressed in fewer words. In some, one word can be substituted for the italicized section. In others, you may have to cut out unnecessary words.

1. *As soon as* he has finished, he will call you.
2. *While we were out playing golf*, we saw two jack rabbits.
3. Turn right *when you come to the corner* of State Street.
4. *In order to play better*, you'll have to practice more often.
5. Work hard *so that you may get* good results.
6. You must read this book *in order to understand* the history of our times.
7. Some people were eating peanuts *while the play was going on*.
8. He did his work in *a manner that showed he did not care*.
9. This passage is *full of beauty*.
10. This is a *type of dog that has no hair*.
11. Bluebeard was a monster *without a heart, without a soul*.
12. He approaches all his problems in a *manner like that of a child*.
13. The car crawled up the hill *at a pace resembling a snail's*.
14. Hitler was *a man completely lacking in mercy*.
15. When I entered the room, my mother greeted me *in an ecstatic manner*.
16. It isn't difficult *to make your home modern*.
17. When you speak, *put emphasis on* the most important words and ideas.
18. *Words that aren't necessary* should be cut out of your writing.
19. This is a sloppy piece of work. You will have *to do it over again*.
20. The trouble with that picture was that *it did not seem to be real*.
21. The painter is coming *to paint the living room over again*.
22. It is your duty to correct *statements which are wrong*.
23. When ice is heated, it *will turn to water*.
24. They bought *a horse that nobody could manage*.
25. The type in the book was *so small that it couldn't be read*.

9 *HOW NOT TO PUZZLE YOUR READER*

> Walking down Fifth Avenue, the Empire State Building glitters in the sun.

What's wrong with this sentence? That's easy: It isn't the Empire State Building that's walking down Fifth Avenue; it's you. The sentence should read: "Walking down Fifth Avenue, I saw the Empire State Building glitter in the sun."

This is a funny example of something that happens ever so often to everyone who writes. It's the kind of sentence that's likely to puzzle a reader. He will have to go back and reread it. In trying to put your ideas on paper in as few words as possible, you have left out something the reader has to know.

As you have learned by now, writing is mostly a matter of putting your minor ideas into subordinate clauses, phrases, and single words, tucked away in your sentences. But be careful! The clause, phrase, or word must be exactly in the right place or the reader will have trouble figuring out where it belongs.

Puzzling Participles

Most often, this sort of mistake happens when you put an idea into a phrase with *ing* in it. You start a sentence with some *ing* word—that is, a present participle—thinking of what you yourself were doing—and then you forget to put yourself into the main sentence. So you start out "Walking down Fifth Avenue . . ." and suddenly it's the Empire State Building that's doing the walking! Here is another example:

> Reading the funny papers, my aunt dropped in for a visit.

Naturally, it was you who were reading the funny papers, not your aunt. So let's rewrite this sentence so that it makes sense:

> I was reading the funny papers when my aunt dropped in for a visit.

Dangerous Prepositions

But the sentence that starts with a participial *ing* phrase is only the most common of these troublemakers. There is the same danger in an *ing* phrase that starts with a preposition. If you don't make sure that the subject of your main clause is also the *ing* person in the *ing* phrase, you will wind up with this type of sentence:

> Every morning before going to school, our dog has to be walked.

(You were thinking of yourself going to school, and before you knew it, you had a scholarly type of dog!)

This sort of thing can happen with any phrase that starts with a preposition, regardless of whether it has an *ing* in it or not. It doesn't matter either whether the prepositional phrase is at the beginning of the sentence or in the middle or at the end. Look at this one, for instance:

> Last night I went to see Clark Gable in a new dress.

What you mean, of course, is:

> Last night I put on a new dress and went to see Clark Gable.

Tricky Infinitives

Now let's look at some other puzzles for the reader. Up to here we have spoken of phrases with *ing* and phrases that start with a preposition. But the same thing will happen whenever you start a sentence with a phrase about yourself or some other person and then carry on with a main clause that has a different subject. It happens quite often when you start with *to*—like this:

> To get to the station, the bus stops right in front of our house.

This reads as if the bus were eager to get to the station and *therefore* stopped in front of your house. In other words, it's nonsense. Let's rewrite it:

> To get to the station, take the bus. It stops right in front of our house.

What Are You Comparing?

Very often when you compare two things with each other, you leave out the most important word. Here is an example:

Frank's bicycle is as tall as Mary.

Well, that could be so, of course—if Mary is still a very little girl. But if she isn't, and her bicycle is of the same height as Frank's bicycle, then let's write:

Frank's bicycle is as tall as Mary's (bicycle).

You see what a difference an s can make?

Squinting Modifiers

Another troublemaker is an adverb or a modifying phrase that is wedged into the middle of a sentence so the reader can't be sure whether it belongs to the words before or after it. This is the kind of thing we are talking about:

We keep our radio going often without paying any attention to it.

The chances are that the reader won't stop to reread this sentence. He will think either that you often have your radio on but pay no attention to it or that you have your radio on all the time but often pay no attention to it. Actually, the sentence may mean either of these two things. To be quite sure the reader won't misunderstand, you again have to add something. Here's the least you will have to add—a dash in one case and a but in the other:

We keep our radio going—often without paying any attention to it.
We keep our radio going often, but without paying any attention to it.

Or how about rewriting the whole thing to avoid any trouble?

We often keep our radio going. But we pay no attention to it.
We keep our radio going, but often pay no attention to it.

Puzzling Pronouns

The trouble with squinting modifiers is that the reader doesn't know which of two things the word refers to. This sort of confusion creeps in very often when you use *pronouns*. You write something that starts with it or he or they and the reader can't tell what you mean because there is more than one possible it or he or they in the sentence before. Look at this, for instance:

> The garden wedding was spoiled by rain. It lasted for a whole week.

What was it that lasted for a whole week—the wedding or the rain? You can figure out the answer, of course, but the way the sentences are written, the it can mean either. Let's rewrite:

> The garden wedding was spoiled by rain. The rain lasted for a whole week.

In this way, you have to repeat the word rain. But there's no harm in that, and it is much better than the troublesome it.

Here is another example, this time with an ambiguous he:

> Willy went with Daddy to the village. He was riding his new tricycle.

How can you rewrite this without putting Daddy on a tricycle? It's simple if you repeat the word Willy:

> Willy went with Daddy to the village. Willy was riding his new tricycle.

This sounds a little monotonous because both sentences start exactly the same way with Willy. Let's see what else we can do:

> Willy was riding his new tricycle when he went with Daddy to the village.

Now everything is clear. (We have made good use of a subordinate clause.)

So watch out for those puzzling pronouns that can refer to two things at the same time. Or let's say, just watch out for puzzling pronouns! Sometimes you may use a pronoun but when you look for the noun it refers to you find that it isn't there. If we are in a hurry, we are all likely to write sentences like this:

> Afterwards I went to the library but she told me the book was out.

Of course *she* here means the librarian, but the sentence simply doesn't say so. It should read:

> Afterwards I went to the library, but the librarian told me the book was out.

Watch Out for "Then," "There," "That"

Some other words and expressions are dangerous, too. Then, there, that for instance, are likely to crop up in your writing without anything else to tie them to. You *think* you have said what then or there means, but you haven't. Instead you have written:

> The subject is not mentioned in the book since there were no airplanes at that time.

At what time? At the time the book appeared? Or at the time it was written? Or at the time it deals with? The reader can't tell. Probably you had one of these things in mind when you wrote the sentence, but you didn't say so. The sentence should have been written like this:

> The subject is not mentioned in the book since there were no airplanes in 1893.

Now the reader knows—no more puzzle.
Here is another example with a puzzling **there.**

> The mail comes regularly, but we don't live there any more.

Again there is something left out. Probably what was meant was:

> The mail comes regularly to our old address, but we don't live there any more.

Don't Leave Your Reader in Doubt

We could go on giving you examples, but we know that you have caught on to the principle by now. The principle is this: *Don't puzzle your reader* by leaving out things he must know in order to understand what you mean. *Don't puzzle your reader* by combining your words in such a way that they seem to say what you don't mean. In one way or another, this principle holds true for all the mistakes we have shown and for a number of others we haven't mentioned. You can easily avoid these as long as you remember the principle that *you mustn't leave your reader in doubt.*

Of course we know that this is not quite as easy as it looks; otherwise people wouldn't keep on making those mistakes. The trouble is that while you are writing you know what is going on in your mind and can't put yourself in the place of the reader who has nothing to go by but what he sees on the page. But that's just the point. The only way to avoid these puzzles to the reader is to become a reader yourself. In other words, when you are through with writing, *be sure to read over what you have written.* Of course, you can't quite forget that you wrote it yourself, but you can do your best to read it *as if* it were new to you.

We haven't mentioned this point until now because we wanted to tell you first how to go about writing. But it's very important. Nobody—not even the greatest writers—has ever done any good writing without reading it over after it was finished. Or we should really say, "before it was finished," since writing simply isn't finished before you have read it over.

So read over everything you write and check whether it says what you mean.

Don't leave your reader in doubt about what you mean:
1. Look out for sentences starting with a participial (*ing*) phrase not related to the rest of the sentence. This is called the dangling participle.
2. Look out for puzzling prepositional phrases.
3. Look out for sentences starting with an infinitive (*to*) phrase.
4. When you compare things, make sure you are comparing the right things.
5. Look out for squinting modifiers.
6. Look out for pronouns that may refer to two things, or pronouns that do not refer to anything.
7. Look out for the puzzling *then, there, that.*

Exercise 1. There are two stories in the following 30 sentences: the real story (what actually happened) and another story (that never happened and never could happen). This feat is performed by people throughout our fair land every day in the year by the simple and maddening use of *dangling constructions,* constructions that say one thing and mean something else.

Revise the following sentences. Eliminate all dangling constructions and make the sentences say what they should mean. There are five correct sentences among the 30.

1. Gradually dozing off at my desk, a new girl entered the room.
2. Introducing her to the office staff, we were told by Mr. Marvin, our office manager, that she had moved to our city last week and that this was her first day at work.
3. Upon seeing her, my desire for sleep abruptly vanished.
4. Knowing none of the other people in the office, I thought that she seemed rather lonely.
5. To make her acquaintance, a clever plan entered my mind.
6. Waiting impatiently for the morning to end, at last the noon bell rang.
7. Hurrying over to her, I introduced myself and offered to help her become acquainted with the routine in the office.
8. Smiling graciously, my offer was accepted.
9. A few weeks later, after becoming good friends, the time seemed ripe to ask whether I might call on her at her home.
10. Smiling graciously, she said yes.
11. Delighted, a date was arranged for Saturday evening.
12. Making liberal use of my new after-shave lotion and wearing the hand-painted tie I had gotten for Christmas, my mirror told me that I was indeed a well-groomed, handsome young man.
13. Before leaving, my shoes were shined till they glistened.
14. To reach her home, the bus stopped a block away.
15. On entering the door, she introduced me to her mother, her father, and her little brother.
16. Standing on his hind legs, I also shook hands with her collie.
17. Coming into the room, dinner was announced by the maid.
18. Smothered with onions and dripping gravy, we saw a large juicy steak on the table.
19. Admiring my tie, her mother asked me where I had bought it, but her father signaled me not to tell, and I knew that he was afraid that he might receive one as a gift from his wife.
20. After eating our dinner, the radio entertained us for a while.
21. Filled with steak and contentment, I suggested that we go to the movies.
22. Reaching into my pocket, the realization suddenly struck me that I had left my wallet at home and had only fifty cents.
23. On explaining my predicament to her, she laughted good-

naturedly and suggested that we take a long walk instead.
24. Returning from a brisk walk of about three miles, the glider on the porch looked very inviting.
25. Sitting there in the moonlight, her little brother was noticed crouching behind a chair.
26. To encourage him to leave us alone, a small bribe of fifty cents was the only solution.
27. Having at last persuaded her brother to leave, her parents decided to come out on the porch for a chat.
28. After talking for two hours, the clock struck eleven, and it was time for me to go home.
29. After waiting half an hour for the bus, I remembered that I had given her little brother all my money.
30. To reach home, a two-mile walk had to be taken.

Exercise 2. All of these sentences have pronoun trouble. In some, it isn't quite clear what the pronoun is referring to. In others the pronoun is referring to something—but the something isn't in the sentence. Rewrite the sentences making clear what the pronoun refers to. Reread the section in this chapter that deals with the puzzling pronoun if you aren't clear about what is wrong with these sentences.

1. She wore an orchid in her hair. It was an unusual shade of green, speckled with brown.
2. The mailman passed my house at ten o'clock, but he didn't have one for me.
3. Father told his brother that he was wrong.
4. When my uncle patted Fido on the head, he wagged his tail violently.
5. Bill told Jim that his dog had run away.
6. The baseball broke one of Mr. Cooper's windows. This cost the team three dollars.
7. Mrs. Burgess was the last passenger to enter the plane. Then, with her propellers whirling, she sped across the field.
8. After the policeman arrested the thief, he was put in jail.
9. In my apartment house they have self-service elevators.
10. As soon as the boys came in with the eggs, the girls started to boil them.
11. As a child, he loved to browse through the old medical books in the attic. When he grew older, he decided to become one.
12. If your child doesn't like spinach, try smothering it in an appetizing sauce.
13. I have humored him, threatened him, and tried to reason with him, but it is useless.
14. The canary's wing is healed now, and you may take it home.
15. The clambake was lots of fun while it lasted, but we ate too many of them and we all felt ill later.

Exercise 3. There are a number of things the matter with the following sentences. They aren't clear because they contain comparisons that don't really compare, misplaced modifiers, and squinting modifiers. Reread the sections of this chapter dealing with these errors and then correct the sentences.

1. We devoured the pie that Mother had baked for us in less than a minute.
2. The climate here is like Southern California.
3. The sailor who had risen to his feet angrily sat down again.
4. My aunt kissed me as I was leaving on my forehead.
5. The fragrance of this perfume resembles gardenia.
6. I want to paint that landscape very badly.
7. He bought a soda for the little girl with whipped cream on top.
8. The bear that started running across the ice quickly was pursued by the dogs.
9. Her appetite is like an anaconda.
10. I want to buy a gift for a boy that doesn't cost very much.
11. He stopped the thief who was escaping with his lasso.
12. She was discovered by a policeman sitting on her heels in the park.
13. She was discovered sitting on her heels in the park by a policeman.
14. Is it true that the skin of a rhinoceros is thicker than an elephant?
15. Mrs. Meredith was injured this morning while preparing breakfast very seriously.
16. As the tide crept in slowly he regained consciousness.
17. Drink a teaspoonful of this tonic after you lie down tonight in a cup of tea.
18. The kitten arched her back as the puppy ran playfully over to her in defiance.
19. The waitress spilled the soup all over the suit I had borrowed with a sudden, awkward gesture.
20. She reached out to me as she walked toward the door with her left hand.
21. Her neck seemed as long as a giraffe.

10 HOW TO SAVE YOUR READER EXTRA WORK

Sometimes you can confuse your reader no end by simply leaving out a comma. You don't believe it? Look at this sentence:

The old farmer was raising sheep dogs and turkeys.

Does this mean the old farmer was raising sheep? It does not. If you want to tell your reader that, you'll have to write the sentence like this:

The old farmer was raising sheep, dogs, and turkeys.

The comma after **sheep** makes everything clear. And the second comma after **dogs** will help your reader even more. Now he can't miss the idea that the old farmer was raising (1) sheep, (2) dogs, and (3) turkeys.

Let's take another example:

I go to the movies by myself with a friend or with the whole gang.

You can see that this doesn't make sense. You can't go to the movies by yourself with a friend. Quick, let's put commas where they belong:

I go to the movies by myself, with a friend, or with the whole gang.

Both these examples deal with *items in a series.* They contain a number of things in a row, things that are listed one after the other. If you don't want to puzzle your reader, you must put commas between the items to show him that this is a list of things. As long as you follow this simple rule, you will never make mistakes like **sheep dogs** or **by myself with a friend.**

Slow

When you read the **sheep dog** example and the **movie** example aloud, you will notice that you pause slightly between words that are separated by a comma. The comma tells you: "Slow down." If it isn't there, you run the words together in reading aloud and, naturally, you run them together in your mind.

So the comma is a *slow-down* sign. That's why you need it wherever you want to keep the reader from running on at the same speed. For example:

> I had to sign for that special delivery letter with my feet bare and the water running in the bathroom.

There's no danger here that the reader will misunderstand what is meant; but without a comma after the word letter, he is bound to read **I had to sign with my feet**, and will be puzzled until he is quite sure that isn't what you meant to write.

Introductory Phrases and Clauses

Most often, you get into this kind of trouble when there is a clause or phrase at the beginning or end of a sentence and the reader needs a signal that tells him where the main clause starts or ends. For instance, here is a sentence that starts with a clause:

> When you started sawing Grandma woke up from her nap.

We don't have to tell you that a comma after **sawing** will make all the difference here to Grandma. Expressions like **sawing Grandma** make readers feel uneasy—even those who are quite unsentimental about their family.

Or, for a sentence beginning with a phrase, try this:

> In short pants are practical garments.

Nobody can read this without thinking of short pants. Let's help the reader:

> In short, pants are practical garments.

In short, put commas between words you don't want the reader to run together.

Wedged-In Ideas

If you leave out *two* commas in a sentence, you will naturally have double trouble. Two commas usually mean that there is something wedged into the sentence—an idea that is different from the rest of the sentence. This is called a *parenthetical expression*. For example:

> The landlord paid promptly every month was always smiling.

Does this mean that landlord paid every month? Of course not. Two commas are needed to clear things up:

> The landlord, paid promptly every month, was always smiling.

The words **paid promptly every month** are parenthetical. In this example they modify the noun **landlord**. They are a thrown-in thought; without them, the sentence **The landlord was always smiling** would still make sense.

Another common example of a parenthetical expression is the *direct address*. Somewhere in a sentence you name the person you are talking to. This can be quite funny, too, without the proper commas—like this:

> Don't eat Henry before everyone is downstairs.

The commas make it a little less gruesome:

> Don't eat, Henry, before everyone is downstairs.

And especially dangerous, of course, are those sentences that contain *either* a direct address *or* an apposition—depending on whether you use a comma. Here is one:

> Mike, the author of Hamlet, has been dead for three hundred years.

With the comma after *Hamlet, the author of Hamlet* is an appositive to Mike and the sentence says that Mike wrote *Hamlet*. We can't do that to Shakespeare. Let's take out that comma:

> Mike, the author of Hamlet has been dead for three hundred years.

Restrictive and Non-Restrictive Clauses

In some types of sentences, commas are even more important. They are needed not just because they save the reader the extra work of going back and slowing down at the right spot—they actually make a difference in meaning. For instance:

> All the people in the auditorium who had enough of classical music started to leave.

Now read the same sentence with two commas:

> All the people in the auditorium, who had enough of classical music, started to leave.

You see the difference? Without the commas, there are still some people left who are staying on in the auditorium, ready to enjoy more Bach and Beethoven; with the commas, the auditorium will be empty in no time. To use the grammatical term, *without* the commas the words who had enough of classical music form a "restrictive" relative clause—your remark is restricted to those people who had enough. *With* the commas, these same words are a "non-restrictive" relative clause: You are talking without restriction about all the people in the auditorium. What you mean to say is: "All the people in the auditorium started to leave." In other words, the commas around a group of words mean that the reader can skip them and still get the right meaning of the sentence.

Here is another example of the same rule:

> Wienies that you eat with a knife and fork don't taste right.

We have used no commas in this sentence. This means that the words that you eat with a knife and folk are a restrictive relative clause. Our remark is restricted to wienies eaten with a knife and fork. Wienies eaten outdoors, in a roll, are delicious.

Now let's use commas:

> Wienies, which you eat with a knife and fork, don't taste right.

With commas, we have made the words which you eat with a knife and fork into a non-restrictive relative clause. Now we are talking about wienies in general. We have said, bluntly, that you eat wienies with a knife and fork and that they don't taste right. That's what happens if you use commas in a sentence where they don't belong.

By the way, you may have noticed that we started the restrictive relative clause with that and the non-restrictive clause with which. The reason is this: When a relative clause refers to people (like the people in the auditorium), then it must always start with who (or whose or whom) and the reader has to rely solely on the commas to tell a restrictive clause from a non-restrictive one. But when a relative clause refers to *things* (like wienies), then you have a choice between that and which. It's a good idea to use that for all restrictive relative clauses and which for all non-restrictive ones. This sounds better and helps the reader to tell the two kinds of clauses apart and to understand your meaning.

Stop

The comma, as we said, is a "slow-down" signal; it tells the reader to step on the brake. If you want the reader to stop altogether, you have to use another signal: *the period.* The period means "Stop." (In telegrams, the word stop is sometimes used instead of a period.) Without periods, writing becomes utterly confusing, like this:

> I have never read any play that was so silly besides Shakespeare's Hamlet I have read only a few plays written as a novel the book might have been better.

You can see that this doesn't make sense. But with two periods it does:

> I have never read any play that was so silly. Besides Shakespeare's Hamlet, I have read only a few plays. Written as a novel, the book might have been better.

If you want to be quite sure where to put a period, listen to yourself as you are reading the sentences aloud. *The period marks the point where you drop your voice and pause.* For instance, if you read our example aloud, it will sound about like this:

I never read any play that was so   Besides Shakespeare's
                                                                silly.
Hamlet, I have read only a few   Written as a novel, the
                                                           plays.
book might have been
                                       better.

Of course, some of you will say now that you *don't* drop your voices in these places. That's quite possible. Not everybody speaks alike. But *as a rule*, it's true that at the end of a sentence you drop your voice and that's where you should put a period in writing.

Run-On Sentences

The trouble is that some people, after some types of sentences, drop their voices a *little*. Then, when it comes to writing, they feel that a period isn't quite called for and put in a comma instead. They write what's called "run-on" sentences. Here's an example:

> I was thinking about what Dad had told me, before I knew it the bus had passed our corner.

You may feel that this sounds good when you read it. But that's not the answer. A reader who reads it for the first time, will probably read

> I was thinking about what Dad had told me, before I knew . . .

and expect the sentence to end with

> . . . what was going to happen later.

or something of the kind. After finding out that the word before starts a new sentence, he will have to go back and read it again in the right way. By inserting a comma, you have told him to step on the brake instead of stopping and shifting gears. The only way to save your reader this extra work is to write the two sentences like this:

> I was thinking about what Dad had told me. Before I knew it, the bus had passed our corner.

So stick to the rule: *Never use a comma instead of a period.*

Sentence Fragments

Some people have just the opposite trouble with periods. They drop their voices at a point where they really shouldn't, and put a period where it doesn't belong. For instance, do you make the mistake of putting a period after this kind of phrase at the end of a letter?

> Hoping to hear from you.

That's wrong. It's a "sentence fragment." You haven't yet answered the question: What is happening while you are *hoping to hear* from him or her? Maybe all that's happening is that you are *cordially* his or hers; but even so, you can't separate the two thoughts by a period. You'll have to write it like this:

> Hoping to hear from you, I am
> > Cordially yours,
> > > Ebenezer

The best advice we can give you is to think of a phrase that is built the same way but uses different words, like:

> Stopping to look at you.

We are sure you can see that the period here isn't right. **Stopping to look at you**—and then what? This needs a comma and a main clause that will complete the thought. Let's do it:

> Stopping to look at you, I recognized you at once.

What all this comes down to, of course, is that periods belong at the end of sentences. A sentence must have a subject and a predicate—a person or thing it is about, and something that is said about this person or thing. **Stopping to look at you** has no subject; it doesn't say *who* is stopping. Therefore it is no sentence and you can't put a period after it. On the other hand, in our *run-on* example, the words **I was thinking about what Dad had told me** have a subject (**I**) and a predicate (**was thinking . . .**); they are a complete thought, a sentence. Therefore, the comma is wrong and the period is right.

Semicolons

What about other punctuation marks? you may ask. If the comma is a slow-down signal and the period a stop sign, what are semicolons and colons? The answer is simple: They are stop signs, too, and are used *instead of* periods for certain purposes. The period, you see, is a "full stop." It says: "Here one idea ends and another one starts." The semicolon is a shorter stop. It says: "Here one idea ends and another one starts *that has something to do with it.*"

Here's an example to show what difference a semicolon can make:

Margaret has many friends. Her parents are very rich.

In this example, with a period between the two sentences, there is nothing to show whether the two ideas are connected with each other. Now look at it with a semicolon:

Margaret has many friends; her parents are very rich.

You see what the semicolon does? It says that there is a connection between Margaret's many friends and the fact that her parents are very rich. It has turned a simple statement into a nasty remark.

In other words, a semicolon points up the connection between two ideas without the use of a single extra word. It's a very fine tool of writing if you know how to use it; it helps the reader to read "between the lines."

Here are a few more examples:

Separated by period:	*Tied together by semicolon:*
Bob is going to go to college. He just won a scholarship.	Bob is going to go to college; he just won a scholarship.
It took us an hour to get there. We have a 1931 Ford.	It took us an hour to get there; we have a 1931 Ford.
I like Janet. She doesn't use lipstick.	I like Janet; she doesn't use lipstick.

As you see, in each of these examples, the semicolon shows the connection between two ideas. Without the semicolon, the two sentences just stand by themselves and it is up to the reader to draw his own conclusions.

The Colon

The colon is a stop and a curtain-raiser. It points toward something that follows. It says: "There is something missing in this sentence and here it comes." It is mainly used for two purposes: to introduce direct quotations (as in the previous sentence) and to introduce listings of two or more things (as in this one).

To sum up punctuation would be unnecessary if we didn't write for readers without the use of voice and gestures we must use punctuation to make our written ideas clear.

We mean, of course:

To sum up, punctuation would be unnecessary if we didn't write for *readers*. Without the use of voice and gestures, we must use punctuation to make our written ideas clear. (See what punctuation does?)

---

1. Put commas between items in a series.
2. Put commas where you want the reader to slow down.
   Be sure to put commas after introductory phrases and clauses.
3. Put two commas around parenthetical expressions, appositives, and words of direct address when they come in the middle of a sentence.
4. Put two commas around non-restrictive relative clauses.
   Do not put commas around restrictive relative clauses.
   Start non-restrictive clauses about things with *which*, restrictive clauses with *that*.
5. Don't write run-on sentences.
6. Don't write sentence fragments.
7. Don't forget to use semicolons to tie your ideas together.

Exercise 1. Copy the following sentences, labeling each sentence as follows:

> 0. for a sentence fragment
> 1. for a complete sentence
> 2. for a run-on sentence

1. Stop!
2. One evening, when I was all alone in the house and a fierce storm was raging outside.
3. It was the third week in April, and the forsythias were in bloom.
4. It was the third week in April, the forsythias were in bloom.
5. The bell rang.

6. Although he had only five cents in his pocket.
7. A little kitten that she had found in an alley.
8. He paused a moment, the mushrooms had a suspicious odor.
9. Where is he, what is he doing?
10. In Hunter, New York, there is an unusually shaped mountain, it is called the Colonel's Chair.
11. Listening at the top of the stairs, Ethel heard her father talking to the stranger in loud, argumentative tones and demanding to know who he was, where he had come from, and how he had heard about the ruby.
12. Hurry, it's late.
13. So that government of the people, by the people, and for the people shall not perish from the earth.
14. He is trampling out the vintage where the grapes of wrath are stored.
15. Therefore, do not send to know for whom the bell tolls, it tolls for thee.
16. She walked out onto the stage, her face was white.
17. I am no more lonely than the Mill Brook or a weathercock or the north star or the south wind or an April shower or a January thaw or the first spider in a new house.

Exercise 2. Copy the following sentences, inserting commas where necessary.

Give your reason for putting in commas.

1. As the baker chewed every eye in the room watched him.
2. He cried out for the nurse had not heard him ringing the bell.
3. The girls fed the hogs and chickens and the boys milked the cows.
4. While the baby was eating Mother told him a story.
5. With no friends there to help Jim turned and ran.
6. In his home in his office in the street the doctor always heard the strange noise.
7. We shall have to pay for this piece of metal is essential to the success of our plan.
8. As soon as the fish started nibbling Helen's toes curled with excitement.
9. A few weeks before the opera season had started.
10. "Look at this, you miserable baker!" roared the king furiously pointing at the fly.
11. When we had finished eating my uncle rose to his feet.
12. On leaving the child cried.
13. She bathed her doll and her brother played with his electric trains.
14. Take my bracelet; if you wear Ruth's people will suspect that you have stolen it.
15. When I came in the door shut behind me.

16. John on the other hand found it difficult to read.
17. Jack our president will not be present because he is ill.
18. Our Allies will no doubt understand why we acted as we did.
19. Come here Mother and see what I've done.
20. For breakfast we had ham eggs rolls and coffee.

Exercise 3. Copy the following sentences, labeling each italicized clause as *restrictive* or *non-restrictive*. Insert commas where they belong.

1. A climate *that is too damp* is not very healthful.
2. All books *that deal with science* are on the top shelf.
3. These three men *who worked ten hours a day for the last week* have solved your problem.
4. Alexander Hamilton *who was born in the West Indies* was not eligible for the Presidency.
5. The Winston Churchill *who wrote The Crisis and The Crossing* is not the same Winston Churchill *who was Prime Minister of England during World War II.*
6. Stephen Crane *who wrote The Red Badge of Courage* had never been to war.
7. The climate here *which is very damp* is not recommended for sufferers from sinus trouble.
8. Jim who was *hiding in the apple barrel* overheard the pirates' plans.
9. Be careful not to drink any water *that is polluted.*
10. My aunt will not wear a dress *that costs more than thirty dollars.*

11 HOW TO GET THE MOST OUT OF WORDS

A few chapters back we told you about how to save words. We showed you how you can use little syllables like ing or able to make one word out of four or five or six. We told you how to *build* time-saving words.

But that trick works only up to a certain point. In our language you can use the syllable able to build a word readable that means easy to read, but you can't write doable for something that's easy to do. You can't do it because English *already has* a different word that means the same thing, namely, feasible. And whenever there is a word in the language for a certain idea, you have to use *that* word and not one that you might want to make up yourself.

The reason for this is that English has taken over and adapted thousands and thousands of words from Latin, Greek, French, and a dozen other languages. So if you want to save words and use a single word instead of a phrase or clause, the chances are that millions of old Romans, Greeks, and Frenchmen hit upon the same idea before you and there is a ready-made word for it in English.

Why Increase Your Vocabulary?

And that's where that old question of vocabulary building comes in. Probably you have a notion that you could write beautifully if you only had a large enough vocabulary—that writing would be easy if you only knew the meaning of all those big words. We don't think so; we think that in writing, a great many things are more important than vocabulary. But a large vocabulary does help. Without it, you will forever use six words instead of one.

For instance, suppose you want to write: "The captain was a big man who was easy to talk to." That's a good clear sentence. There's nothing wrong with it except that you might want to say the same thing in fewer words. How can you do that? You can't do it by building a word with ing or able or some other syllable; there's no such thing as an easy-to-

119

talk-to-ing man or an easy-to-talk-to-able man. So you can
save words only if you know a ready-made word that means
easy to talk to. If your vocabulary is large enough, you *will*
know such a word, and you will write: "The captain was a
big, *affable* man."

Or let's take another example. How can you shorten this
sentence: "He stood and watched me with his hands on his
hips and his elbows turned outwards." Naturally, there is
nothing you can do unless you know a word for this posture.
If you do, you can save seven words and write: "He stood
and watched me with his arms *akimbo*."

Now we don't mean to say that affable and akimbo are
particularly fine or beautiful words. But they are extraordi-
narily useful. If you know enough such words, you can pack
anything you write brimful of meaning.

And that brings us back to vocabulary building. How do
you go about learning all these thousands and thousands of
useful words? How can you build up your vocabulary so that
you will have affable and akimbo on tap whenever you need
them?

The Best Way

Let us tell you what we think is the best way. Of course,
you can build up your vocabulary in many different ways,
and we don't mean to say that other ways won't help you.
But we think that these five steps will help you most:

Step One: Read. You can't build a vocabulary without
reading. You can't make friends if you never meet anybody,
but stay at home by yourself all the time. In the same way,
you can't build up a vocabulary if you never meet any new
words. And to meet them, you must read. The more you read,
the better. A book a week is good, a book every other day is
better, a book a day is still better. There is no upper limit.
Keep on reading. Keep on meeting unfamiliar words on
printed pages. Keep on getting acquainted with the faces
of words. *Read.*

Step Two: Look up unfamiliar words in the dictionary. Read
carefully *everything* the dictionary says about the word. Study
the way the word is pronounced, where it comes from, what it
means, and what other words are connected with it. *Be sure
you find the meaning that fits exactly into the sentence in
which you found the word.* Remember that meaning. Remember the way it was used in the sentence. Compare the word

with the words you would have used if *you* had written the sentence.

For instance, suppose you are looking up the word *genial*, which you found in the following sentence: "Doris was a genial hostess." In your dictionary you find this:

gen·ial[1] (jēn′yəl), *adj.* **1.** sympathetically cheerful; cordial: *a genial disposition, a genial host.* **2.** enlivening; supporting life; pleasantly warm, or mild. **3.** *Rare.* characterized by genius. [t. L: s. *geniālis* festive, jovial, pleasant, lit., pertaining to generation or to marriage] **—gen′ial·ly,** *adv.* **—gen′ial·ness,** *n.* **—Syn. 1.** friendly, hearty, pleasant, agreeable. **—Ant. 1.** sullen.

This tells you that the word **genial** has three meanings; but since the dictionary says that the third meaning is rare, you don't have to bother with that one and study only the first two. You read carefully the first definition ("sympathetically cheerful; cordial") and find that it is clearly the one you are looking for: it even gives "a genial host" as an example. But the second meaning ("enlivening; supporting life; pleasantly warm, or mild") also tells you much about the word and helps you to understand more fully the first meaning. The synonyms (similar words) and the antonym (word opposite in meaning) round out the picture: a *genial* hostess is "friendly, hearty, pleasant, agreeable" and *everything but* "sullen." After you have read all the dictionary says about the word, you know the *feeling* of the word and the exact shade of meaning it carries with it.

Now you go back to the sentence where you found the word. You read it over: "Doris was a genial hostess." Now you know exactly what this means. Try to remember Doris in that sentence. Next time you want to describe some hostess like her, **genial** may be just the right word.

And remember: Looking a word up in the dictionary won't get you anywhere if you don't remember what you found. If you really want to do something about your vocabulary, keep a notebook and put down the word you didn't understand, the sentence in which you found it, and everything in the dictionary that will help you remember what the word means.

Step Three: Say the word. Get used to the way it is pronounced. The pronunciation is printed right after the word in the dictionary. If you are not familiar with the pronunciation symbols, look at the explanation at the bottom of the page. (Sometimes the dictionary shows two pronunciations for a word; that means you have a choice, but the one printed first is preferred. Stick to that one.) Pronounce the word the way the dictionary says you should, and say it aloud often enough to be sure you won't stumble over it when you use it the first time.

Step Four: Use the word. Reading, looking up, and pronouncing is not enough. To add a word to your vocabulary, you have to use it. Next time you get a chance to work it into a conversation, do it. This is the most important step: *Get the word off in speaking as if it had always been yours.* Never mind whether your friends will think you are showing off. They won't. Either they know the word anyway, or they will just see that you know something they don't know. And don't worry about not using the word correctly. If you use the word in just about the same way it was used where you first saw it, there is little danger of that. And even if you do say something like "a genial party," there's no great harm done. It isn't quite right, because genial is ordinarily used only for people, but after a while you will get straightened out on that point by your reading, and in the meanwhile genial will have become part of your vocabulary.

Step Five: Keep in touch with your vocabulary. Remember, knowing words is like knowing people. If you don't keep in touch with them, you lose them. After a while, you may even forget their names. So keep up with your latest word acquaintances. Watch out for them in what you read, look them up again in the dictionary if necessary, keep saying them and using them. This is easy. In fact, you will find that the words you have just added to your vocabulary will keep cropping up in your reading and your speech. Never mind that; just keep on using them and watch your vocabulary grow.

Maybe you wonder why, in a book on writing, we are teaching you how to build a *speaking* vocabulary. But we are doing that on purpose. If you really want to add a word to your writing vocabulary, there's no better way than to add it to your speaking vocabulary first. A word isn't really yours until you have *said* it. Then, when it comes naturally in your speech, it will slip into your writing naturally too. Often you won't even notice that you have used a new word.

Fun With Words

And that's all we have to say about vocabulary building—except for one thing: We think vocabulary building is fun. It's fun to find out where words come from and what makes them tick, and it's even more fun to take a new word and use it to say exactly what you *mean* to say. For example, do you know the word tantalize? It means "torment or tease by keeping something desired in sight but out of reach, or by holding out hopes that are repeatedly disappointed." That's a lot of meaning packed into one word, isn't it? And there's a whole legend behind the word, about the Greek king Tantalus who was punished terribly for his sins. He had to stand up to his chin in water, under branches laden with fruit, but whenever he tried to drink or eat, the water or fruit went out of reach. Tantalize is a useful and picturesque word. When you say that the display behind the drugstore counter is tantalizing, you are really saying *something!* Or do you know the word meander? Doesn't it sound beautiful? It means "wander aimlessly, following a winding course"—like the winding river Meander in Asia. Instead of merely *walking* through the park, try *meandering* sometime. Well, your dictionary is full of words like that. And they are worth knowing.

Word Flavors

Most new words in your vocabulary will be word-savers. But many of them will do even more: They will make it possible for you to say two things at the same time. You think that can't be done? Let us give you an example:

> When it was time for lunch, Johnny devoured two peanut-butter sandwiches.

You see what the word devoured does here? First of all, it says that Johnny *ate* the two sandwiches; that's what the sentence is about. But in the second place, the word devoured shows also *how* Johnny ate those sandwiches. It tells you that he ate them *fast* and *hungrily*. So it does say two things at the same time: it gives you the main meaning plus something else.

How is it possible that a word can mean two things at once? The explanation is simple: The word has been used so often together with certain other words that it has taken on some of their flavor. For instance, to devour has been used so often in speaking and writing about animals that by now it means not only *eating*, but *eating like an animal*. And so with thousands of other words; they have been used so often in a certain way that they carry with them all sorts of *overtones*—things that are not said but understood by anyone who knows something about that word.

This is why vocabulary building is only the first step in getting the most out of words. Once you have a large enough vocabulary so that you can pick and choose your words, it's even more important to know the *flavor* of each word. Then you can use words that not only save half a dozen others in the sentence but add another, extra meaning to it.

Suppose, for instance, you have written this sentence: "After the party, Tony stayed for another half hour." That's the shortest way to put it, to be sure, but there is no particular flavor about the word stayed; it doesn't mean anything else but that Tony was still there when the other guests had gone. But maybe you want to stress that everybody else had left? How about "After the party, Tony *remained* for another half hour"? Or do you want to drop a hint that he should have gone home too, but didn't? Here's how you can do that: "After the party, Tony *tarried* for another half hour." Or did Tony stay behind on purpose? Would it be true to say that "after the party, Tony *lingered* for another half hour"?

So you see that you can make many of your words do double duty. If you know the right words, you can express your thoughts and at the same time, *between the lines*, tell the reader a little more. There's no magic about this; in fact, you are doing this sort of thing all the time without knowing it. But you can try to do more and more of it and to tell your reader with each word as much as you possibly can.

A Taste for Words

How do you learn about all these different word flavors? Exactly the same way you learn about words. You pick them up in your reading, look them up, use them, and keep on using them. The only difference is that in looking for *word flavors*, you have to find the difference in meaning between *several* words instead of the meaning of just *one* word. For this you need a *dictionary of synonyms* rather than an ordinary dictionary. Let's say, for instance, you have come across the word **amble** in your reading, in a sentence, "I looked out and saw Uncle Geoffrey ambling toward our house." You know that ambling means some kind of leisurely walk, but you don't know *exactly* its flavor and that's why you have never used it in your speaking or writing. To learn the exact flavor of ambling, you now look it up in a dictionary of synonyms. You find that it is discussed together with the words saunter and stroll:

> saunter. Saunter, stroll, amble agree in meaning to walk slowly and more or less aimlessly, especially in the open air. Saunter suggests a leisurely pace and an idle and carefree mind; as, "*sauntering* about the streets, loitering in a coffeehouse" (*Fielding*). Stroll differs from *saunter* chiefly in its implications of an objective, such as sight-seeing, exercise, or the like, pursued without haste and with wandering from one place to another. "Then we *strolled* For half the day thro' stately theatres" (*Tennyson*). "The notables of the town . . . *stroll* past with the dignity of Roman senators" (*A. Huxley*). Amble occasionally conveys the same implications as *saunter* or, sometimes, *stroll*, but it far more often suggests merely an easy, effortless gait comparable to that of an ambling horse. In older use, it usually was applied to dancing, especially to formal step dancing; as, "you jig, you *amble*, and you lisp" (*Shak.*); in modern English, it sometimes connotes slow mincing steps and at other times, a casual, jaunty gait.

By permission. From Webster's Dictionary of Synonyms, copyright, 1942, by G. & C. Merriam Co.

To remember the flavor of ambling from here on, you do exactly what we told you to do in vocabulary building. You go back to the sentence where you found the word, make notes about that sentence and about what you found in the dictionary of synonyms, and make an effort to use the word with its exact flavor in speaking. And pretty soon, you will distinguish between amble, saunter, and stroll without giving it a second thought.

Once you have a good stock of synonyms, be sure to use them correctly. Particularly, don't use a synonym just because you are afraid to repeat the same word. Don't write:

I noticed a book with a blue cover and took the volume from the shelf. It was a work I had read before.

That's artificial and stilted. There is nothing wrong with repeating the word **book**, which fits exactly, or using the pronoun it—like this:

> I noticed a book with a blue cover and took it from the shelf. It was a book I had read before.

In other words, if you have used a word which you think was the right word, don't shy away from using it again. Don't use a different word just because it's different. For instance, suppose you have written:

> I looked at my watch and said: "It's half past nine."
> Jim looked at his watch and said: "Your watch is slow; it's 9:35."

It doesn't matter that you have used **looked** and **said** twice, since that's what you meant and that's all the reader needs to understand your meaning. It would again have been artificial and stilted to write something like this:

> I looked at my watch and said: "It's half past nine."
> Jim gazed at his watch and uttered: "Your watch is slow; it's 9:35."

This sort of thing just shows that you thought you had to avoid repetition at any price; so you used synonyms regardless of their flavor. If you had looked up **gaze** in a dictionary of synonyms, you would have found that it means a long, admiring look; and **uttering** means voicing a cry or a sigh rather than words. These words just aren't appropriate to describe a quick look at a watch and a simple statement about the time of day. So, if you *had* to use synonyms, it might have been a good idea to make sure of the right word flavors first and write:

> I looked at my watch and said: "It's half past nine."
> Jim glanced at his watch and remarked: "Your watch is slow; it's 9:35."

In short, don't be afraid of repeating a word; and if you do use another one, be sure it has the right flavor. Don't just hunt for synonyms; and *never, never* pick a synonym at random from a book of synonyms (like *Roget's Thesaurus*) where words with different flavors are listed but not explained.

Use words that fit your thoughts exactly.
To build up your vocabulary,
1. read;
2. look up in the dictionary all words you don't know;
3. say those words;
4. use those words; and
5. keep using them.
To learn the flavors of words,
1. read;
2. look up in a dictionary of synonyms all words whose flavor you don't know;
3. say those words;
4. use those words; and
5. keep using them.
Never use synonyms at random.

Exercise 1. Read the following selection by E. V. Lucas, from *Twixt the Eagle and the Dove.* Look up in the dictionary the meaning of the words in black type. Some of these words have more than one meaning. Select the meaning that fits the words as they are used in these sentences in the paragraph. This is the way to build your vocabulary through your reading.

On Finding Things

Finding things is at once so rare and pure a joy that to **trifle** with it is peculiarly heartless. Yet there are people so **wantonly** in need of **sport** as to do so. Everyone knows of the purse laid on the path or pavement beside a fence, which, as the excited passer-by stoops to pick it up, is twitched through the **palings** by its **adherent** string. There is also the coin attached to a string which can be dropped in the street and instantly pulled up again, setting every eye at a pavement **scrutiny**. Could there be lower tricks? I fear so, because some years ago, in the great days of a **rendezvous** of **Bohemians** in the Strand known as the Marble Halls, a wicked **wag** (I have been told) once nailed a bad but **plausible** sovereign to the floor and waited for events. In the case of the purse and string the **butts** are few and far between and there is usually only a small audience to rejoice in their **discomfiture**, but the denouement of the cruel comedy of which **acquisitiveness** and cunning were the warp and woof at the Marble Halls was only too bitterly public. I am told, such is human resourcefulness in **guile**, that very few of those who saw the coin and marked it down as their own went for it right away, because had they done so the action might have been noticed and the **booty** claimed. Instead, the discoverer would look swiftly and **stealthily** round, and then gradually and with every **affectation** of **nonchalance** (which to those in the secret, watching from the corners of their wicked eyes, was so funny as to be an agony) he would get nearer and nearer until he was able at last to place one foot on it. This accomplished, he would relax into something like real naturalness and, practically certain of his prey, take things easily for a moment or so. Often, I am told, the poor dupe would, at this point, whistle the latest tune. Even now, however, he dared not abandon **subterfuge**, or his prize, were he seen to pick it up, might have to be surrendered or shared; so the next move was to drop his handkerchief, the idea being to pick up both it and the *sovereign* together. Such explosions of laughter as followed his failure to do so can (I am informed) rarely have been heard.

Exercise 2. For each expression in parentheses in the following paragraphs by Henry David Thoreau, find the correct word among those listed below. Then rewrite the paragraph, substituting the words for the parenthetical expressions.

From *A Plea for Captain John Brown*

No man has appeared in America, as yet, who loved his fellow man so well and treated him so tenderly. He lived for him. He took up his life and he laid it down for him. What sort of violence is that which is encouraged, not by soldiers, but by peaceable citizens, not so much by (persons not of the clergy) as by ministers of the (first four books of the New Testament), not so much by the fighting (religious denominations) as by the Quakers, and not so much by Quaker men as by Quaker women?

This event advertises me that there is such a fact as death—the possibility of a man's dying. It seems as if no man had ever died in America before, for in order to die you must first have lived. I don't believe in the (coaches for carrying the dead) and (covered coffins) and funerals that they have had. There was no death in the case, because there had been no life. . . . No temple's veil was (torn asunder), only a hole dug somewhere. Let the dead bury their dead. . . . I hear a good many pretend that they are going to die; or that they have died, for aught I know. Nonsense! I'll defy them to do it. They haven't got life enough in them. They'll (become liquid) like (molds or toadstools) and keep a hundred (persons who speak in praise of others) mopping the spot where they left off. Only half a dozen or so have died since the world began. Do you think that you are going to die, sir? No! there's no hope for you. You haven't got your lesson yet. You've got to stay after school. We make a needless (fuss) about (involving the loss of life) punishment—taking lives, when there is no life to take. *Memento mori!*[1] We don't understand that (solemnly impressive and noble) sentence which some (person of eminence) got sculptured on his gravestone once. We've (explained the meaning of) it in a (cring-

[1] Remember that you must die!

ng, abject, and debased) and (fretfully complaining) sense; we've
wholly forgotten how to die.

1. palls	7. laymen	13. sects
2. worthy	8. hearses	14. capital
3. sublime	9. rent	15. deliquesce
4. ado	10. eulogists	16. sniveling
5. fungi	11. sloughed off	17. Gospel
6. interpreted	12. groveling	

Exercise 3. In the following groups choose the word from the left
column that fits each description in the right column.

Ways of talking:

1. cajole
2. expostulate
3. harangue
4. quibble
5. whine
6. rant
7. babble
8. stammer
9. mumble
10. expatiate
11. gibber

a. to deliver a noisy oration
b. to speak falteringly and hesitantly
c. to bluster vehemently
d. to evade the truth or the point at issue by arguing over trifles
e. to speak indistinctly
f. to express oneself at considerable length
g. to reason earnestly with someone in an attempt to have him correct his faults or turn from the course he is taking
h. to talk coaxingly and flatteringly
i. to complain in a childish, fretful manner and in a nasal tone
j. to chatter continuously in a child-ish or foolish way
k. to talk rapidly, incoherently, or nonsensically

Policies:

1. conservative
2. utopian
3. reactionary
4. radical
5. liberal

a. favoring a return to former conditions; opposed to social advancement
b. favoring progress and measures extending democracy and promoting social welfare
c. hoping for ideal perfection, impossible of attainment
d. tending to favor things as they are and to oppose change
e. favoring extreme and rapid change or reform; revolutionary

Describing literary style:

1. bombastic
2. colloquial
3. rococo
4. pithy
5. precious
6. hackneyed
7. pedestrian
8. lucid
9. archaic
10. punning
11. vivid
12. erudite
13. obscure

a. clear
b. difficult to understand, not clear
c. affected and artificial
d. antiquated, belonging to a bygone age; using words no longer in common use
e. so elaborate and flowery as to be in bad taste
f. producing pictures in the mind
g. pompous; using high-sounding language
h. trite, commonplace, lacking in originality
i. informal, conversational
j. slow-moving, dull, lacking in imagination
k. brief and full of meaning; saying much in a few words
l. playing on words; using words similar in sound but different in meaning
m. scholarly and learned

Describing people:

1. astute
2. impecunious
3. articulate
4. pompous
5. obsequious
6. prim
7. ruthless
8. visionary
9. parsimonious
10. ebullient

a. pitiless, cruel
b. enthusiastic, of a bubbling disposition
c. self-important and pretentious
d. extremely neat and exact
e. able to express oneself clearly and fluently
f. stingy
g. always without money
h. fawning and servile
i. not practical or realistic
j. keen, acute, cunning

Exercise 4. One of the tests of an effective vocabulary is the ability to use synonyms with a discriminating sense of differences in shades of meaning. In each of the following, select the appropriate synonym to complete the sentence:

1. aromatic, fragrant, perfumed, redolent
   a. He gazed at the classroom for the last time, a room _____ with memories of his youth.
   b. The _____ odor of freshly brewed coffee greeted my nostrils as I descended the stairs.

c. As I sat next to her in the theater, her strongly _____ hair began to give me a headache.

d. The _____ honeysuckle blossoms filled the night air with sweetness.

insisted, persisted, persevered, urged

a. He _____ that bigotry is immoral, irreligious, and un-American.

b. We _____ that he treat his unfortunate father more generously.

c. Though he tried to convince her how unjust she was, she _____ in believing him guilty.

d. Despite the difficulty of the work, he _____ until he had completed the assignment.

insurrection, mutiny, revolution, sedition

a. Wordsworth inaugurated a _____ in literary taste.

b. Several times these oppressed slaves have risen in _____ against their tyrannical masters.

c. Can we accuse a man of _____ simply because he holds unpopular opinions?

d. Captain Bligh harshly suppressed the _____ of his sailors.

4. abate, decrease, diminish, dwindle

a. Unless he shows more prudence, his estate will _____ to nothing in a few months.

b. If the storm does not _____, we shall have to spend the night in this cabin.

c. Your painful memories will gradually _____ if you occupy yourself with other interests.

d. As she grew better, the doctor instructed her to _____ her daily dose of the medicine.

5. avaricious, economical, frugal, niggardly, thrifty

a. The _____ youngster found a job as a delivery boy and had soon saved enough to purchase the equipment.

b. We had a _____ meal of black bread and potato peelings.

c. How can we build a playground with such a _____ allotment of funds?

d. His _____ management of the factory has greatly increased our profits.

e. The _____ guide looked greedily at the bags of gold on the floor.

6. accomplice, ally, associate, colleague, partner

a. My accountant is not a personal friend of mine, merely a business _____.

b. Our love deepened in intensity until that fateful night when she was my _____ in a bridge game at the Pellers'.

c. The thief was caught, but his _____ escaped.

d. Japan was our _____ in World War I, but our enemy in World War II.

e. My English professor introduced me to a _____ of his, young instructor of physics at the university.

7. color, hue, shade, tinge
   a. I should prefer a lighter _____ of green for the walls for th dining room.
   b. Blue is my favorite _____.
   c. As she drank the tea, a slight _____ of pink appeared in he pale cheeks.
   d. The wings of this butterfly are a metallic green of a bluis _____.

We were going fifty miles an hour when suddenly I saw an animal crossing the road. Almost at the same time Marion cried, "Watch out for the dog!" and Walter stepped on the brake. When the car stopped, we discovered we had missed a fine old St. Bernard by just a few inches.

Did you notice something interesting about the words used in this paragraph? Did you notice that the same creature is referred to three times—once as an animal, once as a dog, and once as a St. Bernard? What do you think is the reason for this?

The explanation is simple as soon as you realize that the story is told by someone sitting in a car that was moving *toward* the St. Bernard. At first, the St. Bernard is just *something crossing the road*—something that from the distance looks like an animal. It may be a horse, a calf, a dog: the distance is still too great to see what kind of animal it is. But immediately afterwards, Marion cries out, "Watch out for the dog!" She has seen the animal too; but by the time she cries out, she is near enough so she can tell it's a dog. Finally, when the car has stopped a few inches from the dog, everybody can see what kind of dog it is: it's a *St. Bernard.*

Faraway and Close-up Words

So the words we use tell something not only about the things we are talking about but also about the distance between us and those things. In almost anything we say or write, we have a choice between *faraway* words, *nearer* words, and *close-up* words. In our St. Bernard example, it works out like this:

faraway	animal (horse? calf? dog? cat?)
nearer	dog (collie? bull dog? St. Bernard? police dog?)
close-up	St. Bernard

In other words, for everything there is a word that means just *that thing*, and another word that means *that thing* and

133

a number of other things of the same kind, and another word
that means *still more things of the same kind,* and so on and
on like the address someone once wrote on an envelope:

> Mr. John Smith
>   223 Maple Street
>   Chicago
>   Illinois
>   U.S.A.
>   Western Hemisphere
>   The Earth
>   The Universe

Of course, nobody addresses a letter like that. We don't
bother the post office with unnecessary generalities. We realize that a vague expression like "Western Hemisphere"
won't help the mailman a bit.

Words to Get Close

But in ordinary writing, we make that kind of mistake all
the time. We overuse the in-between and the faraway words.
Sometimes we use them because we think they are bigger
and therefore better, but more often simply because we are
too lazy to think of the proper close-up word. So the reader,
naturally, never gets a clear picture of what we are talking
about. Instead of letting him look over our shoulder, we hand
him the wrong end of a telescope. This is the kind of thing
we write:

> The next corner is that of a tree-lined street that goes down
> to the river. Usually it is noisy with traffic, but early in the
> morning it is quiet. I often walk down there to a point where
> I can see the river.

But what the reader needs is a close-up picture like this:

> Right next to the big old Methodist Church is the corner of
> Main and Lafayette Streets. Lafayette Street is a steep, cobble-
> stoned street that winds its way down to the Hudson between
> one-hundred-year-old elms and pleasantly neglected, rambling
> framehouses. During the day it clatters with delivery trucks
> and taxicabs, but at 7 a.m. it is sleepy and silent. That's the
> time of day when I like to stroll downhill. My goal is always
> the same: the second bend in the road where suddenly the
> view opens and the wide, wide river valley stretches in the
> morning sun.

We don't mean to say that everything you write should be cluttered up with detailed description. There can be too much of it in the wrong places. But ordinarily, every writer should make an effort to steer away from vague, general words and give the reader exact word pictures. There's no reason why we should write

> We have had some crazy weather here lately.

when we might as well tell the reader

> Yesterday it was freezing cold and pouring all day long. Today there hasn't been a cloud in the sky and the thermometer has hit 80.

And why write

> When I came into the room, he was reading.

if we have a chance to be more specific—like this:

> When I came into the room, he was lying on the floor, flat on his stomach, utterly absorbed in **The Original Scotland Yard Magazine.**

The principle is easy to understand: The right word is the word that will give the reader the idea—the word that is neither too wide nor too narrow, but just right. The way to find that word is simply to describe what you have in mind— not vaguely, but exactly. If it's important for the reader to know that the house you are talking about has green shutters, then you can't expect him to *see* those green shutters after reading something about "a typical colonial house." If you want the reader to get a close-up view, you have to use close-up words.

Ideas Into Pictures

So far, we have talked about the right words to use in *describing* things. We have told you that in writing you are likely to use words that are too far away and that you should always try to find words that give a close-up picture. But what about words that deal strictly with thoughts—words that don't give the reader any picture at all? What about words like independence, success, obstacle, courtesy, or rumor?

It's true that such words are so general and abstract that there doesn't seem to be any way of getting closer to the idea. But that's only so at first sight; it only looks that way when you take those words *by themselves* and try to find more colorful and picturesque expressions. As soon as you use them in actual sentences in your writing, you will find that there is some way of giving the reader a better grip on the idea. Here are some examples:

Faraway:	*Close-up:*
I like independence in my work.	I like having no boss over me.
He had great success in his business.	He reached the top of the ladder in his business.
The fact that he did not know the language was a great obstacle.	The fact that he did not know the language was a great stumbling block.
Customers are served with courtesy.	Customers are served with a smile.
There have been rumors that she is engaged.	It's been whispered around that she is engaged.

Actually, what have we done in these examples? We have taken the *abstract*, faraway word that might give the reader only a vague impression, and replaced it by something that will give him an exact picture—exactly as we did when we switched from the word animal to the word St. Bernard. The only difference is that here the close-up word does not naturally come to mind as soon as we take a good look at the thing we are talking about. We have to make an effort to find a more colorful expression for an abstract word.

How do we do this? There are various ways. We may think of the actual situation we are talking about (independence to me means that I have no boss). In other words, we illustrate a general idea by showing how it applies to a specific case. Or we may talk about some outward sign of the idea (a smile is a sign of courtesy) or something colorful that is *similar* to the idea (success is like reaching the top of a ladder, an obstacle is like a stumbling block, a rumor is like a whisper). In other words, we give the reader something to see or hear that will make him think our thoughts.

The last way—comparing an idea with another, similar one —is the most important. This is how most abstract, vague, general thoughts can be made lively, dramatic, and interesting. And this is how all writers and speakers have made readers read and listeners listen ever since language was invented. **Obstacles** have been called **stumbling blocks** and **rumors** have been called **whispers** for hundreds and thousands of years. In fact, you can hardly use the English language without making such comparisons all the time; so you had better make the most of that feature of our language and find the most forceful, lively comparisons for your abstract thoughts. Comparisons will always help in driving home your ideas; but if you use nothing but trite old stand-bys like **happy as a lark, sick as a dog,** or **dead as a doornail,** then you haven't done much to bring your ideas closer to your reader. The best way to write about any abstract or general idea is to think up *by yourself* a clear, concrete illustration or a vivid, dramatic comparison. If you write "The lecture was dull," you have simply stated an abstract idea and your reader will hardly notice what you have said. If you write "The lecture was as dull as dishwater," you have used a trite old comparison, but you have at least added some vividness to your thought. But if you write "The lecture went on and on like a dripping faucet," you have used a new word picture of your own that will make the reader's mind jump. Now he *really* knows what you are talking about.

To show the difference clearly, let's end this chapter with two paragraphs dealing with the same subject—one written in faraway words, the other in close-up words. Read them both and see how pale and weak the left-hand passage is, and how much more vivid and forceful is the one on the right:

Faraway words:	*Close-up words:*
The Declaration of Independence contains the sentence "All men are created equal." There has been much discussion as to how these words should be interpreted. Obviously, the physical features of human beings are not the same. It is now the accepted interpretation that the words refer to the place of people in the community and their rights as citizens. With these words, the Declaration of Inde-	When Thomas Jefferson wrote the draft of the Declaration of Independence, he put in the words "All men are created equal." Just what do these words mean? Volumes have been written about this question and it has been argued hotly for thousands of days and nights ever since 1776. Naturally, if you just look at people, you can see that they are not "created equal": they all have

pendence rejects the concepts of nobility and of social inequality.

different hands and eyes and noses. Some have dimples in their cheeks and some others have no earlobes whatever. So, surely, that isn't what Jefferson meant. Most textbooks and professors now say that "All men are created equal" means this: No matter who a man is, he is just as good as anybody else and shouldn't have to fight against a handicap all his life. Nobody should spend his life pounding against locked doors just because his parents couldn't afford to buy him fine clothes or send him to expensive schools. What Jefferson had in mind was the difference between the common people and the noblemen of his time. His idea was that it shouldn't matter whether you are born in a log cabin or in a castle.

Don't overuse faraway words; try to find close-up words for your ideas.

To put abstract ideas into close-up words, use concrete illustrations and comparisons.

Whenever you can, use illustrations and comparisons of your own.

Exercise 1. Rewrite each of the following sentences. Substitute more concrete, specific, picture-making words for the italicized words. You may have to rephrase the sentence or add a few ideas to the original—as in the following example.

Example: Women will soon take over many jobs formerly held by men.

Women will soon wield the welder's torch, sit in overalls at the tractor's wheel, and issue orders in crisp tones from behind the executive's desk.

1. The maid was in the kitchen *preparing* our meal.
2. The audience applauded the actor as he *came* out on the stage.
3. The county fair was full of many *interesting sights*.
4. The firemen *worked* as the *crowd watched the fire*.

5. The animal *approached me in a menacing way*.
6. She *came* down the stairs beautifully dressed, a *look of happiness on her face*.
7. It was a beautiful spring morning when we *got* into our car and *drove* off for the picnic.
8. A strangely dressed young man was *performing unusual antics* on the street corner. Evidently he was being initiated into a college fraternity.
9. All men, regardless of race or religion, are alike in being human beings; *they all have the same kinds of feelings, the same hopes, and the same fears*.
10. Her actions showed me that *she was in the habit of henpecking her husband*.

Exercise 2. List the words in the following passage that seem especially vivid because they are specific and concrete:

The cognomen of Crane was not inapplicable to his person. He was tall, but exceedingly lank, with narrow shoulders, long arms and legs, hands that dangled a mile out of his sleeves, feet that might have served for shovels, and his whole frame most loosely hung together. His head was small, and flat at the top, with huge ears, large green glassy eyes, and a long snip nose, so that it looked like a weathercock perched upon his spindle neck to tell which way the wind blew. To see him striding along the profile of a hill on a windy day, with his clothes bagging and fluttering about him, one might have mistaken him for the genius of Famine descending upon the earth or some scarecrow eloped from a cornfield.
—*The Legend of Sleepy Hollow* by Washington Irving

Exercise 3. The following sentences are statements of general truths. The language, as you will see, consists of vague, "faraway" words. The thought of each is clear, but the sentence is pale and colorless. In your own words, restate the ideas in each sentence using more colorful, more specific, more concrete words. You may have to use more than one sentence to achieve the effect of "close-up" writing.

Example: The influences and experiences of our youth determine the kind of adults we shall be. (Vague, faraway words.)
As the twig is bent, so the tree is inclined. (Concrete, specific, close-up words.)

1. The evil that men do lives after them.
2. Day follows day in monotonous sequence.
3. Experience is the best teacher.
4. Democracy guarantees and respects the rights of the individual.

5. Freedom of speech, freedom of assembly, and freedom of religion are among our most precious possessions.
6. The best way to prevent great troubles from overwhelming you is to take care of the little ones when they occur.
7. It is sometimes wiser to keep quiet than to speak your mind.
8. We all desire something more than the bare necessities of life.
9. If all the nations of the world do not learn to live harmoniously, then humanity will come to a tragic end.
10. Those who violate the laws of society will in the end have to answer to the forces of justice and order.

Exercise 4. Copy each of the following. Complete each, using a comparison that will make the subject more vivid and concrete to your reader. Try to think of an original and effective comparison.

Example: A road at night.
The road was a ribbon of moonlight.
1. She was in love. Her heart was fluttering like _____.
2. The large, staring, blue eyes of the stern old general were like _____.
3. She is as unresponsive as _____.
4. The nostrils of the angry woman pointed at me like _____.
5. Old age is like _____.
6. Frank Sinatra is like _____.
7. As he trudged through the snow storm, the snow falling on his face felt like _____.
8. It was the first day of spring. The air felt like _____.
9. The water dripping into the rain barrel sounded like _____.
10. She danced as gracefully as a _____.

Exercise 5. Copy the following sentences, using a verb that will express a comparison.

Example: Compare the employer to a bird of prey.
Mr. Jones *swooped down upon* the clerk who had just slipped a package of candy into his pocket.
1. Her eyes _____ with anger. (Compare her look to a fire.)
2. The sight of the puppy _____ my heart. (Compare the sight of the puppy to the effect of sun on ice.)
3. The office _____ with rumors. (Compare the office to a beehive.)
4. The poverty, the endless toil, the squalid surroundings _____ years from his life. (Compare these disadvantages to a knife.)
5. The male chorus _____ out on to the stage. (Compare the chorus to a herd of horses.)
6. He _____ with the problem until he solved it. (Compare what he did with the problem to two men engaged in a physical contest.)
7. "Good morning," she _____. (She sounds like a cricket.)

8. "What do you want, Smith? Another day off?" the boss
_____. (Some bosses do sound like dogs, don't they?)

9. "Everybody is always picking on me," Jenny _____. (What
animal makes this sound that we always associate with the
chronic complainer? What is the name of the sound?)

10. He took off his shoes, opened the door quietly, and _____
into the room. (He's really a very respectable fellow who
stayed out too late. But he doesn't act like one. Whom is he
acting like?)

Exercise 6. Starting with one of the following sentences, create a
picture for your reader. Use concrete, specific language, and vivid
comparisons wherever possible.

1. When Richard opened the door, I looked into one of the most
disorderly, untidy rooms I had ever seen.

2. By the time I arrived, the house was a mass of flame.

3. The average young man (no matter what he thinks) is just
not a dashing Romeo, and Mal Phillips is no exception to the
rule.

4. But at night the beach was a place of quiet enchantment.

5. As soon as the game ended, the crowd poured out onto the
field.

6. The entire city seemed crowded into Times Square on New
Year's Eve.

7. Their hearty appetites sharpened after a day's work in the
fields, the horde of farmhands burst into the fragrant kitchen.

8. Women's hats are generally odd, to say the least. But this one
was like nothing I had ever seen before or hope to see again.

9. If you've never seen a typical bobby-soxer, you have missed a
great experience. There are really no words to describe her, but
I'll try.

10. There on the hill it stood—the typical haunted house.

13 HOW TO MAKE IT FUN TO READ

Suppose you go to your library and take a book from the shelf. You want to know whether it will be fun to read. How can you find out? You know the answer: You have done it dozens of times. You look through the pages to see whether they are full of solid paragraphs or broken up by printed dialogue. Most people do the same thing; almost everybody secretly agrees with *Alice in Wonderland,* who said: "What is the use of a book without pictures or conversations?"

Since this is a book about writing, we are not going to say anything here about pictures. But we do want to say something about written conversations.

Say It With Quotes

In general, direct quotations are a good way to tell almost anything you might want to write about. If you are telling a story, and part of your story is what people said, then direct quotations are the only natural way to write—like this, for instance:

> "How about a picnic on Sunday?" Mother asked.
> Everybody agreed it was a good idea.
> "Let's!"
> "Fine!"
> "We haven't had a picnic for ages!"
> But Father was against it, as always.
> "Why crouch among the ants if you can eat comfortably at home?"
> There followed the usual discussion. Everybody knew, of course, what the outcome would be.
> Afterwards Mother smiled.
> "Dad just has to have his little struggle. He really likes to go on picnics . . ."

You can see that the story would be completely spoiled if you had written it without direct quotations, like this:

> Mother suggested a picnic on Sunday. Everybody agreed with enthusiasm, but Father was against it, as always. He

142

argued that he preferred to eat comfortably at home, and that he disliked ants. There followed the usual discussion, the outcome of which everybody knew in advance. Afterwards Mother remarked that Father habitually opposed such proposals, but that he really liked to go on picnics.

Direct quotations are useful not only for stories, but for almost everything else, too, as we said before. Suppose, for instance, you are writing about something that seems to be nothing but dry facts:

> The President of the United States is elected at a fixed date for a fixed period of four years. He remains in office even though a Congress may have a majority of members of the opposite party. In most other countries, for example in England, the system is entirely different. The British Prime Minister has to resign as soon as Parliament refuses to give the Government a "vote of confidence."

Can you turn this into written dialogue? Of course you can! Here it is:

> We usually take our system of elections for granted. But as soon as we talk to a foreigner, an Englishman for instance, we realize that other countries have other ways of doing things.
> "Why, of course, our President is elected on the first Tuesday after the first Monday in November," we would say to our British friend, "and then he stays in the White House for four years. If Congress doesn't agree with him about things, that's just too bad."
> "Well, I never!" our Englishman would answer. "But that doesn't seem to make sense, old boy! In our country, if there is a parliamentary vote of no confidence against the Government, the Prime Minister resigns and a new one comes in, naturally. Don't think we would take to that four-year system you have over here. Seems rather rigid, doesn't it?"
> "Come to think of it, it does. But, after all, at least we know what's what . . ."

And so on. It is an easy trick to put what you have to say into the mouths of people—and your reader will be grateful for the little added fun in reading.

Make It Sound Natural

You notice that we have tried to make our Englishman sound a little British. That's important. If you write conversa-

tion, it has to sound the way people talk—in particular, th
people you are writing about. If those people are describe
as rather formal in their speech, then there wouldn't be an
point in making them use slang words; and if you are writin
up a leisurely dialogue across the back fence, it shouldn
sound like a lecture. And, of course, don't mix different way
of talking. Don't write this kind of thing:

> "I cannot agree," the speaker continued, "to making eve
> the slightest concessions in this matter or to accept any con
> promise. I can only repeat what I have said many times be
> fore: Nuts!"

Similarly, be sure of a dialect or other special type c
speech before you use it. For instance, the English tal
slightly differently from the way we do. They say all rigl
rather than o.k. and they call the underground what we ca
the subway. So don't write:

> "O.K.," said the King, "let's take the subway."

Most people don't use enough direct quotations in the
writing simply because they are not quite sure how it
done. Of course they know that direct quotations are sup
posed to be put between quotation marks, but they hav
trouble in using punctuation marks and quotation marks *to
gether,* and so they shy away from the whole thing. Actually
the rules for writing dialogue are quite simple, and you ca
learn them once and for all in a few minutes. (You'll fin
them on pages 279-84 of this book.) And when you *do* knov
the rules, put what you have to say into direct quotation
whenever you have a chance.

The Conversational Touch

But even without using direct quotations, there is much yo
can do to loosen up your writing. After all, you can alway
write *as if you* were engaged in conversation with *you
reader.* There's no reason why an essay or a theme shoul
sound impersonal or stiff. The tone you use in writing can an
should be the one you would use in *talking* to your reade
How can you make your writing sound like conversation
The most important thing is to use the types of sentences use
in conversation. When we talk, we don't put all our thought
into subject-predicate sentences—one following the other i

pretty much the same pattern. We vary our sentences. We start one sentence with the subject, the next one with a prepositional phrase, the next one with an infinitive; then we ask a question or answer one with a word or two; then we interrupt ourselves with a casual side-remark; and so on. Our sentences don't follow a single pattern, but come out of our mouths in a variety of shapes and sizes. So to make our writing more conversational and more fun to read, we need *sentence variety*.

Vary Your Sentences

Sentence variety means mainly three things:

1. questions and answers;
2. short sentences sandwiched between longer ones; and
3. no sentence built exactly like the one before.

Suppose, for instance, you have written:

> There was a lively debate among the students. There was great enthusiasm for the idea. There was hardly a dissenting voice. There was full agreement on the project in the end.

Now this doesn't sound like conversation at all. There are no questions and answers; all sentences are about the same length (between six and ten words); and all of them start with There was. Let's try to do something different:

> The debate was lively. Were the students enthusiastic? They certainly were. Hardly a dissenting voice was heard, and in the end, everybody agreed on the project—yes, every one of them.

Or let's take these sentences:

> I am sorry for this long delay. I have not written for four weeks. But I have some excuse for my behavior. I have been working at the store all these week ends and evenings.

Again, all these sentences start with I am or I have. (The one but doesn't really make much difference.) And they are all built on the same simple subject-predicate pattern. Let's see how much sentence variety we can get into this paragraph:

What a long delay! Is it really four weeks since I have written? I am sorry—but there is some excuse for my behavior. All these week ends and evenings I have been working at the store.

How about using some participles, infinitives, or prepositional phrases to add variety? Let's try this passage:

I went to the library in the afternoon. I took out a book that was on the reading list. Then I went home to eat supper. I did not open the book until after supper. Then I discovered that it was the wrong volume. I was greatly annoyed. I should have looked at the book when I took it out. I had nobody to blame but myself.

Now let's rewrite it, beginning each sentence with a participle, a preposition, or an infinitive:

In the afternoon, I went to the library to take out a book on the reading list. Then, armed with my book, I went home for supper. Opening the book after supper, I was greatly annoyed; it was the wrong volume. To take out a book without looking at it was just like me. I had nobody to blame but myself.

It's not hard to follow these three simple rules and put variety into your sentences. The main thing is to pay attention to the pattern of your sentences. Two or three similar sentences in a row have a way of cropping up by themselves, so to speak. The trick is to *see* these boring repetitions, and to weed them out.

The Personal Touch

Direct quotations and sentence variety are good because they will keep the reader interested. He will also be interested if he reads about people or, at least, if he gets the feeling that the writer himself is a person talking to him, the reader, *personally*. That's why it is always a good idea to give what you write a personal touch; that's why you should keep writing about your own experiences and your own thoughts. If you are writing a letter to a friend, this will be natural. But there should be a personal touch in whatever you write, whether it's addressed to one specific reader or not.

It's hard to give you an illustration of this. But suppose, for instance, you are reading a book written by two people, like this one. Wouldn't it be interesting to know how two people work together on a book? You know, of course, that for popular songs one fellow usually writes the music and the other the lyrics. But a textbook? Do the authors write the paragraphs and sentences together? Or do they split the work, one working on the odd chapters and the other on the even ones? If you want to know the answer, here is how we worked on this book. We planned it together; we decided together what should go in and what shouldn't; and we planned each chapter together. Then one or the other wrote a first draft of a section or chapter, and finally we worked together again in putting the book into final shape. And do you think we did our work in a school office? If you do, you're wrong. It so happens that we both live in or near New York City, but one of us lives in Westchester County, one hour's train ride north, and the other in Brooklyn, one hour's subway ride east. So to work on this book, we met each Tuesday evening in the Manhattan apartment of a friend of ours, a radio director who was never at home at that time. There we went over what each one of us had prepared during the week—and occasionally we stopped to raid the well-stocked icebox of our friend.

Well, to come back, if you want to make something fun to read, try to give it a personal touch. Or at least try to show that you are interested in what you are writing. If you are not interested, how can you expect the reader to be? Nothing is as boring and tiresome to read as something with which the writer was bored to begin with. Show the reader that writing isn't just a chore for you. Don't make him feel that you dislike putting words on paper.

The Humorous Touch

If you add a little humor to whatever you are writing, that's, of course, even better. Every reader appreciates an opportunity to laugh or smile—not just in reading humorous stories and jokes, but even more so in serious matters. A dash of humor may make all the difference. The following story about the late Dwight Morrow neatly illustrates this point:

> When Dwight Morrow was United States Ambassador to Mexico, he once went over some documents that had been prepared by a new young attaché.

"I think you did very well," he said to the young man, "but next time you come to my office, don't forget Rule Seventeen."

Somewhat perturbed, the young attaché went back to his desk. He had never heard about numbered rules for the Embassy staff. Finally, he approached an older colleague and asked for an explanation.

"No, we don't have numbered rules," was the reply. "Rule Seventeen is the only one. It reads: 'Don't take yourself too darn seriously.'"

In other words, a little humorous quotation or anecdote will add a touch of something to almost any topic. We say *almost;* naturally, there are many subjects where humor would be out of place. You wouldn't use anecdotes in writing about a tragedy or a disaster; and you wouldn't let humor spoil the effect of something you're really serious about.

But otherwise humor in writing is useful, and sometimes even necessary. Most formal, official speeches start with an anecdote or two, to "break the ice." It's the same with writing. Something is needed to break the ice between writer and reader, and later little anecdotes and humorous asides will help keep it broken.

Naturally, there must be a point to whatever anecdotes or humorous quotations you use, and the point must be related to your subject. Just the fact that something is funny is no excuse for dragging it in. On the other hand, an anecdote or humorous quotation is often more convincing than the most telling argument. You could not find a stronger argument against statistical evidence than Oscar Wilde's: "There are three kinds of lies: ordinary lies, white lies, and statistics." You couldn't describe the relationship between England and America better than Bernard Shaw did when he called them "two countries separated by the same language." And you couldn't characterize the old-fashioned idea of education better than in Finley Peter Dunne's words: "I don't care what ye larn thim so long as 'tis onpleasant to thim."

And if you write about everyday life, you might do worse than quote this remark: "What can you expect from a day that starts with getting up in the morning?"

Use direct quotations whenever you can, and be sure to make them sound natural.

Use questions and answers.

Vary your sentence length and structure.

Add, whenever you can, a personal touch or a touch of humor.

Exercise 1. The following anecdotes would be more fun to read if some of the indirect statements were turned into direct quotations. Rewrite them, using direct quotations. Try to make each punch line as effective as possible.

1. Andy, who had a reputation for being stingy, asked his sweetheart whether she enjoyed moving pictures. She quickly replied that of course she did. Andy then suggested that maybe she would like to help him move a few down from the attic.

2. A stranger in a new automobile drew up in front of the town post office and asked two men who were lounging there whether they knew where the spaghetti factory was. Zeb replied that he had never heard of any spaghetti factory in those parts and that he hadn't the faintest idea where it was. The stranger drove off. Then Luke turned to Zeb and asked whether the stranger might perhaps have meant the macaroni factory. Zeb slapped his thigh and said that he'd bet that Luke was right. He suggested that the two of them run after the stranger and try to catch him.

   The two men shouted at the top of their lungs. Hearing them, the stranger stopped his car and waited until they caught up with him. Zeb asked him whether it might have been the macaroni factory that he was looking for. The stranger replied that he guessed that Zeb was right, and he asked where the macaroni factory was. Zeb answered that they didn't know where that was, either.

3. The man settled himself into the barber chair. As the barber approached him, razor in hand, ready to shave him, the man asked the barber if he had another razor. The barber asked why he wanted to know. The man replied that he wanted to defend himself.

4. A woman went into a pet shop to buy a dog. After looking over the various dogs in the kennels, she decided on one that she wanted. The owner told her that she was very lucky to get such a valuable, thoroughbred bloodhound. The woman then asked how the owner knew that the dog was really a thoroughbred bloodhound. In answer to her question, the owner turned to the dog and asked him to bleed for the lady.

5. The startled waiter looked hard at the customer who had just ordered one rotten egg and two slices of burnt toast for breakfast, and asked him why he wanted such a dish. The man replied that he had a tapeworm and that this was good enough for him.

Exercise 2. The following topics might be developed into interesting essays through the use of dialogue. For each topic, suggest two or more characters who might participate in the conversation.

Example: The Hudson River in the American Revolution
This might be developed in the form of a conversation between Rip Van Winkle and a fellow townsman after Rip had returned from his twenty-year nap.

1. Contributions of Immigrant Groups to American Life
2. Advertising on the Radio
3. Tips for Safer Driving
4. Developments in Cancer Research
5. Peacetime Uses of Atomic Energy
6. What Would Atomic War Be Like?
7. Double Features
8. G.I. Joe Returns
9. Do Women's Fashions Make Sense?
10. Prejudice in America
11. Sports Make Men
12. The Case for (or Against) Compulsory Military Training
13. Accident Prevention
14. Will Airplanes Take the Place of Automobiles?
15. The G.I. Bill of Rights
16. Who Should Go to College?
17. Problems of Modern Youth
18. Parents, Too, Need Education
19. Classical Music versus Jazz Music
20. Getting the Most out of Your Education

Exercise 3. Which of the two following letters is more fun to read? Which is more interesting? Which one makes better use of the devices discussed in this chapter?

Try to improve the style of each one of these letters. Look out for a series of sentences that follow the same pattern. Combine some of the shorter sentences into longer ones. Save the most important idea for the end of the sentence. Use direct quotations where you can. Use questions and answers where they would be appropriate.

Change the wording if you wish. Add something here and there to give the letter humor or more personal interest. Don't change the meaning of the original.

1.

I am enjoying a very pleasant, lazy summer up here in Middle Falls. I rest most of the time. I am recuperating very rapidly. The days go by very peacefully. Only three things ever happen in this little town. They are morning, afternoon, and night.

The sole activity is the constant passing to and fro of a group of young girls on their way to the ice-cream parlor around the corner. They congregate there to sip sodas and wistfully eye me whenever I come in to buy a magazine or a book. I pretend not to notice them. But I have noticed one. She is a pretty little thing with long blond hair, lots of dimples, and very blue eyes. I may bestow upon her the honor of making my acquaintance if my present inertia grows monotonous.

I sit on the vine-covered porch most of the time. I reread Thoreau. I listen to the radio, and just loaf. Should I desire variety, activity, or something to eat, I arise slowly from my rocking chair and filch a few tomatoes from our neighbor's garden. I can't think of anything so luscious as large, ripe, fresh tomatoes, with plenty of salt, between two thick slices of pumpernickel. But I certainly despise the saboteur who first thought of spoiling their flavor with lettuce leaves. I think that lettuce is a vile vegetable. I think it is fit for consumption only by cows and caterpillars. Anyway, I'm rapidly becoming a man of great wisdom and fatigue, what with all the reading and radio-listening I'm doing.

2.

I shall now describe my latest job for you, as you asked about it in your letter. I don't know whether you have ever examined a man's bedroom slipper. The back of the slipper is held erect by something inside it. This is called a counter. I am the little girl who pastes the counter between the outside of brown imitation leather and the inside of blue plaid. I have several objections to this kind of work. First, I hate it. Second, I have to use rubber cement to paste the counters in. I find that my hands are soon encased in rubber-cement mittens. Last, I cannot quit until I have saved enough to buy myself a new fall outfit. I hope that you will shed a tear for me. I remember that, when we last saw each other, you remarked that I looked discontented and tired. I wonder what you would say now. I am up here, careworn, hungry, and penniless, for I haven't received my first week's pay yet. I also have long hair and short teeth. The dentist said yesterday that my teeth were too long. He did something to shorten them. I look quite different now. All this happened after three days at the Cosmopolitan Counter Company. I wonder what I'll be like after three weeks.

14 HOW TO GIVE IT PUNCH

This chapter is called HOW TO GIVE IT PUNCH. Do you think it would have been better to call it HOW ADDED PUNCH CAN BE GIVEN TO YOUR WRITING? No; you can easily see that it wouldn't. But just why is HOW TO GIVE IT PUNCH better than HOW ADDED PUNCH CAN BE GIVEN TO YOUR WRITING? Let's look a little more closely at the two titles. First of all, HOW TO GIVE IT PUNCH is shorter. It has five words, and the other title has nine. In the second place, the verb is in the active voice (give) in one title and in the passive voice (be given) in the other. Third, HOW TO GIVE IT PUNCH has the main word punch at the end and the other title buries it in the middle. So our title is better than HOW ADDED PUNCH CAN BE GIVEN TO YOUR WRITING because it follows these three rules:

1. Be brief.
2. Use active verbs.
3. Wind up with a bang.

We have already said enough in other chapters about saving words and being brief. So let's go on to the second and third of these points.

Live Writing

In writing, the difference between the active and the passive voice makes all the difference in the world. The active voice, which shows who is doing something—as in I hit Johnnie—makes a sentence strong; the passive voice, which shows who is being acted on—as in Johnnie is being hit by me—makes a sentence weak. A sentence that is cast in the active voice hits the mind of the reader and makes him sit up and take notice. A passive-voice sentence passes through his mind without much trace.

One reason for this may be that the passive voices of all verbs are formed with some such word as is or was or are or being. These words are so common in our language that they mean very little to a reader. He hardly notices them on a page. By using the passive voice too often, we stuff our writing with dozens and dozens of is's and was's and are's and make it dull and uninteresting, instead of making it interesting by using live, kicking verbs.

We don't mean to say, of course, that the passive voice should never be used. There is a place for it whenever you want to draw the reader's attention to the person who suffers or gets something. It is natural to write:

Mr. Miller was killed in an accident.

or

Billie was showered with birthday presents.

But these are exceptions. As a rule, if you switch a sentence from the passive to the active voice it will read better.

As an example, here are a few paragraphs translated from the passive voice into the active voice. Look at the active-voice passage on the right. Doesn't it have more punch?

Passive voice:	Active voice:
It is well known that advertising is designed to sell merchandise. But it is usually not realized how much planning and work is being put into it. No effort is spared by manufacturers to get our minds used to their products. Once it was considered enough to be better known than the closest competitor. Now advertising slogans are being built into our everyday life.	Everybody knows that advertisers want to sell merchandise. But not everybody realizes how much planning and work they put into it. They spare no effort to hammer the names of their products into our minds. Once they considered it enough to beat the closest competitor. Now they build their advertising slogans into our everyday lives.
Many complaints are heard about this. Advertising is being attacked because our press is too dependent on advertising income. It is also said that our radio entertainment is being cheapened since practically all of it is sponsored by advertisers. Even the beauty of our country is considered spoiled because our highways are lined by billboards.	Many people are complaining about this. They attack advertising because our press depends too much on advertising income. They say that the advertisers who sponsor practically all of our radio entertainment have cheapened it. They point to the billboards that line our highways and spoil the beauty of our country.

These complaints have been answered by a strong counter-argument: Thanks to advertising, our standard of living has been made the highest in the world . . .

But these complaints provoke a strong counter-argument: Advertising has made our standard of living the highest in the world . . .

Build Up to the End

How about the third rule: *Wind up with a bang?* It's the most important of our rules for giving our writing punch. If you are like most people and save the frosting on your cake until the end, then you won't have much trouble with it. The principle is exactly the same: You take the most important or most effective word or idea and save it up until the end of the sentence. Naturally, if you are greedy and always start with the choice bits, then you won't have any icing left to top off your sentences and each one of them will taper off into measly, left-over *word-crumbs*. But if you pay a little attention—and particularly if you are the frosting-at-the-end kind of person—then you will naturally build all your sentences *up*.

We cannot give you any general rule for doing this. You must know which word or idea in each sentence you want to lead up to. You must make up your mind what word to put at the end—where it will stick in the reader's mind. You must decide which is the cake to eat and the frosting to save.

Suppose Jim is your best friend. He is the youngest vice-president and he has a beautiful sister, Betty. Now you want to write something about Jim. Naturally, you will want to say all these things about him. But the question is, "In what order?" The choice depends on you—on the thing you consider most important and most remarkable about Jim, the thing you really want to *tell* your reader about him. Whatever it is, the trick is to put it last.

This is how you write about Jim, the youngest vice-president:

My best friend, Jimmy—Betty's brother—is our youngest vice-president.

This is how you write about Jim, the brother of Betty:

My best friend Jimmy, our youngest vice-president, has a beautiful sister, Betty.

And this is how you write about Jim, your best friend:

> Betty's brother Jimmy, our youngest vice-president, is my best friend.

Add a Dash

Sometimes a dash (—) before the last word will add even more force to it. That's a good thing to remember. If you want to underline the last word in a sentence, don't underline it but put a dash in front of it. That may sound odd, but actually the position of a word at the end of a sentence, after a dash, makes it stronger than any underlining could make it. In fact, underlining doesn't help much if you want to stress a word or phrase; and there is always the danger that you will fall into the "underlining habit" and write every second or third word at the top of your voice, so to speak. Compare

> I got a sweater, a couple of books, and an accordion for Christmas.

with

> For Christmas I got a sweater, a couple of books, and—an accordion.

The Exclamation Point: Handle with Care

Exclamation points, too, should be used with care. Don't try to use them to dress up a sentence that isn't exciting in the first place. The punch must come from the inside—that is, from the words. If you haven't built up to an idea, then you can't expect it to make an impression just because it is followed by an exclamation point. In this sentence, for instance, the exclamation point doesn't help at all:

> There were blooming magnolia trees I noticed when I was walking through Elm Street last Wednesday!

But if you build up your idea properly, you don't need the exclamation point:

> Walking through Elm Street last Wednesday, I had an unforgettable experience: I saw it lined with magnolia trees in full bloom.

Word and Sentence Patterns

But you can add more punch by other means. You can build up to your final word by preparing the reader's mind for what's going to come. You can form your words and sentences into patterns so that the idea you want to play up comes at a natural high point. You can arrange your words in such a way that they add up in power.

There is no one single rule for this. You can build word patterns in many different ways. You can form a pattern by repeating a word or phrase; or by following three or four long sentences with a short one; or by putting a few short sentences before a long one; or by writing your words in a rhythmical pattern; or by doing several of these things together. In other words, you can play with your language and make it do tricks. Of course, you wouldn't want to do this always, but for special occasions it's useful to know how to make your words twice or ten times or twenty times as effective.

Suppose you are writing about the first time you were flying in an airplane. There wouldn't be much punch in it if you wrote it this way:

> Then the plane turned and left the ground and I thought that this was the first time I was flying and looked out of the window. I had to be strapped to my seat with a belt.

But here is how we can build the idea up by repeating the word flying:

> The plane turned and left the ground. We were in the air. All my life I had been thinking about flying. I had been reading about flying. I had been dreaming about flying. The moment was here. It was 12:35 p.m., Sunday, April 27, 1947. I was flying.

Or let's put the idea into a short sentence that follows three long ones like the crack of a whip:

> Strapped to my seat with a belt, I sat tense and excited and looked out of the window. Now the plane made a sharp turn and, with the engines roaring, gathered speed and finally left the ground. The moment had come of which I had been thinking and dreaming ever since I could remember. I was flying.

And now let's show our excitement by the rhythm of the words:

> Gathering speed, the plane rolled on. It left the ground and was up in the air. The moment had come: I was flying.

Finally, here are a few tricks in combination: word rhythm, a repeated phrase, and a crack-of-a-whip ending:

> The plane turned, the engines started roaring again, and up we went. The airport buildings sank away. "This is it"; I said to myself, "this is it at last. I am flying."

We are sure that you'll get the point from these five versions. But maybe we should give you another example. Let's use this opportunity to tell you with as much force as we can the main thing about writing:

> Writing isn't just spelling; it's much more than spelling. Writing isn't just grammar; it's much more than grammar. Writing is grasping ideas, seeing images, harnessing words—giving shape and form to thoughts. What matters most in writing is not the rules and conventions for putting words on paper. What matters most in writing is the writer's mind.

To give your writing punch,
1. be brief;
2. use active verbs;
3. wind up with a bang;
4. arrange your words and sentences effectively.

Exercise 1. Rewrite any of the following sentences that can be made more forceful by substituting the active for the passive voice. Do not change any sentences where the passive is satisfactory.

1. We left at dawn, and the hotel was reached early in the afternoon.
2. Many new apartment houses are being built in my neighborhood.
3. As he was strolling through the woods, a cry for help was suddenly heard from the direction of the lake.
4. First read the entire paragraph. Then any errors that are found should be corrected.

5. Our plans were changed abruptly when his message was received by us.
6. The snow fell steadily, and in a short time his tracks were completely obliterated.
7. Helen asked my brother to her party, but I wasn't invited.
8. We took our fishing equipment with us, but our tennis rackets were left at home.
9. After the soup, the turkey was served.
10. If your feet are wet, your shoes and stockings should be changed as soon as you arrive home.
11. The Great Dane playfully ran to greet me, and I was knocked over.
12. The book was read from cover to cover before I went to bed.

Exercise 2. Rewrite the following sentences. Arrange the ideas so that the idea you want to emphasize comes last. "Wind up with a 'bang'!"

1. We returned from the hike chilled, almost starved to death, and footsore.
2. He has burnt our towns, destroyed the lives of our people, ravaged our coasts, and plundered our seas.
3. The man I marry must be considerate, he must be a Dodger fan, he must have an attractive appearance, and he must share my interests.
4. He had sacrificed his very life for her, as well as his career and his wealth.
5. We found the little girl in the attic, sleeping peacefully, after we had searched for hours and had notified the police.
6. The tornado left ruin and death in its wake and tore down every building in the village.
7. The mysterious visitor had stolen the ruby, rifled my desk, and broken open the safe.
8. The flowers appear on the earth, the rain is over and gone, the time of the singing of birds is come, and winter is past.
9. Temptation is the only thing that I cannot resist.
10. A cynic is a man who knows the value of nothing, although he knows the price of everything.

Exercise 3. The following essay contains some entertaining ideas, but it lacks punch. Rewrite it, and try to improve it through the devices suggested in this chapter. Substitute the active for the passive voice wherever possible. Save the most important, most dramatic idea for the end of the sentence. Use the dash or the exclamation point to highlight an idea. Use the kind of sentence and word patterns that will make the writing more interesting and effective.

Why I Committed Suicide

I led a rather normal life until the day I committed suicide. I hated singing commercials, homework, and spinach. I went into raptures over Duke Ellington, chow mein, and Frank Sinatra, just as any normal person does. Then my entire future was changed because of something that happened.

I arose about ten o'clock one Saturday morning, in keeping with my usual habits. I discovered that it was raining when I looked out of the window. The bad weather did not annoy me too much, however. I was not even disturbed when I found that my breakfast consisted of some lukewarm coffee and some stale bread. I was still in a rather genial mood when a rip was discovered in my one remaining pair of nylon stockings. I admit that my smile became a trifle forced when I was informed that my younger sister had emptied my perfume all over the dress I had planned to wear that evening. My spirits did not even sink when a telegram arrived and I was informed by it that my date for that evening had enlisted in the Marines. I decided to spend a quiet evening at home, my good humor only slightly damaged.

I decided to prepare some fudge in a fit of ambition. The experiment turned out rather badly. The fudge wouldn't set, a bottle of milk spilled, and the dish I made it in split. Accidentally I slipped in the milk, overturned the garbage pail, twisted my ankle, and ripped my dress. But I set my teeth and decided to keep my temper at all costs.

I settled down with a good mystery novel. I congratulated myself that at last something was turning out well. When the next-to-the-last chapter was reached, the suspense became unbearably strong. I chewed my nails in excitement, my hair stood on end, and my pulse quickened. I finished the last page of the next-to-the-last chapter overjoyed that nothing disastrous had happened to ruin my pleasure. I turned the page fearfully. I found that the final chapter was missing. Someone had torn out the pages.

I decided then and there that there was nothing more to be done, because I was human and because there was a limit even to my endurance. I felt devoid of emotion. I slowly arose, turned, and walked to the nearest window. It was opened by me. I then jumped out.

15 HOW WRITERS WRITE

Whenever you write, you try to imitate what you have read.
You do it without knowing it; everybody does it, more or less.
Some people go so far in this imitation that in answering the
telephone they use the accent of whoever happens to be calling; but almost everybody follows in his writing the kind of
English he is ordinarily exposed to. So the way you write
depends largely on what you read; and that's why we have
added this chapter on how writers write.

If you want to write well, you must read good writing. Naturally, if you spend all your time reading bad, clumsy, ineffective writing, then you will never get away from bad
clumsy, ineffective writing yourself; if you read nothing but
good writing, your writing will automatically improve.

Good and Bad Writing

How can you tell good writing from bad writing? Actually,
it's easier than you think. The good writer knows the tricks of
his trade—those you have learned in this book and a good
many more—and uses them to make you, the reader, think
and feel the way he wants you to; the bad writer, since he
doesn't know his business, never really touches your mind or
heart.

By "good writing" we don't mean something that is dull or
old-fashioned, or something that you are supposed to read
because it has been declared a classic a long time ago. We
mean writing that is rewarding, writing you can get your
teeth into, writing that is fun to read. (If you read a classic
for this reason rather than because it's a classic, you will
usually be surprised at how much you will get out of it.) If
you stick to this kind of writing, you will learn to appreciate
good writing, and you will improve your own writing.

Building Writing Skill

But, of course, you should not rely entirely on this natural
effect of reading. Building up writing skill works exactly the
same way as vocabulary building. If you just read and don't

o anything else about it, the gain is very, very slow. If you
want to be sure to increase your vocabulary, you have to
study closely the new words you find in your reading, look
them up in the dictionary, and make an effort to use them.
In the same way, if you really want to profit from reading
good writing, you must pay attention to the way writers do
things, study their methods, and try to apply them yourself.
Naturally, if you are reading something you really like, you
won't want to interrupt yourself to see how the author builds
his sentences and paragraphs; but when you have finished
something that has made a deep impression on you, you can
go back and try to find out how it was done.

If you make it a habit to do this, then you'll soon learn
more about writing than we or anybody else can ever teach
you. You will learn to appreciate more deeply what a writer
sets out to do and how he does it. You will begin to understand what makes writing an art.

But, you will ask, what is there to know? Why don't we
just tell you the secret of good writing?

We wish we could. But unfortunately there's no substitute
for reading, observing, and finding out for yourself. All we
can do is to end Part One with a few examples of good writing. They are not selections of masterpieces (you will find
those in other books) but just ten well-written modern short
pieces—simply to show you what we are talking about. Read
them, enjoy them, and then study them, see how they are
written and what makes them enjoyable and worth reading.
And then go on hunting for equally good writing for the
rest of your life.

But before you read the examples, let us say a few words
about them. Why did we pick them? What do these ten passages have in common?

As you will see, they couldn't be more different in subject
matter. Some are humorous, some are descriptive, one deals
with democracy, one with free speech, and one with central
heating. What makes them all qualify as models of good
prose?

We think that these passages have three things in common.
One of them is invisible, the other two you can see.

Writing Is Rewriting

The invisible thing is the fact that each of these passages
is all of a piece, that it flows evenly without a break, that the

writer takes you along and never lets you down. This is invisible because you can't pin it down to any single sentence or paragraph; it marks the piece of writing as a whole. It is also invisible because this effect is usually achieved by taking things *out*. It is the result of the habit of editing and revising. Almost every writer rereads what he has written—to smooth out transitions and, particularly, to strike out all unnecessary and unclear words. Read each one of the passages and see how smoothly it flows.

Simplicity

The second thing about our examples is their simplicity. Of course, not all of them are equally simple, but none of them is really difficult to read. You may think that we picked samples of simple writing because this is a book on how to write, but that isn't so. They are simple because most good writing is simple, because simplicity is the most natural quality of good prose. A writer, if he has something to say, usually finds that the simplest way of saying it is the best. It is the strongest and the most effective. Take, for instance, the simple sentence "He himself never did this" in the passage by Stephen Leacock. Or take the reference to Dix Hill in the little story about Uncle Dockery. If you had to explain to a reader what Uncle Dockery meant by Dix Hill, you would probably say it indirectly, or throw out a dark hint, or go into an elaborate half-page description. But Joseph Mitchell writes simply: "Dix Hill is a suburb of Raleigh, where the North Carolina State Asylum for the Insane is located."

Personality and Style

The third thing our examples have in common is that each bears the unmistakable stamp of the writer's mind. There is something about each of them that nobody else could have written but the man who wrote it. It may be something he saw more clearly than anybody else, or some idea he understood better because of his own experience, or the putting together of two ideas nobody else thought of putting together before. Look for these flashes of the writer's unique personality and imagine how much each passage would lose without them. For example, take the words so flat and cold in the little sketch by Robert Benchley, or we were fishing Little Rump River for blue bream in the piece about Uncle Dockery by Joseph Mitchell; or the last paragraph in Stephen Vincent

Benét's description of Doc Mellhorn; or the last sentence of the piece by Somerset Maugham; or Stephen Leacock's brilliant idea of comparing a sense of humor with an ear for music. Look at Aldous Huxley's use of the words solemn symbolical charades and pompous ballets. Enjoy Carl Sandburg's inspired idea of quoting from Edward Everett's speech but not from the Gettysburg address. Savor E. B. White's nine-word sentence It is the line that forms on the right.

Then, when you come to the selection from Joseph Conrad, feel the majesty of the line . . . as if traced by an unsteady hand on the clear blue of the hot sky.

And in the last passage, read and reread the tremendous sentence: They believed liberty to be the secret of happiness and courage to be the secret of liberty.

THE WRECK OF THE SUNDAY PAPER

by Robert Benchley

What is to be done with people who can't read a Sunday paper without messing it all up? I just throw this out as one of the problems with which we are faced if we are to keep our civilization from complete collapse.

There is a certain type of citizen (a great many times, I am sorry to have to say, one of the "fair" sex) whose lack of civic pride shows itself in divers forms, but it is in the devastation of a Sunday newspaper that it reaches its full bloom. Show me a Sunday paper which has been left in a condition fit only for kite flying, and I will show you an antisocial and dangerous character who has left it that way.

Such a person may not mean deliberately to do the things to a newspaper that he or (pardon my pointing) *she* does. They really couldn't achieve such colossal disarrangement by any planning or scheming. It has to come from some cataclysmic stroke of a giant force, probably beyond their control. Let them but touch a nice, neat Sunday edition as it lies folded so flat and cold on the doorstep, and immediately the rotogravure section becomes entwined with the sporting section and the editorial page leaps out and joins with the shipping news to form a tent under which a pretty good-sized child could crawl. The society page bundles itself up into a ball in the center of which, by some strange convulsion, the real-estate news conceals itself in a smaller and more compact ball. It is the Touch of Cain that these people have, and perhaps we should not blame them for it.

From *No Poems*, published by Harper & Brothers.
Copyright, 1932, by Robert Benchley.

UNCLE DOCKERY

by Joseph Mitchell

I often find it comforting to think of Uncle Dockery Fitzsim
mons, a serene old bright-leaf tobacco farmer who lives in Blac
Ankle County, about six miles from Stonewall. He is the only ma
I have ever known who has absolutely no respect for the mechar
ical genius of Western civilization. One day, when I was abou
fifteen, we were fishing Little Rump River for blue bream and
motorboat chugged by, scaring all the fish to the bed of the rive
and Uncle Dockery said, "Son, the only inventions that make sens
to me are the shotgun, the two-horse wagon, the butter chur
and the frying pan. Sonner or later such contraptions as the moto
boat will drive the whole human race into Dix Hill." Dix Hill i
a suburb of Raleigh, where the North Carolina State Asylum fo
the Insane is located.

Uncle Dockery is still opposed to the automobile. "I don't wan
to go nowhere," he used to say, "that a mule can't take me." Hi
hatred of automobiles embraces people who ride in them. On
summer afternoon we were sitting on his veranda, eating a water
melon, when a neighbor ran up the road and said, "There's beer
a terrible auto accident up on the highway, Mr. Fitzsimmons."
The news pleased Uncle Dockery. He placed his rasher of water
melon on the rail of the veranda, smiled broadly, and asked, "Hov
many killed?" "Four," said the neighbor. "Well, that's just fine,'
said Uncle Dockery. "Where were they going in such a rush?"
"They were going to the beach for a swim," said the neighbor
Uncle Dockery nodded with satisfaction and said, "I guess the
figured the Atlantic Ocean wouldn't wait."

Reprinted from *McSorley's Wonderful Saloon,* by permissio
of Duell, Sloan & Pearce
Copyright 1938, 1939, 1940, 1941, 1942, 1943, by Joseph Mitchell

DOC MELLHORN

by Stephen Vincent Benét

Doc Mellhorn was seventy-odd when he left our town; but whe
he came, he was as young as Bates or Filsinger or any of the boy
at the hospital. Only there wasn't any hospital when he came. H
came with a young man's beard and a brand-new bag and a lo
of newfangled ideas about medicine that we didn't take to much
And he left, forty-odd years later, with a first-class county healt
record and a lot of people alive that wouldn't have been alive i
he hadn't been there. Yes, a country doctor. And nobody eve
called him a man in white or a death grappler that I know of

though they did think of giving him a degree at Pewauket College once. But then the Board met again and decided they needed a new gymnasium, so they gave the degree to J. Prentiss Parmalee instead.

They say he was a thin young man when he first came, a thin young man with an Eastern accent who'd wanted to study in Vienna. But most of us remember him chunky and solid, with white hair and a little bald spot that always got burned bright red in the first hot weather. He had about four card tricks that he'd do for you, if you were a youngster—they were always the same ones—and now and then, if he felt like it, he'd take a silver dollar out of the back of your neck. And that worked as well with the youngsters who were going to build rocket ships as it had with the youngsters who were going to be railway engineers. It always worked. I guess it was Doc Mellhorn more than the trick.

But there wasn't anything unusual about him, except maybe the card tricks. Or, anyway, he didn't think so. He was just a good doctor and he knew us inside out. I've heard people call him a pigheaded, obstinate old mule—that was in the fight about the water supply. And I've heard a weepy old lady call him a saint. I took the tale to him once, and he looked at me over his glasses and said, "Well, I've always respected a mule. Got ten times the sense of a—horse." Then he took a silver half dollar out of my ear.

Well, how do you describe a man like that? You don't—you call him up at three in the morning. And when he sends his bill, you think it's a little steep.

From *Doc Mellhorn and the Pearly Gates*. Copyright, 1938, by Stephen Vincent Benét.

ORDINARY PEOPLE

by W. Somerset Maugham

I have always wondered at the passion many people have to meet the celebrated. The prestige you acquire by being able to tell your friends that you know famous men proves only that you are yourself of small account. The celebrated develop a technique to deal with the persons they come across. They show the world a mask, often an impressive one, but take care to conceal their real selves. They play the part that is expected from them and with practice learn to play it very well, but you are stupid if you think that this public performance of theirs corresponds with the man within.

I have been attached, deeply attached, to a few people; but I have been interested in men in general not for their own sakes, but for the sake of my work. I have not, as Kant enjoined, regarded each man as an end in himself, but as material that might be useful to me as a writer. I have been more concerned with the obscure than with the famous. They are more often themselves. They have had no need to create a figure to protect themselves from the world or to impress it. Their idiosyncrasies have had more chance to develop in the limited circle of their activity, and since they have never been in the public eye it has never occurred to them that they have anything to conceal. They display their oddities because it has never struck them that they are odd. And after all it is with the common run of men that we writers have to deal; kings, dictators, commercial magnates are from our point of view very unsatisfactory. To write about them is a venture that has often tempted writers, but the failure that has attended their efforts shows that such beings are too exceptional to form a proper ground for a work of art. They cannot be made real. The ordinary is the writer's richer field. Its unexpectedness, its singularity, its infinite variety afford unending material. The great man is too often all of a piece; it is the little man that is a bundle of contradictory elements. He is inexhaustible. You never come to the end of the surprises he has in store for you. For my part I would much sooner spend a month on a desert island with a veterinary surgeon than with a prime minister.

SENSE OF HUMOUR

by Stephen Leacock

All that I dare claim is that I have as much sense of humour as other people. And, oddly enough, I notice that everybody else makes this same claim. Any man will admit, if need be, that his sight is not good, or that he cannot swim, or shoots badly with a rifle, but to touch upon his sense of humour is to give him a moral affront.

"No," said a friend of mine the other day, "I never go to Grand Opera," and then added with an air of pride—"You see, I have absolutely no ear for music."

"You don't say so!" I exclaimed.

"None!" he went on. "I can't tell one tune from another. I don't know *Home Sweet Home* from *God, Save the King*. I can't tell whether a man is tuning a violin or playing a sonata."

He seemed to get prouder and prouder over each item of his own deficiency. He ended by saying that he had a dog at his house that had a far better ear for music than he had. As soon as his wife or any visitor started to play the piano the dog always began to howl—plaintively, he said, as if it were hurt. He himself never did this.

When he had finished I made what I thought a harmless comment.

"I suppose," I said, "that you find your sense of humour deficient in the same way: the two generally go together."

My friend was livid with rage in a moment.

"Sense of humour!" he said. "My sense of humour! Me without a sense of humour! Why, I suppose I've a keener sense of humour than any man, or any two men, in this city!"

From that he turned to bitter personal attack. He said that *my* sense of humour seemed to have withered altogether.

He left me, still quivering with indignation.

From *Laugh with Leacock* by Stephen Leacock.
Coypright, 1930, by Dodd, Mead & Company, Inc.
Reprinted by permission of Dodd, Mead & Company.

CENTRAL HEATING AND THE FEUDAL SYSTEM
by Aldous Huxley

Another essential component of modern comfort—the adequate heating of houses—was made impossible, at least for the great ones of the earth, by the political structure of ancient societies. Plebeians were more fortunate in this respect than nobles. Living in small houses, they were able to keep warm. But the nobleman, the prince, the king, and the cardinal inhabited palaces of a grandeur corresponding with their social position. In order to prove that they were greater than other men, they had to live in surroundings considerably more than life-size. They received their guests in vast halls like roller-skating rinks; they marched in solemn processions along galleries as long and as draughty as Alpine tunnels, up and down triumphal staircases that looked like the cataracts of the Nile frozen into marble. Being what he was, a great man in those days had to spend a great deal of his time in performing solemn symbolical charades and pompous ballets—performances which required a lot of room to accommodate the numerous actors and spectators. This explains the enormous dimensions of royal and princely palaces, even of the house of ordinary landed gentlemen. They owed it to their position to live, as though they were giants, in rooms a hundred feet long and thirty high. How splendid, how magnificent! But oh, how bleak! In our days the self-made great are not expected to keep up their position in the splendid style of those who were great by divine right. Sacrificing grandiosity to comfort, they live in rooms small enough to be heated.

From "Comfort" in *Proper Studies*,
published by Harper & Brothers.
Copyright, 1928, by Aldous Huxley.

LINCOLN AT GETTYSBURG

by Carl Sandburg

At least 15,000 people were on Cemetery Hill for the exercises next day when the procession from Gettysburg arrived afoot and horseback. The President's horse seemed small for him. One of the commissioners, riding just behind the President, noted that he sat erect and looked majestic to begin with, and then got to thinking so his body leaned forward, his arms hung limp and his head bent far down.

The parade had begun to move at eleven, and in 15 minutes it was over. But the orator of the day had not arrived. Bands played till noon. Mr. Everett arrived. On the platform sat state governors, Army officers, foreign ministers, Members of Congress, the President and his party.

When Edward Everett was introduced, he bowed low to Lincoln, then stood in silence before a crowd that stretched to limits that would test his voice. Around were the wheat fields, the meadows, the peach orchards and beyond, the contemplative blue ridge of a low mountain range. He had taken note of these in his prepared and rehearsed address. "Overlooking these broad fields now reposing from the labors of the waning year, the mighty Alleghenies dimly towering before us, the graves of our brethren beneath our feet, it is with hesitation that I raise my poor voice to break the eloquent silence of God and Nature."

He proceeded: "It was appointed by law in Athens—" and gave an extended sketch of the manner in which the Greeks cared for their dead who fell in battle. He gave an outline of how the war began, traversed decisive features of the three days' battles at Gettysburg, denounced the doctrine of state sovereignty, drew parallels from European history, and came to his peroration quoting Pericles on dead patriots: "The whole earth is the sepulcher of illustrious men." He spoke for an hour and 57 minutes. It was the effort of his life, and embodied the perfections of the school of oratory in which he had spent his career.

When the time came for Lincoln to speak he put on his steel-bowed glasses, rose, and holding in one hand the two sheets of paper at which he occasionally glanced, he delivered the address in his high-pitched and clear-carrying voice. A photographer bustled about with his equipment, but before he had his head under the hood for an exposure, the President had said "by the people and for the people," and the nick of time was past for a photograph. The nine sentences were spoken in five minutes, and the applause was merely formal—a tribute to the occasion, to the high office, by persons who had sat as an audience for three hours.

That evening Lincoln took the train back to Washington. He was weary, talked little, stretched out on the seats and had a wet towel laid across his forehead. He felt that about all he had given the audience was ordinary garden-variety dedicatory remarks. "That speech," he said, "was a flat failure, and the people are disappointed."

As condensed in *Reader's Digest* from *Abraham Lincoln: The War Years* by Carl Sandburg, copyright, 1939, by Harcourt, Brace and Company, Inc.

WHAT DEMOCRACY MEANS
by E. B. White

We received a letter from the Writers' War Board the other day asking for a statement on "The Meaning of Democracy." It presumably is our duty to comply with such a request, and it is certainly our pleasure.

Surely the Board knows what democracy is. It is the line that forms on the right. It is the don't in don't shove. It is the hole in the stuffed shirt through which the sawdust slowly trickles; it is the dent in the high hat. Democracy is the recurrent suspicion that more than half of the people are right more than half of the time. It is the feeling of privacy in the voting booths, the feeling of communion in the libraries, the feeling of vitality everywhere. Democracy is a letter to the editor. Democracy is the score at the beginning of the ninth. It is an idea which hasn't been disproved yet, a song the words of which have not gone bad. It's the mustard on the hot dog and the cream in the rationed coffee. Democracy is a request from a War Board, in the middle of a morning in the middle of a war, wanting to know what democracy is.

From *The New Yorker*, and included in "The Wild Flag," Houghton Mifflin Company, Copyright 1943 E. B. White.

NOON
by Joseph Conrad

Before going down to his boat Babalatchi stopped for a while in the big open space where the thick-leaved trees put black patches of shadow which seemed to float on a flood of smooth, intense light that rolled up to the houses and down to the stockade and over the river, where it broke and sparkled in thousands of glittering wavelets, like a band woven of azure and gold edged with the brilliant green of the forests guarding both banks of the Pantai. In the perfect calm before the coming of the afternoon breeze the irregularly jagged line of tree-tops stood unchanging, as if traced by an unsteady hand on the clear blue of the hot sky. In the space sheltered by the high palisades there lingered the smell of decaying blossoms from the surrounding forest; a taint of drying fish, with now and then a whiff of acrid smoke from the cooking fires when it eddied down from under the leafy boughs and clung lazily about the burnt-up grass.

FREE SPEECH AND ASSEMBLY

by Louis D. Brandeis

Those who won our independence believed that the final end of the State was to make men free to develop their faculties; and that in its government the deliberative forces should prevail over the arbitrary. They valued liberty both as an end and as a means. *They believed liberty to be the secret of happiness and courage to be the secret of liberty.* They believed that freedom to think as you will and to speak as you think are means indispensable to the discovery and spread of political truth; that without free speech and assembly discussion would be futile; that with them, discussion affords ordinarily adequate protection against the dissemination of noxious doctrine; that the greatest menace to freedom is an inert people; that public discussion is a political duty; and that this should be a fundamental principle of the American government.

16 *BEST FOOT FORWARD*

Do you eat peas with a knife?
Do you pick your teeth at the table?
Do you wear slacks to a formal?

You won't be jailed if you do any of these things. But you won't be invited again. For our social code turns "thumbs down" on this kind of social behavior. If you want to belong, if you want people to think you are well-bred, you'll avoid the *wrong* things and do the *right* things.

Do you say:

> I ain't coming.
> This here book is mine.
> I busted my balloon.
> He took it off of me.
> She is dark-complected.

If you do, **You're a Marked Man!**

In our language there are certain expressions that brand you immediately as *uneducated,* or *uncultivated,* or *illiterate.* Take your choice. But remember: Once these labels are put on your speech or writing, they're very difficult to get rid of. People judge you by what you say and *how* you say it.

"It's not fair," you say. "We shouldn't judge a book by its cover. We shouldn't judge a person's education by a few expressions." There's something in what you say. You have a heart of gold. You're a faithful friend. You're a "square-shooter," a "good sport." You do your work faithfully every day. You take part in all your community's charitable activities. You're kind, generous, considerate. You say "Please" and "Thank you." You're respectful of your superiors. You're everything you should be as a citizen and as a human being. And merely because you write, "I should of gone," society will point the finger of scorn at you and say, "Uneducated! Illiterate! Uncultivated!"?

Yes, that's exactly what will and does happen. Maybe it's

171

a little unreasonable. But it's one of the hard facts of life. Certain expressions (like those five above) are, in the eyes of society, just as undesirable as eating peas with a knife or wiping your lips on your sleeve, or making music with your soup. Of course, you'll be *understood*, but you'll be something of an outcast at the same time. What you want to be is *clear* and *correct*.

The sensible thing for you to do is to find out what these socially unacceptable expressions are and then to get them out of your writing and speaking. (It won't be so difficult as you think. You know many of them by now. And you avoid them, too.)

What Do You Know?

Test Yourself—A. On a sheet of paper write the numbers from 1 to 25. Read each of the following sentences. If the sentence is correct put a + after the corresponding number. If it is incorrect put a *o*. When you have completed the test, check your answers with the explanations that follow. The number at the end of each of the test sentences tells you which section to refer to.

1. It isn't going to rain today. (2)
2. An apple a day will keep the doctor away. (1)
3. Because there was too much air in it, the tire bursted. (4)
4. The frog in the fable blew so hard that he burst. (5)
5. We should have made our reservations a month ago. (7)
6. Ain't he your boss? (2)
7. The horse is supposed to be one of the cleverest animals. (8)
8. The fisherman caught a eel. (1)
9. Men, as a rule, don't spend much time thinking about their clothes. (6)
10. If he eats any more, he'll bust. (5)
11. If you put a pin into a balloon, it will bust. (5)
12. Aren't I going to get a chance to get a raise? (2)
13. He was suppose to be on duty from midnight to dawn. (8)
14. Isn't this your first appearance before the club? (2)
15. Jim ordered an apple pie. (1)
16. The dog will lick your hand if it don't fear you. (6)
17. Without interruptions, he could have finished on time. (7)
18. Were you suppose to collect the tickets for the dance? (8)
19. I'm pretty clever, ain't I? (2)
20. He could of made that touchdown very easily. (7)
21. This is all the farther you have to travel. (3)
22. When I was young, I could of licked my weight in wild cats (7)
23. Spring is busting out all over. (5)
24. If he don't study, he won't pass his examinations. (6)

25. After I left, I knew I should've given him fuller instructions. (7)

Don't Write:	*Write:*
1. I ate a apple.	I ate an apple.

The rule here is very simple:
Use a where the noun begins with a *consonant:*

a *hat*   a *book*   a *car*   a *storm*

Use an where the noun begins with a *vowel:*

an *apple*   an *eel*   an *itch*   an *olive*

Don't Write:	*Write:*
2. The children ain't playing today.	The children aren't playing today.
Aren't I the best player?	Am I not the best player?
I ain't going.	I'm not going.

This whole matter of ain't is a difficult one for some people to decide. It's true that it is frequently used. But that doesn't make it correct. Educated people don't use it, or, if they do, only when they are poking fun or imitating the speech of illiterate or uneducated people.
The correct forms are:

I'm not or I am not.
He, she, it isn't or is not.
We, you, they aren't or are not.

What about ain't I? Is there any other way of saying it? There is: Am I not? It sounds a little stiff, but the English language doesn't have any other substitute. Amn't I? and Aren't I? are attempts to get around this difficulty. But both sound somewhat silly. Aren't I doesn't even make sense. (Aren't I = Are I not?)
So you had better avoid Ain't I? Say Am I not?

Don't Write:	*Write:*
3. That is all the farther I can go.	That is as far as I can go.

All the farther is just pure invention. It sounds awkward too.

Don't Write:	*Write:*
4. The bubble bursted.	The bubble burst.

Bursted is no word at all. The verb is **burst**. Its principal parts are: **burst, burst, burst.**

Don't Write:	*Write:*
5. Handle the baloon carefully or it will **bust.**	Handle the balloon carefully or it will **burst.**

Bust isn't a verb. Don't use it instead of **burst.**

Don't Write:	*Write:*
6. It really **don't** matter at all. He **don't** care what happens to him.	It really **doesn't** matter at all. He **doesn't** care what happens to him.

Here's a very simple way to avoid this error. **Don't** is a *contraction*, a combination of two words: **Do + not.** The apostrophe (') is inserted between the **n** and **t** to show that a letter has been omitted. There are many such contractions in our language. **Don't,** for some strange reason, seems to create more difficulty than the others.

When you are in doubt, just break the contraction up into its two parts, like this:

> It really don't (= **do** not) matter at all. (You wouldn't say that, would you?)
> It really doesn't (= **does** not) matter at all. (That's better.)
> He don't (= **do** not) care what happens to him. (You never say "He **do** not," do you?)
> He doesn't (= **does** not) care what happens to him. (Of course, you say he **does** not.)

Don't Write:	*Write:*
7. I could **of** come earlier. I should **of** done it another way.	I could **have** come earlier. I should **have** done it another way.

People fall into this error because they write these words the way they *think* they *sound*. When we speak, we tend to run certain words together. Thus, we say and write:

could've for could have
should've for should have
would've for would have

This is a perfectly correct and natural kind of streamlining, in our *spoken* English. We, therefore, carry much of it over into our written English, too. But when we do this, we must be careful to write these *contractions* down correctly. Could've *sounds* like could of. But could of doesn't mean anything; could've does (could have). See SPELLING, pages 67-68, for a list of common contractions.

Don't Write:	*Write:*
Was I suppose to run after I hit the ball?	Was I supposed to run after I hit the ball?

Here too, the error is a matter of not hearing or not pronouncing all the sounds in the word. There is a d at the end of supposed. If you pronounce it correctly, you'll write it correctly.

What Do You Know?

Test Yourself—B. On a sheet of paper, write the numbers from 1 to 25. Read each of the following sentences. If the sentence is correct, put a + after the corresponding number. If the sentence is incorrect, put a o after the number. When you have completed the test, check your answers with the sentences and explanations that follow. The number at the end of each test sentence tells you which section to refer to.

1. If you didn't do anything, why were you called in to explain? (12)
2. Don't you think you had ought leave now? (18)
3. The dancer was light-complected. (10)
4. The dresser is so heavy I can't hardly move it. (14)
5. I was so tired I couldn't scarcely move. (16)
6. After paying his fare, he discovered he hadn't but one cent in his pocket. (17)
7. Where do you live at? (9)
8. Haven't you got nothing to do this evening? (12)

9. My father hasn't never neglected his duties. (15)
10. You've worked hard enough. You ought to rest now. (18)
11. You can't hardly blame me for not trusting him. (14)
12. Some people believe in the motto, "Every man for himself." (20)
13. I says to him, "You'd better not try that again." (11)
14. As the enemy moved up, Private Roark discovered he had bu one bullet left. (17)
15. They have no one to blame but theirselves. (19)
16. Do they agree that they ought to behave more considerately (18)
17. Where are you staying at? (9)
18. We had hardly begun walking when it started to rain. (13)
19. He can hardly run around the block. (14)
20. Jack hurt hisself in football scrimmage. (20)
21. Arabs are generally dark-complexioned. (10)
22. He turned to me and says, "Stop that foolish talk." (11)
23. Jack was so shocked he could scarcely speak. (16)
24. "You're the man for this job," I said to him. (11)
25. "I didn't do nothing," the criminal cried. (12)

Don't Write:	Write:
9. Where is his home at?	Where is his home?

The at isn't necessary in this sentence.

Don't Write:	Write:
10. The doctor was a dark-complected man.	The doctor was a dark-complexioned man.

Complected isn't a word.

Don't Write:	Write:
11. I looked at him and says, "Haven't we met before?"	I looked at him and said Haven't we met before?"

Don't use says for said. The past tense of say is said.

Don't Write:	Write:
12. He didn't do nothing.	He didn't do anything.
13. My sister hadn't hardly started practicing when the doorbell rang.	My sister had hardly started practicing when the doorbell rang.
14. She can't hardly hum a melody.	She can hardly hum a melody.

15. I **haven't** never done this   I **have** never done this before.
    before.
16. He **couldn't** scarcely move   He **could** scarcely move after
    after the accident.   the accident.
17. The hunter **hadn't** but one   The hunter **had** but one bullet
    bullet left.   left.

These are extremely common errors called *double negatives*. The rule here is to avoid using **not, can't, don't, haven't** or any of these forms with such words as **scarcely, hardly, but, nothing, never.**

Don't Write: *Write:*

18. I feel I had **ought** to rest   I feel I **ought** to rest now.
    now.

Ought should never be used with **have** or **has** or **had.**

Don't Write: *Write:*

19. Little children play better   Little children play better by
    by **theirselves.**   **themselves.**
20. He has no one to blame   He has no one to blame but
    but **hisself.**   **himself.**

There's nothing difficult about these forms. **Hisself** and **theirselves** just aren't recognized as socially acceptable words.

What Do You Know?

Test Yourself—C. On a sheet of paper write the numbers from 1 to 20. Read each of the following sentences. If the sentence is correct, put a **+** after the corresponding number. If the sentence is incorrect, mark it **o.** When you have completed the test, check your answers with the sections and explanations that follow. The number at the end of each test sentence tells you which section to refer to.

1. Is this pair of skates yours? (27)
2. This here house is for sale. (24)
3. I'm sure you'll like the party who is moving next door. (29)
4. Here in our town we see exhibits like you see in the large cities. (32)
5. There are signs of spring everywheres. (23)
6. Hold the banjo like Jim holds it if you want to play correctly. (33)
7. He played first like Lou Gehrig. (33)
8. I like them people because they are kind. (26)

9. He was dressed like Napoleon. (33)
10. Somewheres there must be a copy of the book you want. (21)
11. That boy which just left is my nephew. (28)
12. Before the man could object, the policeman took his license off of him. (34)
13. Men which want to write must have some training in journalism. (28)
14. He sounded like he was being tortured. (30)
15. It's very warm in here. Take your coat off. (34)
16. Take your hands off me. (34)
17. I can't find my pen anywhere. (22)
18. I like songs like those I heard in Mexico. (32)
19. The Colonel lives in that there apartment house. (25)
20. Tie this package like I told you. (31)

Don't Write:	*Write:*
21. You'll find him **somewheres** in the neighborhood.	You will find him **somewhere** in the neighborhood.
22. Have you seen him **any-wheres?**	Have you seen him **anywhere?**
23. **Everywheres** you go, you'll find sparrows.	**Everywhere** you go you'll find sparrows.

These words have only one correct form: **somewhere, any-where, everywhere, nowhere.** There is no **s** at the end of these words.

Don't Write:	*Write:*
24. **This here** book makes interesting reading.	**This** book makes interesting reading.
25. George Washington lived in **that there** house.	George Washington lived in **that** house.

You don't say **cold ice** or **hot fire**. That's using two words that mean the same thing. Similarly, you should avoid **this here** and **that there** because **here** and **there** are unnecessary:
This book means the book over here, in *this* place.
That house means the house over there, in *that* place.

Don't Write:	*Write:*
26. **Them** peaches taste delicious.	**Those** peaches taste delicious.

Them is a pronoun used instead of a noun but never before a noun.

Those is an adjective used to describe or tell something about a noun (peaches).

Don't Write:	Write:
27. Is this car yourn?	Is this car yours?

There is no word like yourn.

28. The people which were here asked for you.	The people who were here asked for you.

Which is never used to refer to people. Use who when referring to people.

Don't Write:	Write:
29. Do you know the party who wrote the book?	Do you know the person who wrote the book?

This use of party for person is correct only in legal documents where people are often referred to as "the party of the first part and the party of the second part." Avoid using party when you mean person.

Don't Write:	Write:
30. He looked like he meant to kill the detective.	He looked as if he meant to kill the detective.
He looked like he was going to leave.	He looked as if he were going to leave.
31. Do it like I tell you.	Do it as I tell you.
32. Some of our states have storms like you see in the tropics.	Some of our states have storms like those you see in the tropics.
33. He looks like my uncle used to look.	He looks as my uncle used to look.
He looks as my uncle.	He looks like my uncle.

Generally, like is used as a *preposition*. Therefore, it cannot introduce a clause. Only *conjunctions* and *relative pronouns* introduce clauses.

In the following sentence, like is correctly used as a preposition:

He looks like my uncle.

Uncle is the object of preposition **like.**

But in this sentence, **like** is *incorrectly* used as a *conjunction* to introduce a clause:

> He looks like my uncle used to look.

Avoid the use of **like** for **as** and **as if.**

Don't Write:	*Write:*
34. The conductor took the ticket off of me.	The conductor took the ticket from me.
or	
The conductor took the ticket off me.	

Use **off** when there is something actually *on* a person, and you are removing it. You can say:

> The doctor took my wart off. (He removed the wart.)
> I took my shoes off.

But when you are *taking something away* that belongs to someone, then use **from.** In the first sentence, the teacher took the pencil, which belonged to you, *from* you. Never use **off of.**

What Do You Know?

Test Yourself—D. On a sheet of paper write the numbers from 1 to 19. Read each of the following sentences. If the sentence is correct, mark the corresponding number +. If the sentence is incorrect, mark the number *o*. When you have completed the test, check your answers with the sentences and explanations that follow. The number at the end of each sentence tells you which section to refer to.

1. We'll be grateful for anything you can learn us. (36)
2. Leave us meet next week. (40)
3. If possible, I'd like to lend your car for a day. (38)
4. Leave me alone, you bully. (40)
5. Dad's new car is running good. (41)
6. Borrow me your knife, please. (38)
7. They left the old man standing in the rain. (40)
8. From where I stood, I seen the fire. (37)
9. Being as you'll be away during June, we'll have to postpone our meeting. (42)
10. My father wanted for me to go to college. (35)
11. Bob certainly rides his horse good. (41)

12. Since he wouldn't come in, they let the old man stand in the rain. (40)
13. May I have a lend of your flashlight? (38)
14. Being that we won the war, it is our duty to see that we win the peace, too. (43)
15. Is that gent your uncle? (44)
16. We can win if we co-operate together. (46)
17. Don't let me out when you make up the list for our next party. (40)
18. Before Congress adopts an atomic energy control plan, senators and congressmen will discuss about it thoroughly. (45)
19. Sanders serves the most delicious whip cream sundaes. (39)

	Don't Write:	*Write:*
35.	I want for you to come quickly.	I want you to come quickly.

The *for* isn't necessary in this sentence. It doesn't add anything to the sentence—except an extra word. Words that add nothing to a sentence have no place in it.

	Don't Write:	*Write:*
36.	**Learn** us this dance step.	**Teach** us this dance step.

We're almost ashamed to have to mention these two words here. But it's the sad truth that many people confuse them.

Learn means to get knowledge. **Learning** is something you do when you *get* knowledge.

Teach means to impart or give knowledge. **Teaching** is something *someone else* does.

Your teacher **teaches** you and you **learn**.

	Don't Write:	*Write:*
37.	I **seen** my duty and **done** it.	I saw my duty and did it.
		or
		I have seen my duty and have done it.

Seen and **done** are *past participles*. They should never be used alone without *helping* or *auxiliary verbs* like **have** or **has** or **had**. See pages 204-7 for a fuller explanation of this type of error.

Don't Write:	*Write:*
38. Please **borrow** me your umbrella.	Please **lend** me your umbrella.

When you **borrow**, you *accept* something *from* a person. You will return it in time. When you **lend**, you *give* something to a person. You expect it back in time.

In the following sentences, **borrow** and **lend** are correctly used:

> May I **borrow** your pencil?
> Please **lend** me your pencil.
> I will **lend** you the book for a week.
> You may **borrow** the book for a week.

Don't use **lend** as if it were a noun! It is incorrect to say:

> May I have a **lend** of your bicycle?

Don't Write:	*Write:*
39. Two scoops of **whip** cream for me, please.	Two scoops of **whipped** cream for me, please.

Whip is a verb. It can't modify the noun (cream).
Whipped is an adjective. It modifies the noun (cream).

Don't Write:	*Write:*
40. **Leave** us face the truth.	**Let** us face the truth.

These two verbs are very frequently confused. **Leave** means to allow to remain, or to go away, or to abandon. **Let** means to permit or to allow. The following sentences illustrate correct use of these verbs:

> **Leave** the knife where you found it. (allow to remain)
> "**Let** Me Call You Sweetheart" is a lovely song. (allow me)
> **Let** me do that job. (allow me)

The principal parts of these verbs are different. If you don't know the difference, you are sure to use them incorrectly.

Present	*Past*	*Past Participle*
leave	left	left
let	let	let

Note the difference in these sentences:

He left me alone. (He went away.)
He let me alone. (He didn't bother or pester me.)
They left me out. (They didn't include me.)
They let me out. (They allowed me to go out.)

Don't Write:	Write:
41. He does his work **good**.	He does his well **well**.

Good is an adjective. It can't be used to describe *how* he does his work. In this sentence, we aren't talking about good work but about *how* he does his work. Therefore we use **well** —an adverb telling how. We say:

He fights well, he runs well, he writes well, he wrestles well, he rides well.

Don't Write:	Write:
42. **Being as** you are my friend, how can I refuse?	**Since** you are my friend, how can I refuse?
43. **Being that** he was planning to go on a long trip, his father allowed him to take the station wagon.	**Since** (or **because**) he was planning to go on a long trip, his father allowed him to take the station wagon.

Don't use **being that** or **being as** for **since** or **because**. Don't use **being that** and **being as** at all—ever!

Don't Write:	Write:
44. Who was that **gent** I saw you with?	Who was that **gentleman** I saw you with?

Never use the word **gent** for **gentleman**.

Don't Write:	Write:
45. The Prime Ministers **discussed about** the peace treaty.	The Prime Ministers **discussed** the peace treaty.

Discussed means talked about. So there is no need for adding **about**.

Don't Write:	Write:
46. During the war, all groups **co-operated together**.	During the war, all groups **co-operated**.

Co-operated means worked together. Why use the same word (together) twice?

What Do You Know?

Test Yourself—E. On a sheet of paper write the numbers from 1 to 14. Read each of the following sentences. If the sentence is correct, mark + next to the number. If the sentence is incorrect, mark it o. When you have completed the test, check your answers with the sentences and explanations that follow. The number at the end of the sentence tells you which section to refer to.

1. The guilty are not always suspected. (49)
2. We were lucky to get Dr. Woolsey to operate my mother. (50)
3. Carl used to tease his little sister by hiding on her. (47)
4. Next week, he will graduate Blair Academy. (51)
5. Irregardless of the circumstances, I still think he's innocent. (52)
6. Thomas Edison he was one of the world's greatest inventors. (48)
7. Regardless of the weather, we start out tomorrow. (52)
8. In the midst of the performance, I was taken ill and rushed to the hospital where Dr. Ellen operated me. (50)
9. You can't hide from your conscience. (47)
10. My father graduated from Dartmouth. (51)
11. He acted so queerly we suspicioned him immediately. (49)
12. Dr. Warton operated on the president. (50)
13. One of our presidents was graduated from Princeton. (51)
14. Jim hid his raincoat on his mother. (47)

Don't Write:	Write:
47. Why did you hide the flowers on me?	Why did you hide the flowers from me?

Hiding flowers *on* somebody is the neatest trick of the week. Try to figure that out. How can you hide something *on* someone and still keep it hidden? When you hide something, you *remove it from* sight, so that it can't be easily found.

Don't Write:	Write:
48. My uncle he was decorated for bravery under fire.	My uncle was decorated for bravery under fire.

It isn't necessary to insert he in this sentence. The subject is uncle. Adding he does nothing to make the sentence any clearer.

| *Don't Write:* | *Write:* |

9. I suspicioned him immediately.   I suspected him immediately.

Suspicioned is no word.

| *Don't Write:* | *Write:* |

0. Dr. Stavin operated me for appendicitis.   Dr. Stavin operated on me for appendicitis.

Only machines are **operated**. People are not operated. They re **operated on**.

| *Don't Write:* | *Write:* |

1. Helen graduated Curtis High School.   Helen graduated from Curtis High School.

or

Helen was graduated from Curtis High School.

2. Irregardless of what you say, I'm going.   Regardless of what you say, I'm going.

There's no such word as **irregardless**.

17 WHY GRAMMAR?

Learning to write is very much like learning to drive a car. You can't do either one unless you know a few simple things. Let's take that car first. What must you know before you can drive it?

1. *The parts of the car*—not all, of course, but all the important ones that you will be using all the time when you drive. There's the

a. Steering wheel
b. Clutch
c. Brake
d. Accelerator (gas pedal)
e. Gear shift
f. Gas tank

g. Lights and ignition
h. Self-starter
i. Choke
j. Windshield-wiper
k. Gauges on the dash-board

2. *What each part does* in the running of the car. You don't have to be an expert here—but you must know what happens, for example, when

a. You turn the ignition key
b. You step on the starter
c. You step on the accelerator

d. You step on the brake
e. You put the car into first or second or reverse

If you don't know these few things and a few others, you are sure to get into trouble. You won't know when you're going too fast to stop or turn safely. You won't know how to slow up or how to make the car go faster. Not knowing these things, you will find driving just one disagreeable experience after another. That's how important it is for any driver to know what makes his car tick and what it will do under various conditions.

3. *Traffic rules.* You know all about these and what they are for. "Red light" means stop. "Green light" means go. "Don't speed on streets or highways." "Signal when you are going to turn." "Slow up at crossings." "Keep to the right." "Don't pass cars on a hill."

These are simple rules that all drivers must observe. They are made for the safety of all—drivers and pedestrians. Without these rules, it would be impossible for us to do any driving at all. Some drivers would keep to the left, others to the right. Some would observe traffic signals, others wouldn't. So to make sure that we all do the same things at the same time, we have devised these rules. *They make sense. They make for order.*

Of course, there are some people who manage to drive cars without knowing all these things. But they don't drive well—and many don't drive for long!

Writing and Grammar

What has all this to do with writing? Writing is no different. You can't learn to write unless you know what your language is made up of (sentences, phrases, clauses, participles, infinitives, etc.—they're just as simple to learn as gear shift and brake) and what these parts of our language do (how they operate)—and the rules we must observe when we try to get them all to work together. When we drive a car, we are interested in getting it started and having it take us quickly and safely where we want to go. When we write, we are trying to say something to somebody clearly, simply, and directly so that we can be immediately understood.

And grammar? Don't let it frighten you! It simply tells us what's what about our language, and why we should say certain things in certain ways (the rules) if we want to be clear and correct.

Again, of course, you can write (just as you can drive) without knowing too much about grammar. But you won't write too well. And when your writing breaks down (when you make an error), you won't know how to get it started again or how to repair it unless you know the parts of language and how they work.

In this section on grammar, we shall treat only those things that you will need to know in order to write and speak correctly and clearly. That's what you're interested in—improving your writing and speaking. That's what we're interested in, too. We think that's a big job. We want to help you get all the tools and understanding you need to do that job. So we're leaving out many things about grammar—not because we think you ought not to know about them—but because they won't help you much in your writing and speaking.

A word now about how to use this grammar section. You will find that many of your writing errors are errors in grammar. When you make these errors in your sentences, in your verbs, etc., refer to the part of this section that deals with these errors. You'll find the rules and explanations there that will help you correct them. If your writing is free of grammatical errors, you won't need to refer to this section. But, if you are wise, you will read it anyway, just to keep it fresh in your mind. And do the exercises just to keep in trim. Language is like a muscle. If you keep using it, it remains firm and supple. If you don't use it, it soon becomes flabby and useless.

18 *THE SENTENCE*

If you are a genius, skip this whole section on sentences. You don't need it. You always write complete, correct sentences.

But if you are just an average American who wants to learn to write his language passably well, sit up and take notice. This is for you.

The sentence is the basis of all writing. If you can't write complete and correct sentences, you can't write! You can make black marks on paper, but you can't make sense without sentences.

Do you doubt it? Let's see:

The Boss calls you and says, "Your salary for this week—"

Do you say, "Gee, Boss, thanks. You've made me very happy"?

Probably not. You'd ask, "Do I get that extra five dollars you promised me last week, Mr. Jones?"

Then your boss, looking a bit sadly at you, says, "I'm sorry. Your salary for this week remains the same."

Now you know! Mr. Jones has told you something—not what you wanted to hear, but something that answered your question.

Suppose that Mr. Jones had said to you, "Remains the same."

Would your answer have been: "Just as I thought"?

Or would you have asked, "What remains the same?"

And then he'd have told you, "Your salary for this week remains the same."

Here's your answer again. And the answer to the question:

What Is a Sentence?

Whenever you express a complete thought in which you name something and tell something about it, you've written a sentence.

Now, let's define the sentence again:

A sentence is a group of words (1) expressing a *complete thought* and (2) containing a *subject* and a *predicate*.

The *subject* is *what the sentence is about.*

The *predicate* tells *something about the subject.*

189

When your boss said, "Your salary for this week—" he was naming something (salary), but he wasn't telling anything about it. There was *no predicate*.

When your boss said, "Remains the same," he was telling something about something, but the something wasn't there. There was *no subject*.

But when your boss said, "Your salary for this week remains the same," he had spoken a complete sentence:

Your salary for this week / remains the same.
     (subject)   (predicate)

Now try your hand at the following exercise.

Exercise 1. Pick out the complete and incomplete sentences and tell why each is complete or incomplete. Try asking these questions:

A. To the door. (Who went to the door? *Whom are you talking about?* No sentence. No *subject*.)
B. The boy with red hair. (What about the boy? Have you *told* anything about him? (No sentence. No *predicate*.)
C. I can come at four. (Whom are you talking about? I. That's the subject. What are you telling about the *subject?* Can come at four. That's the *predicate*. Does it make sense? Yes. Does it leave any questions unanswered? No. Then it's a sentence!)

1. Around the room.
2. Told him to come.
3. Young girls.
4. The key to our home.
5. To the theater.
6. Wish you well.
7. A downpour of rain.
8. If it rains.
9. I can do it.
10. Am hoping to hear from you.
11. Winter is my favorite season.
12. Smashing it to bits.
13. To be a football player.
14. Skiing can be dangerous fun.
15. Edison, the inventor.

Never Write a Sentence Fragment

Never write a sentence without a subject and a predicate. This is called a *sentence fragment*—one of the unforgivable sins in writing: *It doesn't make sense.*

There is an apparent exception to this. Actually it is no exception. But it looks like one. When you are writing conversation (or dialogue), you don't always write it in complete sentences because people don't always talk in complete sentences. For example, in answer to the question, "Are you going out tonight?", you answer, "Yes." What you are really saying is "Yes, I am going out tonight." But the reader understands the rest of the sentence even though you haven't put it in. (For a fuller treatment of this point see QUOTATION MARKS, pages 280-81.)

We want to say a few things more about the sentence fragment. But before we do, let's talk briefly about—

The Subject and Predicate

Once you learn to spot the *subject* and *predicate* in a sentence, quickly and habitually, you've gone a long way toward writing correct and complete sentences. Here is a simple method for spotting the *subject* and *predicate* of a sentence.

You know now that:

The subject is *what the sentence is about.*

The *predicate* *tells something about the subject.*

In a sentence like this, it's very simple to pick out the subject and predicate:

| I | am going. |
| (subject) | (predicate) |

But not all sentences are so simple. Take one like this:

1. Evelyn, the girl I am going to marry, will leave from Hollywood Station for New York as soon as she can.

Or one like this:

2. After a few moments, Charles rose from his seat, ran to the telephone, and started dialing frantically as if he were reporting a fire.

These look a little harder, don't they? But they're really not.

In sentence 1, whom are you talking about? Evelyn, the girl I am going to marry. That's your subject—*your whole subject.* You thought only *Evelyn* was the subject and you didn't know what the girl I am going to marry was. That's simple, too. The girl I am going to marry is a *modifier*—any word or group of words added to another word to make the meaning clear or to express the idea more fully, more effectively, more precisely. If we didn't add the girl I am going to marry to Evelyn, we wouldn't have helped the reader get an exact idea of who Evelyn really was. **Evelyn, the girl I am going to marry** is the *complete subject*—the *simple subject*, Evelyn, and all her modifiers!

What about the predicate? That's easy, too.

Every predicate must have a *verb* for its base. This is called the *predicate verb*. What follows are the *modifiers*, which do the same for the *predicate verb* as they do for the *subject*. They give us a fuller, more detailed, more accurate idea of the verb. Together with the *predicate verb*, they tell us something about the subject.

Now, what is the *predicate verb* in sentence 1? **Will leave** is the predicate verb, and the rest of the sentence modifies **will leave**.

From where? From Hollywood Station.

Destination? For New York.

When? As soon as she can.

Now let's look at sentence 2.

Subject—Charles (that's all—no modifier).

*Predicate verb—*rose, ran, and started (there are three here). This is called a *compound predicate*. It contains more than one verb.

After a few moments (modifier) tells when he **rose, ran, and started**. Everything else but Charles is the *predicate*.

And that's all there is to this whole subject and predicate business. Pick out what you are talking about and that's your subject. You may be talking about one or two or a million things. It doesn't have to be just one thing or person to be a subject. Anything and everything the sentence is talking about (together with those *modifiers*) is the subject. The rest is the predicate verb or verbs and modifiers.

And remember, too, that the subject isn't always the first word in the sentence. Sometimes it comes in the middle of the sentence or close to the end. But if you just keep asking yourself, "What or whom is he talking about?" you can't miss.

Exercise 2. Write out the following sentences. Underline the subject in each of the sentences and indicate whether it is simple or compound.

1. Sitting in the corner of the room was my long-lost friend.
2. On the other hand, few men like to shave every morning.
3. Wishing is fun.
4. Present at the graduation were friends and relatives of the graduates.

5. Frank and I went to the ball game last week.
6. To make a mistake is only human.
7. After the bell rang, row after row of men filed out of the factory.
8. When asked where he was going, the boy refused to answer.
9. Present at the convention were some men I had known for a long time.
10. Pleasant are the hopes and dreams of a young man.

Exercise 3. Write out the following sentences. Underline the predicate of each and indicate whether it is simple or compound, using S for simple, C for compound.

1. The day before the vacation, the pupils danced and sang as they left school.
2. Unusual indeed was his hobby of collecting toy locomotive parts.
3. The boxer, shaken by the force of the blows, tottered and staggered around the ring.
4. There were many passengers in the railroad station.
5. Where were you on the night of January 16th?
6. "No," came the reply to my request for an increase in salary.
7. When asked, the politician hemmed and hawed and did not reply.
8. The long lines of miners coming out of the pits seemed endless.
9. Few of the men who attended the party enjoyed themselves.
10. Most men like to swim and to play baseball.

Clauses and Phrases

Now that you understand that a sentence doesn't make sense without a subject and predicate, we're ready to move on to some of the specific things that lead people into this kind of error. You'll recognize all of them at once. But we want you to know exactly what is happening in each of these instances. It may be fun to be fooled but it's even more fun to know why. Once you know where the traps are, and how they work, you won't fall into them so easily. Or if you do, you'll be able to get yourself free with very little effort.

The Clause

When you have paid your dues.

Is that a sentence? Let's apply those tests we spoke of.
Does it have a subject? Yes. You is the subject.
Does it have a predicate? Yes. Have paid your dues is the predicate.

Does it make sense? No. There's a question in your mind, isn't there? What will happen **when you have paid your dues?** There's something missing here. **When you have paid your dues** is incomplete. It needs something else—something like this: When you have paid your dues, *you will get your membership card.* Now it's complete. Now it answers the question: What will happen?

What then is **When you have paid your dues?** It's a *dependent* or *subordinate clause.* It can't stand alone. It leans on something else in the sentence for support. It needs something else to complete its meaning: **You will get your membership card.** This is an *independent* or *principal clause.* It can stand alone. It needs no support. Its meaning is clear and complete. You'll have no difficulty with the independent clause. It's the *dependent clause* that fools so many people because it looks like what it isn't. So let's take another look at it.

A dependent clause—

1. has a subject.
2. has a predicate.
3. is introduced by words like:

a. **when, where, although, because, since, while, etc.** These are called *subordinating conjunctions.* They join the *dependent* clause with the *independent* clause.

b. **who, which, that.** These are relative pronouns and the clauses they introduce are *dependent relative clauses.*

So when you see any of these words, stop and look for a dependent clause and be sure that you don't use this dependent clause as a sentence.

A sentence that contains one independent clause and one or more dependent clauses is called a *complex sentence.*

While he was reading his paper, someone picked his pocket.

Someone picked his pocket (independent or principal clause).

While he was reading his paper (dependent clause).

In Chapter 7 on pages 82-83, we saw how the complex sentence is used to show that one idea in the sentence is more important than another. The correct use of the dependent clause enables you to express yourself more clearly and precisely.

A sentence that contains two or more independent clauses is a *compound sentence*.

In a compound sentence, the independent clauses are generally connected by *co-ordinate conjunctions,* such as and, but, or, nor, etc. Sometimes the conjunctions are omitted and semicolons are used.

> I like tea, but Marjorie prefers coffee. (two independent clauses joined by but)
>
> I like tea; Marjorie prefers coffee. (two independent clauses. Semi-colon used instead of but because the contrast between the two clauses is clear)

Exercise 4. In the following, pick out the complete and incomplete sentences. Where a dependent clause has been used for a sentence, add a principal clause to make the sentence complete. (Look for those telltale *conjunctions* and *relative pronouns.*)

1. Whenever it suits my purpose.
2. Since you cannot come, we'll have to call the meeting off.
3. Because the diplomats couldn't agree.
4. While the cook was out.
5. The boundaries of the various countries will be determined when the diplomats meet.
6. If at first you don't succeed, try again.
7. Whether he will become president.
8. Although it was hot, he continued to wear his overcoat.
9. The team that failed to win.
10. Where there's smoke, there's fire.
11. The men who fought at St. Lo were decorated for valor.
12. The uses of adversity may be sweet, but I prefer prosperity.
13. He was an able man; yet they did not elect him.
14. Either you accept the challenge or I will have to strike your name off the list.
15. If winter comes.
16. You must stop this noise or I shall call the police.
17. While the potatoes were cooking.
18. Since there's no help, come, let us part.
19. Why he did this.

The Phrase

To the door.
To be sick.
Going to the store.

Are these sentences? Of course not. They are our old friends, the fragments, again. They aren't sentences because:

1. They have *no subjects*.
2. They have *no predicates*.
3. They *don't make sense* standing by themselves.

They aren't clauses either because:

1. They have *no subjects*.
2. They have *no predicates*.
3. They aren't introduced either by *conjunctions* or *relative pronouns*.

What are they? *Phrases* are what we call constructions like these. They are *groups of related words* without subjects or predicates. They cannot stand alone. They cannot be used as sentences. They are tacked on to other words in sentences to make the meaning clearer or fuller, or to add variety and emphasis to your sentences. (See pages 88-90, 145-46 for a discussion of how these phrases are used to give variety and meaning and precision to your writing.)

There are three kinds of phrases: prepositional, infinitive, participial.

The Prepositional Phrase

You can tell a prepositional phrase very easily. It is introduced by words like in, into, after, above, etc. These are called *prepositions*. Here are the commonest prepositions:

above	below	by
after	beside	except
among	between	for
at	but (when it	from
before	means except)	in
into	on	under
like	over	upon
near	through	with
of	to	without
off	toward	

The prepositional phrase consists of the preposition and its object (a noun or pronoun). Generally, the prepositional phrase modifies some word in the sentence.

Preposition	+	Object	=	Prepositional Phrase
in		the house		in the house
with		the boys		with the boys
to		him		to him
before		her		before her

The Infinitive Phrase

An infinitive is a verb form consisting of two parts: the preposition **to** and the verb:

Preposition	+	Verb	=	Infinitive
to		come		to come
to		go		to go
to		have gone		to have gone
to		have been killed		to have been killed

An infinitive phrase consists of the infinitive plus its modifiers:

Infinitive	+	Modifiers	=	Infinitive Phrase
to be		sick		to be sick
to have gone		to the country		to have gone to the country
to be called		for jury duty		to be called for jury duty

Infinitives and infinitive phrases may be used in a variety of ways in the sentence but *they never* can be used alone instead of sentences.

The skillful use of the infinitive phrase lends variety and interest to your writing. (See page 90.)

The Participial Phrase

A participle is formed by adding **ing, d, ed, en, n,** or **t** to the main stem of the verb: bringing, parted, spoken, etc. It is commonly used as an adjective.

The participial phrase consists of the participle plus its modifiers or words necessary to complete its meaning.

Participle	+	Modifiers	=	Participial Phrase
going		to the movies		going to the movies
caught		in the rush		caught in the rush
illuminated		by the flares		illuminated by the flares
having driven		to the country		having driven to the country

Participial phrases, like infinitive and prepositional phrases, make your writing clearer and more interesting to read. (See pages 93 and 146.)

The Run-on Sentence

Careless writers often fall into another kind of error—the run-on sentence—the sentence that doesn't know where to stop. In this kind of error, a comma is put where a period should be. Ideas that should be separated, collide and produce confusion:

> Don't worry about Jim's safety, football is a game he knows how to play well.

There are two separate ideas here. They should be kept apart so that the reader can see that they are separate ideas. The period shows where one idea ends and another begins:

> Don't worry about Jim's safety. Football is a game he knows how to play well.

There are other ways than the use of the period to avoid the run-on sentence: If the ideas in the two sentences are closely related, and of equal importance, use a semicolon:

> Meet me at Bill's at six; I'll be there waiting for you.

Or use *co-ordinating conjunctions* like but, and if the ideas are parallel and closely related:

> Many are called, but few are chosen.
> I like coffee, and she likes tea.

Or use *subordinating conjunctions* like because, if, whether, since, etc., if one of the ideas is less important than the other:

> Most savages are content with their lot because they do not know any better.

Exercise 5. Some of the following are complete sentences. Some are run-on sentences. Some are fragments—phrases or clauses used instead of sentences. Write the numbers from 1 to 30. Beside the corresponding numbers write for each sentence:

C. for Complete Sentence
R. O. for Run-on Sentence
F. C. for Fragment—Clause
F. P. for Fragment—Phrase

1. Although you have convinced me.
2. Since you are unwilling to accept the nomination, we shall have to look for another candidate.
3. Come with us, we're sure to have fun.
4. To be a good fellow.
5. Coming up the street.
6. Because he couldn't say, "Yes."
7. There never was a time like the present.
8. Try to do it, you will find it very simple, indeed.
9. To the bathhouse.
10. Hoping to hear from you.
11. Being a Boy Scout is wonderful preparation for adult living.
12. To be thrifty is not easy.
13. Whether you like it or not.
14. Sign on the dotted line, you won't regret it.
15. There are men who will tell you that it is easy to resist such temptations, don't believe them, they are talking sheer nonsense.
16. Slowly but surely the soldiers came out of their foxholes.
17. The airplane going around in circles.
18. In the afternoon.
19. Because my friend likes baseball, we often go to ball games, we go to basketball games too.
20. Since you went away.
21. "To be or not to be" isn't an easy question to answer.
22. While you were in the Army having a difficult time of it.
23. Pasted in the upper left-hand corner of the envelope was an air-mail stamp.
24. You may have the book, I have finished it.
25. And while we are on the subject.
26. Up in Northern New York.
27. Until we get home tomorrow afternoon.
28. When day is done and shadows fall.
29. Never in my life did I see such a mess.
30. Singing and dancing in the breeze.

Exercise 6. Pick out the phrase in each of the following sentences and tell whether it is an infinitive, a prepositional, or a participial phrase.

1. The batter hit the ball into the left-field stands.
2. He would have liked to go to the beach that afternoon.
3. Among the new students, there were many we liked.
4. Hidden in the brush was a frightened rabbit.

5. "To err is human" is a famous quotation.
6. Sleeping in the subway can be restful.
7. Far above Cayuga's waters lies Cornell University.
8. In the evening, many people take a quiet walk.
9. Very few men like to wash dishes.
10. Without a smile, the day seems very gloomy.
11. For those who do not try, writing is difficult.
12. They found the lost puppy nestled deep in the sofa.
13. His parents wanted him to amount to something.
14. To become president is the ambition of most youngsters.
15. We find that walking early in the morning is good for our spirits.
16. He did nothing but laugh uproariously when the Mickey Mouse cartoon was shown.
17. The main purpose of the affair was to demonstrate Inter-American solidarity.
18. Circling the airport very slowly, the airplane flashed the landing signal.
19. In the moonlight, everything seems particularly romantic.
20. It is a good practice to speak only when spoken to.

19 THE VERB

How Are Your Verbs? Some of the following sentences are incorrect because the wrong form of the verb is used. Correct those sentences that are in need of correction.

1. Frank begun to do his work as soon as he come in.
2. Edward had drunk all the soda by the time I arrived.
3. George had eat all the frankfurters before we had any.
4. The tenor sung all my favorite songs.
5. I had to admit that I had never swum across the pool in all my life.
6. Dick had went to all the home baseball games of the Yankees.
7. We seen that movie twice and enjoyed it both times.
8. The cat sprung at the thief but did not succeed in scratching him.
9. Babe Ruth swang at the ball and missed it.
10. The shortstop throwed the ball past the first baseman for an error.
11. During the war, I had wrote many letters to the boys overseas.
12. Did you swore never to tell a lie again?
13. He had ridden many miles on the Baltimore and Ohio railroad.
14. When asked how he became so tall, the youngster replied, "I just growed."
15. The boat sunk beneath the ocean after a torpedo had cut it in two.
16. That the bell had been rung was obvious from the vibrations that continued.
17. Because of the extreme cold, the river had froze up.
18. Leonardo da Vinci has drawn many a fine sketch of the human body.
19. Have you chose all the officers of your club yet?
20. The wind had blown the kite a full mile from where I let it go.
21. My friend is a doctor for the last five years.
22. He was a doctor for three years when I was graduated from high school.
23. I have finished the job three hours ago.
24. They have been going to the movies every Thursday evening for the past five years.
25. The baby drunk his milk from the glass.
26. The landlord asked the boys who rung the bell to stop the noise.

27. My sister washed the floor when I came home.
28. My father had brought a quart of ice cream home when I arrived so I helped him finish it.
29. I want to see a real stage play for three years now.
30. When George finished the book, he took it back to the library.

The Simple Verb

The verbs in these test sentences are the simplest and commonest in our language. It is almost impossible to write or say anything without using them. Just try going a whole day without using verbs like say, do, come, bring, take, drink, eat, etc. You'll see how important they are in your daily speech and conversation. Since they are so important and so common, we are expected to use them correctly all the time.

So let's get them straight. It's really very simple. There are just a few things about verbs you'll have to remember in order to use them correctly.

The verb is a word that says something about its subject. It tells what the subject is doing, feeling, thinking, etc. Sometimes it is called an *action* word. But all verbs do not express action. A verb like sleep, for example, does not express action. It expresses just the opposite. But whether it expresses action or not, the important thing to remember is *that it says something about its subject*. The verb, together with its modifiers and words that complete its meaning, is the *predicate* of the sentence. (See VERB AND SUBJECT, pages 210-15.)

Tense—Present, Past, Future

In addition to telling us what is happening to the subject, the verb tells us *when* it is taking place. The *when* of a verb or the *time* at which the action is taking place is called *tense*. The verb changes its form to show changes in time or tense. Events take place in the:

Time—(Tense)	*Example*
Present—(Now)	I look or I am looking
Past—(Yesterday)	I looked or I was looking
Future—(Tomorrow)	I shall or will look, or I am going to look.

Most verbs are like look. They form the past tense simply by adding d or ed to the *present*. They form the *future* tense by putting shall or will or am going to before the present.

Present Tense	Past Tense	Future Tense
start	started	shall or will start, am going to start
return	returned	shall or will return, am going to return
smoke	smoked	shall or will smoke, am going to smoke
dance	danced	shall or will dance, am going to dance

Present Perfect Tense

The present, past, and future tenses are quite simple. But they do not express *all* the kinds of *time relationships* we commonly talk about. Let's take a specific example:

1. Margaret was here for five years.
2. Margaret has been here for five years.

Do these two sentences mean the same thing? Not at all.

1. "Margaret *was* (past tense) *here* for five years" means she is no longer here. She is now in some other city.
2. "Margaret *has been* here for five years" means that she moved here five years ago and *is still* here.

Has been here is a new kind of *time* we are talking about —a sort of combination of the *present* (she is still here) and the *past* (she moved here five years ago). When we are talking about something that happened in the past and is continuing to happen in the present, we use the *present perfect tense*.

Here are some examples of this use of the present perfect tense:

1. I have been working hard all week. (You worked from Monday to Friday. Today is Saturday and you are still working hard.)
2. How long have you been studying Spanish? (You are still studying Spanish at this present moment.)
3. I have been his friend for many years. (And you are still his friend.)

Another use of the present perfect tense is to tell about something *just completed*, when the feeling is that it happened not too far in the past, and that it still has some effect on the present. You will see this point more clearly in the following examples:

> "John, won't you have some pie?"
> "No, thank you. I have just eaten."

The act of eating is past. But you feel, don't you, that it is in the *immediate past*, not too far in the past, perhaps only an hour ago? And the fact that you *have eaten* has some effect on your *present* feelings: You aren't hungry now.

> "Aren't you coming to work this morning?"
> "I don't think so. I have been ill all week."

You are feeling better now. The illness is *past*. But the *effects* of the illness are still *present*. That is why you don't want to go to work. So we use the present perfect tense in this instance because we are talking about something *just completed* (illness) that still has some effect on the present (you still feel a little weak).

Some more examples:

> I have been punished enough. (I won't take any more.)
> I have done the job you gave me. (Now I'm free.)
> I have read that book. (I don't have to read it again.)

Notice that in all these examples, the *exact time* in the past is not given. It is indefinite—but close to the present.

But when the *exact time* in the past is mentioned, use the *past tense*.

> I ate my lunch at twelve o'clock.
> I dug the ditch last week.
> The caravan arrived on Monday.

Forming the Present Perfect Tense

We form the present perfect tense by adding has or have, to the past participle. These are called *auxiliary* or *helping* verbs.

With the regular verbs, there is no problem about forming the *present perfect tense*. Just put have or has before the *past tense* (which is the same as the past participle).

REGULAR VERBS

Past Tense	Past Participle	Present Perfect
loved	loved	have or has loved
spurted	spurted	have or has spurted
killed	killed	have or has killed
picked	picked	have or has picked

The Trouble Makers

The following are the verbs that cause most of the trouble because they are *irregular verbs.* The *present* and *past* tense are entirely different in *form* and *sound.* They present the same difficulties in the *present perfect* as they do in the *past.*

There is one thing to do about these irregular verbs, and only one thing. *Memorize the tenses.* That's all there is to it —nothing more. There's no rule to help you here as with the regular verbs. That's what makes these irregular verbs a trifle difficult. They're not "regular guys." Each one is a "special case." So the best thing to do is to take them one at a time or maybe two or three at a time, and get them down pat. Once you've learned them, they'll stick with you—and you'll have no more verb trouble.

PRINCIPAL PARTS OF VERBS

Present Tense	Past Tense	Past Participle
am	was	been
beat	beat	beaten
become	became	become
begin	began	begun
blow	blew	blown
break	broke	broken
bring	brought	brought
burst	burst	burst
buy	bought	bought
catch	caught	caught
choose	chose	chosen
come	came	come
do	did	done
draw	drew	drawn
drink	drank	drunk
drive	drove	driven
eat	ate	eaten
fall	fell	fallen
fly	flew	flown
freeze	froze	frozen

Present Tense	Past Tense	Past Participle
get	got	got, gotten
give	gave	given
go	went	gone
grow	grew	grown
hang	hung	hung
hurt	hurt	hurt
know	knew	known
lay	laid	laid
lead	led	led
leave	left	left
lie (recline)	lay	lain
ride	rode	ridden
ring	rang	rung
rise	rose	risen
run	ran	run
say	said	said
see	saw	seen
set	set	set
shake	shook	shaken
shrink	shrank	shrunk
sing	sang	sung
sink	sank	sunk
sit	sat	sat
speak	spoke	spoken
spring	sprang	sprung
steal	stole	stolen
sting	stung	stung
strike	struck	struck
strive	strove	striven
swear	swore	sworn
swim	swam	swum
swing	swung	swung
take	took	taken
tear	tore	torn
throw	threw	thrown
wear	wore	worn
write	wrote	written

Important

1. Don't use the *past participle* alone without **have** or **has** (auxiliary verbs).

Don't Write:	Write:
I done it.	I have done it.
I seen it.	I have seen it.
I drunk my milk.	I have drunk my milk.

2. Don't use the *past participle* alone for the *past tense.*

Don't Write:	*Write:*
Yesterday I run two miles.	Yesterday, I ran two miles.
Last March, I swum the Channel.	Last March, I swam the Channel.

Past Perfect Tense

You won't have as much occasion to use this tense as the others. But there are certain ideas that you can't express unless you use the past perfect tense.

Let's take a few examples to begin with:

1. He counted his money when I arrived.
2. He had counted his money when I arrived.

What's the difference?

In sentence 1, two events *in the past* happened *at the same time in the past:*

The counting of the money (he *counted* the money—past tense).

I saw him count the money (when I *came* in—past tense).

In sentence 2, two events happened in the *past* but one came *before* the other:

He *had counted* the money when I arrived. (I didn't see him do the counting. That happened *before* I arrived.)

Had counted is the *past perfect tense.* When you are talking about two events that take place in the past and you want to show which one happened *first,* use the *past perfect* tense for the event which took place *first.*

Form the past perfect tense by putting had before the past participle. (See PRESENT PERFECT TENSE, pages 203-5.)

Examples:
1. The second feature began as I settled into my seat.
2. The second feature had begun as I settled into my seat.
   (In which sentence did you miss part of the picture?)
3. The train pulled out of the station when I reached the platform.
4. The train had pulled out of the station when I reached the station.
   (In which sentence did you miss the train "by a hair"? In which did you miss it "by a mile"?)

Tense Sequence

In general, the tenses of verbs in a sentence should be the same. That's a sensible rule. Let's see why. Take this sentence:

I **was** at home because I **am** sick.

Now, what happens to the reader of this sentence? He begins by thinking of you in the *past* (was) and then suddenly he finds you talking about yourself in the *present* (am).

I **was** at home because I **was** sick.

Now that makes better sense, doesn't it? To prevent this kind of confusion, keep the tenses of your verbs straight. If you are writing in the present tense, keep your whole composition in that tense. Your reader will be living in the *present* with you as you write. Don't shock him by suddenly writing in the past tense unless you really mean to refer to something that has happened in the past.

Exercise 1. Correct the verbs in the following sentences where correction is necessary:

1. Frank had drunk two ice cream sodas when the gang walked in.
2. She wants to go to the seashore for the past two months.
3. Hardly did she jump from the plane when the parachute opened.
4. We finished the payroll last night.
5. I joined the Boy Scouts when I was younger because I liked to go on hikes.
6. We have eaten our lunch at one o'clock.
7. They saw the movie before I got a chance to go.
8. You should have did your work more efficiently.
9. Gene has been in New York for two years but he doesn't live here any more.
10. I did the dishes when the girls arrived so I was able to leave with them immediately to see a movie.
11. In a flurry of activity, the boys swum across the river.
12. That was the best movie I ever seen.
13. For three years, I would like to go to the country for the summer.
14. After I had asked him to, George set the book on the table.
15. The driver had rode all day and was very tired when he came in.

16. It was easy to see that the coat had lain out in the rain all night.
17. When I came back to work, I discovered that George started his vacation that very day.
18. I had come back East well after the beginning of the year.
19. Ty Cobb stole more bases than any other ball player who ever lived.
20. I laid under the tree for three hours that afternoon.
21. The team was beat by a determined group of players.
22. Last week I had finished my painting.
23. John did not come to the rally yesterday because he has to rest his injured ankle.

20 VERB AND SUBJECT

Do They Agree? Choose the word in parentheses that makes the sentence correct. The number at the end of each sentence refers to the section below that explains it.

1. Neither of you (is, are) correct. (3)
2. Neither of your reasons (is, are) acceptable. (3)
3. One of these books (is, are) mine. (1e)
4. Either Jim or Jack (is, are) eligible for the office. (1f)
5. Neither Jane nor her friends (is, are) ready to leave. (1f)
6. Neither my brothers nor my sister (is, are) at home. (1f)
7. There (is, are) several men waiting for you. (9), (1c)
8. Jim, Henry, and Jack (was, were) present at the game. (1b)
9. I didn't think you (was, were) coming. (8)
10. Where (is, are) your mother and father? (1b)
11. There (is, are) five ways of doing that job. (9), (1c)
12. Capital, as well as labor, (is, are) to blame. (1e)
13. The effects of the new ruling (was, were) apparent to everybody. (1e)
14. I shall be happy to be one of the men who (is, are) chosen to represent the union at the conference. (2)
15. The problem of taxes (demand, demands) the best understanding of our legislators. (1e)
16. All of us (was, were) responsible. (4)
17. All of the honey (was, were) gone. (4)
18. Some of the members (has, have) returned. (4)
19. Every man and woman (was, were) required to pay dues. (3)
20. Where (is, are) the scissors? (7)
21. Civics (is, are) my best subject. (6)

If you got all of these sentences correct, and if you know why, then you don't have any "agreement" trouble. But if you didn't do too well, if you guessed, or if you weren't certain, then read the following sections carefully.

All the sentences you have just tried to correct reveal whether you know a very important thing about your writing and speaking. You've heard it before. But it will bear repeating because the failure to learn it accounts for a great number or errors.

Here It Is

1. The *verb* must agree with its *subject* in *person* and *number*. *Number* shows whether the subject (noun or pronoun) is

		Noun	Pronoun
Singular	one	boy	he
Plural	more than one	boys	they

A singular subject takes a singular verb.
A plural subject takes a plural verb.

How It Works

a. My mother is at home.

Subject—**mother**—singular.
Verb—**is**—singular.
That's simple—no question here.

b. My mother and father are here.

Subject—**mother and father**—plural—more than one person. This is called a *compound subject*.
There's nothing puzzling about this, either. The conjunction **and** shows that one thing is being added to another. That means *plural*.

c. Some mothers are more understanding than others.

Subject—**mothers**—plural—more than one.
Verb—**are**—plural.
This is easy, too.

d. Mother, father, sister are coming along soon.

Subject—**Mother, father, sister**—plural—three people.
Verb—**are coming**—plural.
You weren't fooled by this, were you? It's still a compound subject. There's no and here—but it's quite clear that you are adding **mother** plus **father** plus **sister**.

e. My mother together with my father is coming to the fair.

Are you surprised at the verb **is**? Shouldn't it be **are**? Not at all. Let's see why.

Subject—mother—singular.

What about father? The sentence reads: **together with father. Father** is *object* of the preposition **with**; with **father** modifies **mother**. It's a *prepositional phrase*—not another subject.

Turn the sentence around and you'll see that **father** is really not the subject:

> Mother is coming to the fair **together with father.**

Clear? Let's try another just to make certain. Take sentence 13:

> The effects of the ruling were apparent to everyone.

Subject—effects—plural.

Verb—were—plural.

Were you confused by **of the ruling**? It's just another prepositional phrase. Ask yourself now: What was apparent to everyone? The ruling? Of course not. The effects? Yes.

So watch your subject. Keep asking "How many?" and make the verb agree with it in number. Just a little thought and a little care—that's all. There's nothing very difficult about it.

It doesn't matter how many words come between the subject and its verb. It's the subject itself that counts. Find your subject. Get its number, *singular* or *plural,* and then make the verb agree.

Special Cases

There are some special problems in agreement. The following rules explain them.

    f. John or Mary **is** going.
       Neither John nor Mary **is** going.

A compound subject whose parts are joined by **or** or **nor** takes a singular verb if each of the parts is singular. But *note:* If the parts of the subject *differ* in person or number, the verb agrees with the subject *nearer* to it.

Neither my brother nor my sisters (plural) are (plural) going.

Neither my sisters nor my brother is going.

2. A relative pronoun (who, which) agrees with the word it refers to (its *antecedent*) in person and number. The verb agrees with the relative pronoun in person and number. This sounds a little difficult so let's illustrate it with a sentence.

I was happy to be one of the men who were chosen to represent the union at the conference.

who (relative pronoun) refers to men; men is plural; therefore who is plural and takes were, plural verb.

Let's change the sentence somewhat and see how this relative pronoun relationship works out somewhat differently:

I shall be happy to be the one who is chosen to represent the union at the conference.

who (relative pronoun) refers to one; one is singular; therefore who is singular and takes is, singular verb.

The same principle holds here as in the other examples we have dealt with. Ask yourself:

What does the relative pronoun refer to?

What is its number? Singular or plural?

The relative pronoun then takes its number from the word it refers to—and the verb agrees with the relative pronoun.

3. Words like each, either, every, neither, everyone, anyone, nobody, etc., are singular and take singular verbs.

Every, each, no, attached to a subject make the subject singular.

Every man is welcome to join this organization.

Each man and woman is welcome to join this organization.

4. All, more, some take either a singular or a plural verb depending upon the sense of the sentence.

Some of us are satisfied.

Some here means more than one.

Some of the candy is left.

Some here is singular. The emphasis is on *how much,* not how many.

All of us are home. (plural)
All of the money was spent. (singular)

Just a lump sum—no emphasis on the number of dollars spent.

5. Some nouns that are names of groups (they are called *collective nouns*) take either singular or plural verbs depending on whether you are thinking of the group as a whole, or as individual persons. These are words like **crowd, family, team, army, committee, majority,** etc.

The majority of the members were in favor of the new law.

Here you're thinking of them as individuals.

The majority was in favor of the new law.

Here the group as a whole is considered.

6. Some words like **athletics, news, physics, mathematics, civics, ethics,** though they are plural in form, take a singular verb.

Mathematics is a difficult subject to master.
Athletics gives young people a chance to develop themselves physically.

7. Some words like **scissors, pincers, wages, pants** always take a plural verb. (See PLURALS, page 288, for a fuller list of such words.)
8. The word **you** always takes a plural verb.
9. Sentences beginning with **there** are a little tricky. To make sure that subject and verb agree, just drop the **there** out of the sentence and put the subject before the verb.

There are several men waiting for you.
    (verb)   (subject)
Several men are waiting for you.
    (subject)(verb)

There is a bottle of catsup on the table.
     (*verb*)(*subject*)
A bottle of catsup is on the table.
     (*subject*)   (*verb*)

Exercise 1. Choose the word in parentheses that makes the sentence correct.

1. Neither my sister nor my brothers (is, are) eager for me to prepare for the civil-service examinations.
2. The captain, as well as the entire crew, (is, are) unwilling to make the trip.
3. The main part of the skates (was, were) removed.
4. Neither you nor she (is, are) in the wrong.
5. The entire club (is, are) present for the important voting.
6. Six per cent (is, are) a usual rate of interest for mortgages.
7. The supporters of the change in the Constitution (is, are) in the minority.
8. All of the food (was, were) consumed by the hungry picnickers.
9. The man volunteered to be one of the persons who (was, were) drafting the new by-laws for the club.
10. All of us (was, were) present when the politician made his campaign pledges.
11. (Was, were) you on the committee chosen to run the affair?
12. The dreams of the young man (was, were) in the process of being realized.
13. Who (is, are) the bridesmaid and the best man at this wedding?
14. Either you or I (am, are) eligible for office.
15. None of us knew that the results of the election (was, were) so favorable for our side.
16. Frank will be there and his mother and father (is, are) coming too.
17. Not a single one of the movies (was, were) distinguished for fine acting.
18. The whole question of ground rules (was, were) discussed by the umpire and the captains of the two teams.
19. The boy soon discovered that there (was, were) many obstacles to his attaining his goal.
20. Some of my best friends (is, are) older than I.

21 PRONOUNS

Do They Agree? Choose the word in parentheses that makes the sentence correct.

1. Be sure that everybody brings (his, their) togs along.
2. If anybody calls, tell (him, them) that I'll be back in half an hour.
3. Nobody is required to report (his, their) absence to the supervisor.
4. Each one of us had (his, their) fingerprints taken.
5. No one was able to bring (his, their) instrument along.
6. Each member must show (his, their) card before entering.
7. I'm sure someone has forgotten (his, their) lunch.
8. Every one of the soldiers was able to pass (his, their) tests.
9. Any man who doesn't meet these requirements will have (his, their) name removed from the list.

How did you score on these sentences? Did any of them puzzle you? Did you know why you chose one of the words in parentheses?

Maybe you recognized that these sentences are, in a way, like those on the verb and its subject. They present problems in *agreement*. The rule is the same here:

The pronoun must agree with the word it refers·to (its antecedent) in *person* and *number*.

Number simply shows whether the pronoun is singular or plural.

Person shows whether the pronoun represents

the speaker—first person
the one spoken to—second person
the one spoken about—third person

Examples

I am having a fine time.

First person—the speaker is *I*.

You may come at nine.

216

Second person—someone is talking to *you*.

He is my best friend.

Third person—someone is talking *about* someone else.

The form of the pronoun changes to show difference in person and number—like this:

	Singular Number	Plural Number
First person	I, me, mine, my	we, us, our, ours
Second person	you, your, yours	you, your, yours
	thou, thee, thy, thine	
Third person	he, him, his, she, her	they, them, their, theirs
	hers, it, its	

Now, back to that rule we just mentioned:

A pronoun must agree with its antecedent (word it refers to) in *number* and *person*.

The application of the rule is especially important in the test sentences you have just worked on. Here's why: As you can see from the list above, the English language doesn't have any pronoun in the third person singular that means "his or her" or "he or she"—in other words, that refers to *one* person who may be *either male or female*. So, if we need a pronoun to refer to words like **anyone, anybody, everyone, everybody, someone,** or **somebody** (words that mean a single person of either sex), we would have to say "he or she" or "his or her." But we usually don't do that because it takes too much time. Instead, we use a makeshift device: Ordinarily, we use the masculine pronoun—he, him, his—and just skip the or she or or her; often, in informal talk, we use the plural —they, them, their. The "safe" way out, in writing, is to use the masculine singular form.

Let's see how it works out in some of those test sentences. Take sentence 1:

Be sure that everybody brings ———— togs along.

The togs belong to *everybody*—and *everybody* may be either a boy or a girl. So the foolproof way to write the sentence is this:

Be sure that everybody brings **his or her** togs along.

But that's much too awkward. So we write:

> Be sure that everybody brings his togs along.

That's the usual way to write this kind of sentence. The reader will understand that we mean the girls, too.

In conversation, we would probably say:

> Be sure that everybody brings their togs along.

But in writing this often sounds too informal.

Now try sentence 2:

> If anybody calls, tell _____ I'll be back in half an hour.

It's the same here. We can write either:

> If anybody calls, tell him or her I'll be back in half an hour.

This sounds very awkward. Or we can write this:

> If anybody calls, tell them I'll be back in half an hour.

This sounds very informal. To be on the safe side, let's write this:

> If anybody calls, tell him I'll be back in half an hour.

However, in those sentences where we have a noun to refer to, the situation is different. Take test sentences 8 and 9:

> Every one of the soldiers was able to pass his tests.
> Any man who doesn't meet these requirements will have his name removed from the list.

Here we could never say his or her, and therefore we have no excuse for using the plural their as a makeshift, even in quite informal speaking. A soldier or man is single and masculine; therefore we must use the pronoun his.

Exercise 1. Choose the word in parentheses that makes the sentence correct.

1. Every man must do (his, their) patrol duty every evening.
2. Each one who completes the difficult battery of examinations can consider (himself, themselves) lucky indeed.

3. Not a one was considered fit to adapt (his, their) talents to the audience.
4. If anybody objects, let (him, them) think up a better scheme.
5. Each citizen in a democracy must feel it (his, their) duty to vote every time elections come around.
6. Everybody was urged to do (his, their) utmost to make the affair a great success.
7. Jack was certain that someone had not received (his, their) invitation.
8. Let every one try to carve (himself, themselves) a niche in the Hall of Fame.
9. Any woman who doesn't like cooking must have (her, their) head examined.
10. Each one of us had to present (his, their) ticket at the gate.
11. There wasn't a single person who forgot to bring (his, their) gift for the bride.

22 ADJECTIVES AND ADVERBS

Adverb or Adjective? Choose the word in parentheses that makes the sentence correct. The number at the end of each sentence refers to the section below that explains it.

1. I'll have nothing to do with (these, this) kind of people. (8)
2. (That, These) kind of book does not appeal to me. (8)
3. Do you prefer (those, this) sort of hat? (8)
4. John is the (taller, tallest) of the two. (5)
5. Of all the boys, Jean likes John (less, least). (6), (3)
6. That evening I saw the (strangest, most strangest) sight. (7)
7. The fans liked Bartley's pitching (better, more better) than that of Sorel. (7)
8. I feel (fine, finely) today. (9)
9. If it wasn't your fault, don't feel (bad, badly) about it. (9)
10. He drives a car (well, good). (10)
11. The car runs (good, well). (10)
12. Roses in bloom smell (sweet, sweetly). (9)
13. Gooseberries taste (sour, sourly). (9)
14. He looks (well, good). (10)
15. When you're hungry, food tastes (good, well). (10)
16. Jane is (more beautiful, beautifuler) than her sister. (2)
17. Which class do you like (less, least), Spanish or English? (3), (6)
18. I am (more sad, sadder) than you. (1)

You can't talk or write without *adjectives* and *adverbs*. And of course, you can't talk or write correctly without using adjectives and adverbs correctly. If you got a perfect score on the test, you probably know the difference between adjectives and adverbs. But don't get cocky. Check with each section-number to make sure you didn't just guess the correct form. (It's fairly easy to guess, you know, when you have to choose between two words. You have a fifty-fifty chance of picking the correct one.) If you know why you've chosen the correct form, then you'll always write it correctly when you have to use it. That's the most important purpose this test serves: to help you improve your written and spoken English.

Adjectives and Adverbs—What Are They?
Adjectives and adverbs are alike in one respect. Both tell something about other words.

Adjectives tell something about nouns. Without adjectives your speech and writing would be colorless. Every time you wanted to say something about a *boy* or a *girl* or a *house,* you would have to say just **boy, girl, house.** By using adjectives you can add meaning to the nouns you use:

Bad boy	Pretty girl	Beautiful house
Good boy	Petite girl	Large house
Little boy	Attractive girl	White house
Big boy	Vivacious girl	Shuttered house
Smart boy	Unhappy girl	Roofless house

Adverbs tell something about verbs, adjectives, or other adverbs. If we had no adverbs, we couldn't tell *when, where, how,* or *why* things happened. We would be limited to sentences like: He *walked,* He *ran,* He *stood.* With adverbs, which give fuller and more accurate meaning to the verb, or adjective, or adverb, we can say:

He walked **quickly.**	He ran **swiftly.**
He walked **quietly.**	He ran **there.**
He walked **jerkily.**	He stood **here.**

Comparing Adjectives and Adverbs

Here are three girls: Jenny, Jean, Celia.

Celia is passably good-looking and has occasional dates.

Jenny won a Miss America contest.

Jean never has a date.

You want to say how popular each one is as compared with the other. What do you say?

> Celia is popular. (She has some dates.)
>
> Jenny is the **most** popular girl. (What would you expect? She's Miss America.)
>
> Jean is the **least** popular. (No dates—poor kid!)

Or you can say:

> Celia is **more** popular than Jean. (She has more dates than Jean.)
>
> Jenny is **more** popular than Celia. (She has more dates than Celia.)

And since popularity adds to our happiness, we would say:

Celia is happy. (Just plain happy.)

Jenny is happier than Jean. (She has more reasons for being so.)

Jean would be the happiest, if she had only one date a week.

Now what has happened to those adjectives **happy** and **popular**, and the adverbs **least** and **most**? They've changed their form to show a change in meaning. This change is called *comparison*. It is a characteristic of adjectives (adverbs, too) —the only way they have of changing their meaning to express *differences in degree* (how much—more or less).

The rules of comparison are fairly simple:

Adjectives and adverbs have three degrees: *positive, comparative* (more), *superlative* (most, the highest).

1. Adjectives of one syllable add **er** to form the *comparative* degree, **est** to form the *superlative* degree—like this:

Positive	Comparative	Superlative
sad	sadder	saddest
bold	bolder	boldest
strong	stronger	strongest
fair	fairer	fairest

2. Adjectives of more than one syllable generally form the *comparative* degree by putting **more** before the *positive*, and the *superlative* by putting *most* before the positive— like this:

Positive	Comparative	Superlative
beautiful	more beautiful	most beautiful
intelligent	more intelligent	most intelligent
interesting	more interesting	most interesting

The only reason for writing the comparative and superlative degrees in this way is that it sounds better. Just try saying:

He was the recklessest man I have ever met.
I spent the interestingest evening in the theater.

and you'll see what we mean.

Note: Some adjectives of more than one syllable can be

written either way—more unhappy or unhappier—because either combination doesn't grate on the ear.

3. Some adjectives aren't as simple as the ones we've just spoken about. They are much like the irregular verbs. So you'd better learn them:

Positive	Comparative	Superlative
bad	worse	worst
good	better	best
little	less, lesser	least
much, many, some	more	most

4. Most adverbs are formed by adding ly to the adjective.

Adjective	Adverb
sad	sadly
easy	easily
bold	boldly
courageous	courageously

When we compare adverbs, the procedure is a bit different. We generally put more before the adverb to form the comparative degree, and most for the superlative degree.

Positive	Comparative	Superlative
readily	more readily	most readily
easily	more easily	most easily

5. When comparing *two* persons or things, use the comparative degree.

Jane is the shorter of the two.

6. When comparing *three* or more persons or things, use the superlative.

Wilson is the best of them all.
Quigley is the fastest runner on the team.

Note: Some writers use the superlative in comparing *two* things:

This is the longest of the two sticks.

But the *comparative,* longer, is preferred and considered correct by most authorities.

7. In forming the comparative and superlative, don't use **more** and **er**, or **most** and **est** for the same word. It's just saying the same thing twice.

Don't Write:	*Write:*
The most saddest sight	The saddest sight
The more better book	The better book
The more sillier hat	The sillier hat

8. The adjectives, **this** and **that, these** and **those,** are troublesome only when combined with words like **sort, type, kind. This** and **that** are singular.

Write:

This kind	That kind
This type	That type
This sort	That sort

because **sort, type, kind** are singular, too.

9. In sentences with **look, feel, taste, smell,** and **hear,** people often run into difficulties. Now that you know the difference between the adverb and the adjective, you should have no difficulty using them correctly.
What would you say here?

    1. The steak looks tender.

or

    2. The steak looks tenderly.

Sentence 1 makes sense. **The steak looks tender** means that it looks as though it will be tender when we're ready to eat it. **Tender** is an *adjective* that tells us something about the kind of **steak** (noun) we're going to eat.

Sentence 2 is a little strange and confusing, to say the least. Why? **Tenderly** is an *adverb.* (Remember that telltale **ly** ending of the adverb.) **Tenderly** tells us something about *how* the steak is *looking* at something or somebody. *Before* the steak became a steak (when it was a cow) it might have *looked* *tenderly* at its calf or at its owner. But when the cow becomes a steak, it can't *look tenderly* any more. It is just steak—and steak *is* (looks) or is *not* (does not look) *tender* (good to eat).

What we have said about looks holds true for **smell, taste, feel**. When these words say something about the subject (noun), use the adjective form after them. When they tell *how* an action is being performed, use the **ly** or *adverb* after them.

Examples:

The flower smells **sweet**. (The flower isn't smelling anything. It is a **sweet** flower.)

The orange tastes **sour**. (The orange isn't tasting anything. It is just a **sour** orange.)

The stove feels **hot**. (It's a **hot** stove.)

Here's a simple and handy way to remember when to use the adjective form: If you can substitute **is**, then use the adjective:

The apple tastes (is) sour.
The flower smells (is) sweet.
The pot feels (is) hot.

Use the **ly** (adverb) form with these words when someone is actually feeling, tasting, hearing, or smelling something, when he is using his hands, his tongue, his ears, or his nose. Then the adverb will describe *how* he is feeling, tasting, etc.

The dog sniffed (smelled) the bone suspiciously. (How? In a **suspicious** manner.)

He tested the wine cautiously. (How? In a **cautious** manner.)

The doctor touched the injured arm gently. (How?)

10. **Good** is always an adjective, **well** an adverb. Never use **good** to describe how something is done.

He's a good boy.

Well is an adverb describing *how* something is done.

He works well.
He runs well.
He plays well.

Note: When well means in good health, then it is an adjective.

> I feel well.
> My father is well.

You will see the difference between well and good more clearly in the following sentences:

> This is a good car. It runs well.
> She has a good voice. She sings well.

11. There are a few adverbs that have two forms. One ends in ly. The other doesn't. It is permissible and, in some instances, preferable to use the form without the ly.

slow or slowly   fair or fairly
quick or quickly   direct or directly
close or closely   deep or deeply
wrong or wrongly   tight or tightly

> Drive slow (or slowly).
> Come quick (or quickly).
> Send your letter direct (or directly) to headquarters.
> He did the problem wrong (preferred to wrongly).
> Hold me tight (tightly).

But notice the difference in these sentences:

> The batter drove the ball deep (not deeply) into center field. (Deep is preferred here.)
> The play moved me deeply. (Deeply is preferred here.)
> Stay close to me. (Adverb showing place—where.)
> Examine the work closely. (Adverb showing how.)
> He played fair with his opponents.
> The money was distributed fairly.

A few short adverbs are most frequently used without the ly ending:

hard   high   low
right   straight

> He hit the ball hard (not hardly).
> Swing high, swing low.
> Drive right.
> The arrow flew straight to the center of the target.

Exercise 1. Did you get the point? Choose the form in parentheses that will make the sentence correct.

1. This bat is the (heavier, heaviest) of the two.
2. This bat is the (heavier, heaviest) of all.
3. Yesterday I witnessed the (most unusual, unusualest) sight of my life.
4. Oil is (more thick, thicker) than water.
5. We have just passed through the (worse, worst) year in our history.
6. Of all the things I have to do, house cleaning is the (less unpleasant, least unpleasant).
7. Do you like (these, this) kind of radio?
8. (This, these) sort of apples taste best when kept in the refrigerator.
9. Outside, they could hear the steady drone of the tractor (plain, plainly).
10. Don't handle those dishes so (rough, roughly).
11. New mown hay smells (delightful, delightfully).
12. She looks (beautiful, beautifully) to me.
13. The perfume smelled (sweet, sweetly).
14. These new fabrics feel (soft, softly).
15. In another month, my injured back will be (good, well).
16. When you are tired, a hot bath feels (good, well).
17. Your new sweater looks (good, well) on you.
18. Brush your teeth (good, well) every morning and night.
19. My car is running (good, well) these days.
20. Two months after his operation, he was (good, well) again.

23 PERSONAL PRONOUNS

What Case Would You Use? Choose the word in parentheses that will make the sentence correct. The number at the end of each sentence refers to the section below which will tell you whether you have made the correct choice and why.

1. I am sure that it will be (she, her) after all. (2)
2. (Us, we) boys won't be fooled this time. (1, 6)
3. (Him, he) and (I, me) have been close friends for many years. (1)
4. Did you think the boy was (he, him)? (2)
5. There can be no doubt that it was (she, her). (2)
6. It was (they, them) who objected. (2)
7. Let (he, him) and (I, me) go. (3)
8. Did you see (he, him) and (me, I)? (3)
9. Wait for Mary and (I, me). (4)
10. Between you and (me, I), there's really nothing to that rumor. (4)
11. Everyone came but (she, her). (4)
12. Come along with (we, us) fellows tomorrow. (4, 6)
13. Jack, Belle, and (she, her) can be counted on to support our side. (1)
14. I think I'll invite Mary, Jane, and (he, him) to the party. (3)
15. (Who, Whom) are you going to see? (5)
16. (Who, Whom) are you talking to? (5)
17. (Who, Whom) do you think is the hero of the play? (5)
18. (Who, Whom) did you see at the ball game? (5)
19. My brother is taller than (me, I). (7)
20. She wants to sing as much as (I, me). (7)
21. Would you rather have Jack than (I, me) as your co-worker? (7)
22. She was as angry as (we, us), but she wouldn't show it. (7)
23. My cousin invited (her, she) and (me, I). (3)

Perhaps some of those sentences you just did puzzled you a bit. If so, don't fret, and don't think you're stupid. You've been through a trying experience. Those personal pronouns you were trying to place correctly are among the most slippery and tricky of all the parts of speech. Of course you never have the difficulties of that love-smitten Chinese who wrote:

228

I look at she;
Her look at me;
Her see much not;
Me see quite lot.

Nor would you ever write anything like this, found on an old tombstone—a touching sentiment, no doubt, and from the heart, but—well, you be the judge:

Her can never come back to we,
But we will certainly go to she.

But you do have your troubles—other troubles with these personal pronouns. And you aren't alone. Even people who have majored in English will confess (in confidence, of course) that they are occasionally puzzled when they must make a choice among personal pronouns. So you're in good company—but you don't have to stay there unless you want to. You can move into *better* company. You can pick the right pronoun every time if you know a few simple things.

Don't let anyone tell you that the simplest thing to do is just to memorize the correct form—and not worry about reasons, and explanations—grammatical or otherwise. It is true that in some instances you do have to memorize things (principal parts of irregular verbs, for example). But the use of pronouns is governed by sensible and easy-to-understand rules. Get these straight and you'll know exactly which pronoun to use at all times—and why. You'll be intelligent about your language. That's what we all want to be—*correct* and *intelligent*.

Now down to the business at hand.

Your difficulty with pronouns is not that you don't know whether to use he or she. That's easy: He for a man (masculine), she for a woman. It's him or he, she or her that troubles you. And that's because you aren't sure of what *case* to use.

Case is the form of a pronoun that shows how it is related to other words in the sentence. The case of a pronoun changes to show differences in meaning. Nouns have case, too—but they have the same form for all cases except the possessive— and that's no problem at all.

There are *three* cases. (You will have to memorize what these look like.)

	1st Person	2nd Person	3rd Person
Nominative	I, we	you	he, she, it, they, who
Possessive	my, mine, our, ours	your, yours	his, her, hers, its
			their, theirs, whose
Objective	me, us	you	him, her, it, them, whom

What Case Shows

NOMINATIVE CASE
used for
Subject of *sentence*
and
Predicate Nominative

1. Subject of Sentence

He went to the store.
I went to the store.
They went to the store.
We went to the store.

You never get these wrong when you write them in separate sentences. When you use any of the two or all three as subject of sentence, they must still be in the nominative case:

He and I went to the store.

You don't say **him** went or **her** went or **us** went, do you?

2. Predicate Nominative

This is just as simple as the subject. The key here is the verb **be** or any of its forms such as:

am	was	are
were	is	have been

When you use a pronoun after any form of the verb **be**, be sure it is in the *nominative*. For the predicate nominative refers to the *subject*—and the subject is in the nominative case. The predicate nominative actually *stands for* the subject.

Jack (subject nominative) is the **captain** (predicate nominative).
The **captain** (subject nominative) is Jack (predicate nominative).

Take a sentence like this one—number 4, on page 228.

Did you think the boy was **he?**

He is a predicative nominative here—the same case as **boy**, the *subject*, to which it refers. (*He* was the boy—the boy was *he*.)

Now try **him** and see what happens:

Did you think the boy was **him?**

Can you say "him was the boy"?

All the sentences where it is the subject and the verb is am, was, is, etc., follow the same rule because the pronoun is a predicate nominative.

THE POSSESSIVE CASE

This case is used to show possession as in:

my overcoat   **his** book   **your** rainhat   **their** pens

The possessive case of the pronoun presents practically no problems. So let us leave it.

THE OBJECTIVE CASE
is used for
Direct Object of Verb
Indirect Object of Verb
Object of Preposition
Subject of Infinitive

3. *Direct Object*

Whenever a verb *does something* to a person or thing, that person or thing is called a *direct object*.

The *direct object* is in the *objective case*.

He beat **me.**

(Me is the direct object—objective case. He did something to me. He is subject—nominative case.)

So sentence 8 on page 228 should read:

Did you see **him** and **me?**

Him and **me** are *direct objects—objective case*. Try the nominative case and you'll shudder:

> Did you see **he** and **I**?

Nobody talks or writes like this.

Number 14 on page 228 seems to present a problem—but it's no different:

> I think I'll invite Mary, Jane, and **him** to the party.

Him is direct object—objective case.

What you are actually saying is:

> I'll invite Mary. I'll invite Jane. I'll invite **him**.

Don't invite **he**. **Him** won't come. Do you see why?

4. *Object of Preposition*

The objective case is used after a preposition.

> Give that book to **me**.

Sentence 10 on page 228 (the classic stumbling block) is an example of the same thing. It should read:

> Between you and **me**, there's really nothing to that rumor.

The preposition is **between**. In this sentence, it has *two* objects (a *compound* object): **you** and **me**.

Special Problems

5. *Who or Whom*

In *interrogative* sentences (sentences that ask questions), just turn the sentence around and you'll be able to decide very easily whether to use **who** (nominative) or **whom** (objective).

> **Whom** are you calling?

You are calling **whom**—whom is direct *object* of verb. Therefore it is in the *objective case*.

> **Whom** are you talking to?

You are talking to **whom**—**whom** is object of preposition **to**. Therefore it is in the *objective case*.

Now, what about sentence 17? It doesn't seem to fit either of the two cases we've just mentioned. Actually, it does fit— but with a slight difference.

> Who do you think is the hero of the play?

What this sentence is saying is: *Who is the hero of the play?* but **do you think** is wedged into the sentence (a parenthetical expression) and that sometimes tends to throw you off. Just drop **do you think** out of the sentence; it still makes sense—and you'll see more clearly that **who** is the subject of the sentence and therefore is in the nominative case.

6. *Us and We*

Us boys and **we boys** is a constant source of confusion. Just remember that both of these are what we call *appositives* and that they must be in the same case as the word they are related to. But here's an even simpler method of finding out which to use.

Leave out the word **boys** or **girls** or **fellows** and then you'll know.

> We (girls) are at home.

Not **us**, because **we** is subject—*nominative case*.

> They hit **us** (fellows).

Not **we** because **us** is object of verb—*objective case*.

> Talk to **us** (boys) sometime.

Not **we** because **us** is object of the preposition **to**—*objective case*.

7. *Than* and *As*

In all the above sentences with **than** or **as**, there is just one thing to remember. These are clauses, in which something is left out. What you must be certain of is how the pronoun fits into what has been left out.

> He is taller than I.

This really means:

> He is taller than I (subject) am tall.

That's why it's wrong to say me because you wouldn't say me am tall.

> She wants to sing as much as I.

This really means:

> She wants to sing as much as I (subject) want to sing.
> Would you rather go with Jack than me?

That really means:

> Would you rather go with Jack than (with) me (object of preposition, with)?

In all than and as sentences, it's the meaning that counts. Don't just put down me or they or we or any other word until you are sure of what you want to say.

Exercise 1. Choose the word in parentheses that will make the sentence correct.

1. It's (him, he) who should be blamed for the accident.
2. You can't tell (us, we) fellows what to do.
3. (Him, he) and (me, I) know exactly what to do.
4. I thought the man was (him, he).
5. Now I am sure that it was (she, her).
6. Let (her, she) and (I, me) be the first ones to go.
7. Call for Jim and (me, I).
8. Let nothing come between you and (I, me).
9. Everyone was there but (her, she).
10. Susan, Dorothy, and (me, I) are going together.
11. I'm asking Lucille, Evelyn, and (he, him) to come.
12. (Who, Whom) did you see yesterday?
13. (Who, Whom) are you going with?
14. Henry is taller than (I, me).
15. She was as pleased as (us, we) at the result of the election.

24 *THE CORRECT WORD*

You use words, for only one purpose—to make yourself clear to others. If you use words correctly, everybody understands you. But if you use words carelessly or incorrectly, then you run the danger of being misunderstood. Sometimes this misunderstanding may not be too important. Your reader may be kind and charitable, and give you credit for saying something you meant to say but didn't. At other times, if you don't use the correct words, you may get into all sorts of difficult and comic situations.

Do you doubt it? Let's see:

> The doctor said I had no temperature.

Did he really? Then you're dead! If you have no *temperature,* you have no body heat! For *temperature* is a measure of body heat. If your body temperature is 98.6°, you have normal temperature. When your temperature is above 98.6°, you have a *fever*—that is, *more temperature* than is good for you.

So, you see, it's important to know the difference between *fever* and *temperature.*

1. I ran in the room.
2. I ran into the room.

Do both of these sentences mean the same? They do not. In sentence 1 (for some unexplainable reason) you were running around *in* the room.

In sentence 2, you started running *outside* the room and came running *into* the room.

There are many words like those we have just mentioned that will lead you into similar confusion if you don't learn to tell them apart. Here are a list of some of the commonest "confusers." How many can you use correctly?

Do You Know the Difference?

Test A. Choose the correct word from the words in parentheses. Check your answer with the explanations that follow. The number at the end of each sentence refers to the section that will help you understand and correct any error you make.

1. Frank ran (around, about) a hundred yards. (1)
2. Henry Ford owned (around, about) a billion dollars in industrial equipment. (1)
3. Everyone had a good time (accept, except) me. (2)
4. Please (accept, except) this gift as a token of our gratitude for all you have done. (2)
5. Foreigners have difficulty in trying to (adopt, adapt) themselves to our American ways. (3)
6. If you want to be happy, you must learn to (adopt, adapt) a different attitude. (3)
7. The sign read, "Private! No (Admission, Admittance)!" (4)
8. The price of (admission, admittance) is fifteen cents. (4)
9. The witness' (admission, admittance) made it clear that the jury would find him guilty. (4)
10. We have not yet learned exactly how the atomic bomb (affects, effects) human beings. (5)
11. Spoiled food is sure to have a bad (affect, effect) on your digestion. (5)
12. His appeal (affected, effected) the parents deeply. (5)
13. The passage of the English Channel was (affected, effected) with great difficulty. (5)
14. The (amount, number) of high school students going to college is increasing. (6)
15. Year by year we are reducing the (amount, number) of people who cannot read or write. (6)
16. His manners (aggravate, annoy) me. (7)
17. This is the most (aggravating, annoying) thing that has ever happened to me. (7)
18. Running up and down stairs will (aggravate, annoy) even the mildest heart disease. (7)

1. About—Around

About means approximately. When you run *about* four blocks, you cover a distance of approximately four blocks.

Around means starting at one point and coming back to that same point. In mathematics, the word for around is circumference. When you run *around* four blocks, you cover more ground than if you were to run *about* four blocks.

2. Accept—Except

Accept—to receive or take something that is offered.

Except—(1) to take out or leave out anything; (2) otherwise or other than.

To *except* something is to leave it out of consideration.

During the war, all fathers were, for a time, excepted from selective service rulings.

or

During the war, selective service drafted all men except (other than) fathers.

3. Adapt—Adopt

When you *adopt* a child, you take the child as your own.

When you *adopt* a plan, you *take* over the plan and put it into use.

Adopt, then, means to take as your own what was originally not your own. You can never adopt yourself.

But you can *adapt* yourself because **adapt** means to adjust yourself to new conditions.

Note: If you are offered a plan for building a model airplane, you can either adopt the plan (take it over as your own without any changes);

or

adapt the plan (change it in some respects to suit your own needs).

4. Admission—Admittance

Admittance is used almost always in the sense of being allowed to enter. **No admittance** means you can't enter.

Admission means a number of things:

1. A fee paid for being allowed to enter.

Fifty cents is the price of admission.

2. The act of being received or being allowed to enter a group, a society, a college, or a school.

Gaining admission to college these days is difficult.

3. Owning up to an accusation or statement.

He admitted (owned up to) his part in the crime.
His admission of his part in the crime shocked everyone.

5. Affect—Effect

Most students (and grown-ups, too) curse the day when these two words were invented. When faced with the problem of which of these two to use, they are torn by doubt and anguish. There's something almost magical about these words which makes it impossible to *guess* at them. Almost invariably we guess wrong.

There's only one thing to do. Fix the meaning of these words clearly in your mind and when you use them, ask yourself what you mean to say, and then see if your sentence makes sense.

Affect is always a verb—nothing else. It means:

1. To impress or to influence or to move or to act on (generally the mind or feelings).

   Bach's music affects me (moves me) deeply.

2. To assume the character or appearance of—to put on.

   He affects a British accent and manner.

Effect is both a noun and a verb. As a *noun,* it means:

1. A result or consequence or outcome.

   We shall long feel the effects of World War II.

2. Fulfillment or accomplishment.

   We shall do all we can to carry your plan into effect.

3. The making of an impression.

   He did this chiefly for effect.

As a *verb,* it means:
To bring about, to execute—often in the face of difficulties or obstacles.

   The doctor effected a miraculous cure.

Note: **Effects** (plural) means goods or possessions: household effects, personal effects.

6. *Amount—Number*
Use **number** when you can count the things you are writing about.

Every year a large number of people are killed in accidents of all kinds.

Use **amount** when dealing with quantities that can't be counted or when you are just considering the size of things.

There was a tremendous amount of sand on the highway this past week.
Americans spend large amounts of money every year on travel and amusements.

Note: When we speak of money, we use **amount** in this specific sense:

The sales amounted to $500.

7. *Aggravate—Annoy—Irritate*

Aggravate means to make something worse. That's the only sense in which it is used correctly.

Words like **annoy, irritate, exasperate** are not synonyms for **aggravate**.

Do You Know the Difference?

Test B. Choose the correct word from the words in parentheses. Check your answer with the explanations that follow. The number at the end of each sentence refers to the section that will help you understand and correct any error you may make.

1. I am (all together, altogether) at a loss to account for his behavior. (8)
2. After many years of separation, they are (all together, altogether) at last. (8)
3. Before he was committed to the asylum he suffered from the (allusion, illusion, delusion) that he was Napoleon. (9)
4. When you see something that really doesn't exist, you are having an optical (allusion, illusion, delusion). (9)
5. In his writing, he made frequent (allusion, illusion, delusion) to the Bible and Shakespeare. (9)
6. Mother divided the candy (among, between) Jack and Sue. (10)
7. The president divided the prize money (among, between) the members of the club. (10)
8. I (bet, beat) Jimmy that we would win. (12)
9. What is the difference (among, between) *allusion, delusion, illusion?* (10)
10. Stay here (beside, besides) me. (11)

11. (Beside, besides) being an athlete, he is also a good student. (11)
12. The Giants (bet, beat) the Tigers, 12-5. (12)

8. *All Together—Altogether*

Altogether means wholly, completely.

All together means all (of us, of them) together (in one place, with each other).

The clue here is to watch for the word **all** and then you won't confuse these words.

9. *Allusion—Delusion—Illusion*

Allusion is an indirect reference:

> He suffered like Job. (Indirect reference to the Bible. Biblical allusion.)
> There are many Hamlets in the world today. (Indirect reference to Shakespeare's Hamlet—Shakespearean allusion.)

Delusion is a false belief. The common phrase "to labor under a delusion" means believing something that is not true.

Delusion is used in a special sense to describe the false and fantastic ideas of insane people, for example, **delusions of persecution, delusions of grandeur.**

> To delude oneself is to fool oneself.

Illusion is a deceptive appearance, generally an *optical illusion* (seeing something that isn't there, or mistaking what you see for something else).

10. *Among—Between*

The general rule here is that **between** is used with *two* persons or things:

> Between you and me.
> Between father and mother.

Among is used with three or more persons or things:

> She walked among the flowers.
> The cake was divided among all of us.

But when you have a large number of things or persons and you are distinguishing between any *two* of them, the correct word is between.

In sentence 9 on page 239 we say "What is the *difference* between *allusion, delusion,* and *illusion?*" because, although there are three items, we are talking about them *two at a time.* We are distinguishing

> between *allusion* and *delusion;*
> between *allusion* and *illusion;* and
> between *delusion* and *illusion,* etc.

11. *Beside—Besides*

Beside means at the side of.
Besides means in addition to.

12. *Bet, Beat*

Bet—to make a wager.
Beat—to win, to conquer, to defeat

> I'll bet fifty dollars (make a wager) that I can beat you.

Do You Know the Difference?

Test C. Choose the correct word from the words in parentheses. Check your answer with the explanations that follow. The number at the end of each sentence refers to the section that will help you understand and correct your answer.

1. Please (bring, take) this book to the library; it is due today. (13)
2. He asked me to (bring, take) his tennis racket to his home when I came to see him. (13)
3. The New York State (Capitol, capital, capitol) is located in Albany. (14)
4. The (capitol, capital) of California is Sacramento. (14)
5. His parents were eager for him to outgrow his (childish, childlike) behavior. (15)
6. It is difficult to keep our (childish, childlike) innocence as we grow older. (15)
7. The game was called off because the umpires thought the weather was (liable, likely, apt) to be unfavorable. (16)
8. Those drivers who disregard speeding laws are (likely, liable, apt) to have accidents. (16)
9. Because of their long tradition of freedom of speech, Americans are (likely, liable, apt) to be outspoken. (16)

13. *Bring—Take*

Bring is the *opposite* of take.
Bring means "to carry, to come with" something, toward the speaker or listener.

> Bring me the newspaper.
> Bring the hat home this evening.

Take means "to carry something *away* from" the speaker.

> Take this package to the post office.
> Take little Johnny home to his mother.

After the party, you ask:

> May I take you home? (To your home.)

When you are coming home with a friend, you call mother and say:

> I'm bringing Jack home with me.

14. *Capital—Capitol*

Capital refers to the city, the seat of government, as in the sentence:

> Paris is the capital of France.

Capital also means punishable by death—a *capital* crime.

Capitol is a building where a state legislature meets; a state house. When you speak of the building in Washington where our national legislators meet, write it Capitol (capital C).

15. *Childish—Childlike*

Both of these words refer to the behavior of children but with this important difference:

Childish refers to the *unattractive* features of children such as silliness, stubbornness, temper tantrums, etc.

Childlike refers to the *best* and *most attractive* characteristics of children: their sweetness, innocence, faith, etc.

16. *Apt—Liable—Likely*

Apt means having a natural tendency.

> A thoughtless person is apt to say unkind things to people. (He has a natural tendency to do such things because he is thoughtless.)

Likely emphasizes the idea of probability—it may happen.

It is likely to rain.

Apt and **likely** are often used interchangeably. But careful writers distinguish between their meanings.
Liable implies the possibility of something unpleasant happening.

If you don't watch where you are going, you are liable to fall.

Do You Know the Difference?

Test D. Choose the correct word from the words in parentheses. Check your answer with the explanations that follow. The number at the end of each sentence refers to the section that will help you understand and correct your answer.

1. Most of us are flattered when we receive a (complement, compliment). (17)
2. When Frank joined the ship's crew, its (complement, compliment) was filled. (17)
3. Most criminals have no (conscience, conscious). (18)
4. Many of us are not (conscience, conscious) of our faults. (18)
5. Americans out of this country are urged to keep in close touch with their (consul, counsel, council). (19)
6. The New York City (consul, counsel, council) met to vote on important issues of the city. (19)
7. During the football game, Wilson fouled the quarterback. This was a (contemptible, contemptuous) act. (20)
8. It is advisable to seek the best (consul, counsel, council) possible before making a crucial decision. (19)
9. Many persons who are (contemptible, contemptuous) of others have many faults of their own. (20)
10. The prediction of intermittent showers was fulfilled when the rain fell (continually, continuously). (21)
11. For three hours, there was no letup to the rain, which fell (continually, continuously). (21)

17. *Complement—Compliment*
Complement is that portion which fills up or completes:

We received our complement of Easter goods (what we needed to complete our stock, or what we needed to make the order complete).
The complement of an angle is the amount of angle needed to make the angle 90° (to complete the angle).

You aren't likely to use **complement** very frequently in your writing or speaking, but you are likely to confuse it with **compliment**, which means praise, commendation, congratulation.

Compliment may be used as a verb or a noun:

> She blushed when I paid her a compliment. (noun)
> She blushed when I complimented her on her singing. (verb)

18. *Conscience—Conscious*

Conscience is that quality within us which helps us to decide what is morally right and wrong. Our conscience is commonly referred to as "the still small voice."

Conscious simply means aware of.

> If you have a **conscience**, you will be **conscious** of what is right and what is wrong.

19. *Consul—Counsel—Council*

Consul is an official who represents his government in foreign countries.

Counsel means advice (noun) or an advisor, usually a legal advisor (noun), or to advise (verb).

> His father gave him the best of counsel (advice).
> The guilty man's counsel (advisor) tried his best to play upon the emotions of the jury.
> I counsel (advise) you not to go under any conditions.

Council means a body of people serving in a legal, administrative, or advisory capacity.

> The King's Privy Council.
> The Council of Foreign Ministers.
> The Executive Council of the Association.

20. *Contemptible—Contemptuous*

Contemptible means deserving of contempt; despicable; vile.

> Torturing animals is a contemptible act.

A **contemptuous** person regards others as contemptible, looks down on them with disdain and scorn.

21. *Continual—Continuous*

Continual means repeated often.

> Throughout the evening, I was continually interrupted. (Every hour or so.)

Continuous means without a stop.

> From where I lay, I could hear the continuous pounding of the surf.

Do You Know the Difference?

Test E. Choose the correct word from the words in parentheses. Check your answer with the explanations that follow. The number at the end of each sentence refers to the section that will help you understand and correct your answer.

1. The dramatist, S. N. Behrman, is noted for his sparkling (dialect, dialogue). (22)
2. Although the national language of Mexico is Spanish, many a (dialect, dialogue) is spoken in various sections of the country. (22)
3. The world is a better place to live in because of the things Thomas A. Edison (discovered, invented). (23)
4. A walk in the park is sufficient to enable some of us to (discover, invent) the beauties of nature. (23)
5. There is a (dual, duel) reason for doing good work in school: namely, to become a good citizen and to be a success in life. (24)
6. *The Spectator* contains an article that states that the (dual, duel) is an unnecessary relic of bygone days of chivalry. (24)
7. The ambition of most young people is to grow up to become (famous, notorious) citizens of the United States. (25)
8. Pitchers are (famous, notorious) for being unusually weak hitters. (25)
9. Some persons can be happy with (fewer, less) money than others. (26)
10. (Less, Fewer) college students are turning to teaching than ever before. (26)
11. The pilot said that this was the best plane he had ever (flowed, flown). (27)
12. Much water had (flowed, flown) under the bridge since the two friends had seen each other. (27)
13. Many Americans who (formally, formerly) wasted soap are careful to use it economically now. (28)
14. Frank was (formally, formerly) inducted as president of the club. (28)

22. Dialect—Dialogue

Dialect is a variation of the standard language characteristic of groups of people or regions of a country: Negro dialect, New England dialect.

When you write down the actual conversation of people, you are writing **dialogue**. Plays are written completely in dialogue. In novels and short stories, dialogue or conversation is surrounded by quotation marks.

23. Discover—Invent

To **discover** something is to find something that was there before you came upon it.

> Columbus discovered America.

To **invent** something is to create something new.

> Eli Whitney invented the cotton gin.

24. Dual—Duel

Dual means belonging to two or shared by two as in:

> This gadget serves a dual purpose (double purpose or two purposes).

Duel is a contest between two persons, fought with deadly weapons, swords or pistols. Duels are generally fought by agreement, according to fixed rules.

> Hamlet fought a duel with Laertes.

25. Famous—Notorious

Both of these words mean well-known.

Famous means well-known for some admirable, useful, or unusual achievement.

> Edison is famous for his electrical inventions.

Notorious means well-known but in an unfavorable light.

> He is notorious for his rudeness toward his subordinates.

26. Fewer—Less

Fewer refers to *number*.

> I am buying fewer presents this year than last.

You bought twenty-five last year; this year you are buying twelve.

Less refers to *amount* or *degree*.

> This year we had less rainfall than we expected.

You're talking about the *amount* of rain. If you were talking about the *number* of raindrops, you would have to use **fewer**.

27. Flowed—Flown
This error is easy to avoid. Just learn the principal parts of the verbs:

Present	Past	Past Participle
fly	flew	flown
flow	flowed	flowed

If you get these clearly in mind, you won't speak of the flying water or water that has flown under the bridge!

28. Formally—Formerly
Formally means in accordance with certain rules or forms.

> He was formally introduced to the members of the club (in a formal fashion).

Formerly means in the past, at another time.

> Herbert Hoover was formerly President of the United States.

Do You Know the Difference?
Test F. Choose the correct word from the words in parentheses. Check your answer with the explanations that follow. The number at the end of each sentence refers to the section that will help you understand and correct your answer.

1. Babe Ruth and Christy Mathewson are both in the Hall of Fame. The (former, latter) was a great Giant pitcher, and the (former, latter) was a great Yankee home run hitter. (29)
2. How (good, well) you do your work will be reflected in your sales at the end of the year. (30)
3. Her work as a file clerk has been (good, well) for the month just ended. (30)
4. He went to Florida because the climate was (healthy, healthful). (31)

5. Living in the open air made him a (healthy, healthful) young man. (31)
6. The judge rendered a (human, humane) decision in the difficult case. (32)
7. He showed that he had (human, humane) failings when he disappointed his family. (32)
8. During the seventeenth century, many Puritans were forced to (immigrate, emigrate) from England to the United States. (33)
9. Many persons in Europe wish to (immigrate, emigrate) to the United States because of the freedoms we enjoy. (33)
10. Do you mean to (infer, imply) that I am not good enough for the job? (34)

29. *Former—Latter*

Use these words only when you are speaking about *two* people or things.

Former refers to the first of the two mentioned.

Latter refers to the second one mentioned.

> Bill and John were hard workers. But the former (Bill) was more efficient.
> Bill and John were good workers, but the latter (John) was more popular.

30. *Good—Well*

Good is generally an adjective. It must, therefore, modify or complete the meaning of a noun.

> His art work is good.
> His pitching is good.
> Her dancing is good.
> "I got over my cold." "That's good."

Well is used both as an adjective and an adverb. It is an adjective only when it refers to health.

> I am feeling well. (predicate adjective)
> I work as well as I can. (adverb)
> The machine works well (not good). (adverb)

31. *Healthful—Healthy*

> Healthful diet and living habits make you healthy.

(You are *healthy*. The things that promote good health are *healthful*.)

2. Human—Humane

Human means characteristic of man.

> To err is human.

Humane means tender, kind, compassionate.

> He was a humane ruler.

3. Immigrate—Emigrate

Immigrate means to come into another country after leaving your native land.

> Toward the end of the nineteenth century, many Europeans immigrated to America.

Emigrate means to leave your native land.

> During the nineteenth century, many people emigrated from Europe and came to America.

When you leave your own country to settle elsewhere, you are an *emigrant*.

When you enter a new country to settle there, you are an *immigrant*.

4. Imply—Infer

Imply means to hint.

> The speaker implied (hinted) that the commissioner knew more than he had revealed to the attorney general.

The speaker *didn't actually say* that the commissioner knew more than he had revealed to the attorney general, but he made it clear indirectly.

> Though he said they were all honorable men, the sneer in his voice implied that they were not.

Infer means to find out by reasoning, to draw a conclusion from facts.

> On the basis of his past record, it was easy to infer (to come to the conclusion that) he would make a great president.

Do You Know the Difference?

Test G. Choose the correct word from the words in parentheses. Check your answer with the explanations that follow. The number at the end of each sentence refers to the section that will help you understand and correct your answer.

1. Robert was declared (illegible, ineligible) because he had played professionally. (37)
2. The report he handed in was so (illegible, ineligible) that the professor was forced to return it to him. (37)
3. The (latest, last) picture with Ingrid Bergman was a great success. (38)
4. This was her (latest, last) movie before she retired. (38)
5. The boy was (laying, lying) in the gutter after he had been hit by the car. (39)
6. Frank had (laid, lain) the book aside because he was sleepy. (39)
7. (Lay, Lie) down and rest for a while. (39)
8. The very tricky plan thought up by John was (ingenious, ingenuous). (35)
9. A girl with very little experience in life is likely to be (ingenious, ingenuous). (35)
10. The blabbering idiot could not make himself (intelligent, intelligible) to the man who faced him. (36)
11. The parents were delighted when their child turned out to be very (intelligent, intelligible). (36)

35. *Ingenious—Ingenuous*

Ingenious means clever, skillful, resourceful, inventive.

> He had an ingenious mind, always thinking up ways of saving time.

Ingenuous means frank, sincere, honest, open.

> He was of an ingenuous nature.

Note: **Ingenuous** is often used to mean naïve or simple—unsophisticated, not wise in the ways of the world.

36. *Intelligent—Intelligible*

Intelligent means alert, wise.
Intelligible means capable of being understood.

> Some intelligent people, when they write or speak, do not always make themselves intelligible (understood).

37. *Illegible—Ineligible*

When your handwriting is so poor that no one can read it, it is *illegible*.

When you are *ineligible* for a position or office, you do not have the necessary qualifications: schooling, experience, etc.

38. *Latest—Last*

Latest means the most recent.
Last means the final one.

This is my last attempt to win the tennis singles championship match. (There will be no more.)
This is my latest attempt to win the tennis singles championship match. (I'm still trying.)

39. *Lay—Lie*

There are probably no more confusing words in our language than lie and lay. If you have any trouble with them (most people do), there is only one thing to do. Give them a few minutes of concentrated, intelligent attention, and learn what distinguishes one from the other. There isn't any easy, magic formula to apply. Nor is there anything exceptionally difficult about these words.

Lay means to put something down. Lay *must always take an object*.
The principal parts of lay are:

Present	I lay (or am laying) the book on the shelf.
Past	I laid the book on the shelf.
Present Perfect	I have laid the book on the shelf.

Lie means to recline.
The principal parts of lie are:

Present	I lie (or am lying) on the sofa.
Past	I lay on the sofa.
Present Perfect	I have lain on the sofa.

Lie also means to tell an untruth.
The principal parts of lie (to tell an untruth) are:

Present	I never lie.
Past	I lied when I told you I was ill.
Present Perfect	I have never lied before.

Right and Wrong

I lied in bed.

(If you did, then you are a horizontal liar!) Actually, of course, you *lay* (past tense) in bed.

Hens lay eggs.

(That's correct—biologically and grammatically.)

I have laid in bed.

No—you *have lain* in bed (present perfect).

Lay down, Fido.

Fido is a good grammarian, so he will *lie* down instead.

Do You Know the Difference?

Test H. Choose the correct word from the words in parentheses. Check your answer with the explanations that follow. The number at the end of each sentence refers to the section that will help you understand and correct each answer.

1. The boy thought that people were trying to (persecute, prosecute) him. (40)
2. Although the lawyer insisted, the man decided not to (persecute, prosecute) the case. (40)
3. Mr. Bradford is (principal, principle) of Henry Aldrich's school. (41)
4. The (principal, principle) that all men are created equal was stated clearly in the Declaration of Independence. (41)
5. Because she was clumsy, Madeleine happened to (pour, spill) some coffee on the lap of the host. (42)
6. Joan was asked to (pour, spill) the tea because she was most reliable. (42)
7. The plan to invade France didn't seem (practical, practicable) at first, but history proved otherwise. (43)
8. Andrew Mayo was not an idealist, but an extremely (practical, practicable) person. (43)
9. When entering a building, it is always polite to allow older people to (precede, proceed) the younger. (44)
10. The chemist who asked permission to try the experiment was allowed to (precede, proceed). (44)

40. *Persecute—Prosecute*

Persecute means to annoy, to plague, to hunt down, to bring suffering and unhappiness upon someone.

In Germany, Hitler persecuted the Jews and other minority groups.

Prosecute means to carry out a legal action.

The district attorney has vowed to prosecute all offenders against the law.
The lawyer ably prosecuted the case.

41. Principal—Principle

Principal is easy to fix in your mind. He's the head of the school—the pupils' "pal." Principal also means main or most important, as the principal witness, principal city.

Principle means a belief, truth, policy, conviction, rule.

Where a great principle (truth, policy, conviction) is at stake, we must fight.
He was a man of high principles (convictions).
This runs against all my deeply cherished principles (beliefs, convictions).

42. Pour—Spill

When you *pour* a cup of tea, you *fill* the cup.
When you *spill* a cup of tea, you accidentally upset the cup and the tea runs out.

43. Practical—Practicable

Practical means useful and valuable—tried and tested in actual practice.

He is a practical man.

(He acts only on ideas that have been found to work. He doesn't rely on theory alone. He isn't a dreamer.)

Practicable means workable. It is used when speaking of plans or ideas that can be put into practice.

This plan seems practicable even if it is a bit risky.

44. Precede—Proceed

Precede means to go before.

As we enter the room, I will precede you.

Proceed means to go on or forward.

Proceed at your own risk.

Do You Know the Difference?

Test I. Choose the correct word in parentheses. Check your answer with the explanations that follow. The number at the end of each sentence refers to the section that will help you understand and correct your error.

1. The men removed their hats (respectfully, respectively) when the flag passed by. (45)
2. Frank and George were named president and vice-president (respectfully, respectively). (45)
3. The time has come for us to follow the (rout, route) to lasting peace. (46)
4. Once again the bedraggled freshmen suffered a (rout, route) at the hands of the powerful seniors. (46)
5. The man was asked to (sit, set) his materials down on the floor while he waited. (47)
6. The supervisor asked the newcomer to (sit, set) down at the desk near the window. (47)
7. The sick child was told to (stand, stay) at home until he completely recovered. (48)
8. The children (stood, stayed) at camp all summer. (48)
9. Many women like to have their (stationary, stationery) printed with their names on it. (49)
10. Although the winds battered the house, it remained (stationary, stationery). (49)
11. In what play does a (statue, statute) come to life? (50)
12. They all agreed that the (statue, statute) was unenforceable as passed. (50)
13. To his parents' disgust, John was completely (uninterested, disinterested) in becoming an engineer. (51)
14. Umpires in a baseball game must be (uninterested, disinterested). (51)

45. *Respectfully—Respectively*

Respectfully means showing respect or honor to someone.

He addressed his parents respectfully.

When you write a letter to a superior, or to someone in authority, you sign it

Respectfully yours,
John Smith

Respectively refers to a number of items taken in order:

> Harry, Joe, and Jim respectively were elected captain, manager, and coach of the team (Harry—captain, Joe—manager, Jim—coach).

46. Rout—Route

To **rout** means to defeat completely.

> The Marines routed the Japanese on Guadalcanal.

A **rout** is an overwhelming and smashing defeat.

> Saipan was a complete rout for the Japanese.

A **route** is a road.

> On your way to the Rockies, take the northern route.

To **route** means to send by way of a certain road or route.

> After the flood, the postal authorities decided to route the mail through Peoria.

47. Sit—Set

> Set this plant down near the window (put or place).
> Sit down on that chair near the window.

These are two different words. Don't confuse them. Learn the principal parts of both verbs:

Present	Past	Past Participle
set (place or put)	set	set
sit	sat	sat

48. Stand—Stay

> Stand there (on your two feet).
> Stay there. (Don't leave or go away. Remain where you are.)

If you don't use these words correctly, you'll make yourself sound really silly—like this:

> I stood in bed all week.

(That's really remarkable, isn't it? But, of course, you weren't *standing* in bed, although that's what you said! You *stayed* in bed.)

My father stood in New York all winter.

(Does it run in the family? Now, get your poor father off his feet for a while and have him *stay*—remain—in New York for the winter.)

The *past tense* of these verbs is the one most often confused. So learn the principal parts:

Present	Past	Participle
stand	stood	stood
stay (remain)	stayed	stayed

49. *Stationary—Stationery*

Stationary means remaining in one place.

Things that don't move are stationary.
A rock is a stationary object.

Stationery means writing paper, envelopes, etc.

Go down to that new stationery store and get me some letterheads.

50. *Statue—Statute*

A statue is "an image of a person or animal carved in stone or wood, or cast in bronze or clay or wax."

In the city of Washington, you will find statues of our national heroes.

A statute is a law.

Our legislators in Washington are constantly making new statutes.

51. *Uninterested—Disinterested*

A disinterested person is one who has no desire to gain something for himself.

He was chosen judge because we all knew he would be disinterested.

(He would be fair and impartial because he would not favor either side and because he was not interested in personal gain.)

Uninterested means not interested.

If you are uninterested in your work, you will fail.

Do You Know the Difference?

Exercise 1. This test covers all the words in this chapter. See how well you can do now. Choose the word in parentheses that makes the sentence correct.

1. There was nothing he could do but (accept, except) the position.
2. The senator tried his best to (affect, effect) a change in the bill but failed.
3. At the meeting, the club made an effort to (adopt, adapt) the constitution to the needs of the occasion.
4. (Admission, Admittance) into high society often depends on the amount of money you possess.
5. We ran (about, around) five minutes before our wind gave out.
6. There was a large (amount, number) of children in the matinee audience at the theater.
7. The batter cut his finger and (aggravated, annoyed, irritated) the wound every time he swung his bat.
8. (Among, Between) the heroes of the Yankees, Babe Ruth is outstanding.
9. Some people labor under the (allusion, illusion, delusion) that they can get by without doing any work.
10. (Beside, Besides) George, sixteen other boys are going.
11. There are (all together, altogether) 51 sentences in this exercise.
12. Our company bowling team (beat, bet) Consolidated Company in the play-off game yesterday.
13. Every member was asked to (bring, take) his lunch for the picnic.
14. When entering upon a business venture, it is best to have ample (capital, capitol) in reserve.
15. There was something very (childish, childlike) about the simplicity of her decisions.
16. The sight-seer was warned that he was (apt, likely, liable) to hurt himself if he leaned over the edge of the seat.
17. They thought that his nomination was a (complement, compliment) to his outstanding organizational ability.
18. Few persons are high-minded enough to take (consul, counsel, council) when it is offered by those wiser than they.
19. Stopping the game every now and then, the umpire (con-

tinually, continuously) warned the players on the bench to quiet down.

20. The average person is extremely (conscience, conscious) of his shortcomings.

21. The criminal was very (contemptible, contemptuous) of his captors although he had been outwitted.

22. The (dialect, dialogue) of the play was sprinkled with many a witticism.

23. People who live in the city rarely take the trouble to (discover, invent) the beauties of nature.

24. It is a fact that (less, fewer) airplane than railroad accidents are taking place.

25. The textile company was (famous, notorious) for the poor quality of merchandise it put on the market.

26. Many persons maintain that it is impossible to have a (dual, duel) allegiance to the United States and to some other country.

27. Herbert Hoover, (formally, formerly) President of the United States, is now helping with food investigations throughout the world.

28. The scientist noted where the tributary had (flowed, flown) into the river.

29. Franklin D. Roosevelt ran against Wendell Willkie in 1940; the (former, latter) put up a good fight but lost.

30. It was (good, well) that he had completed his work because the inspection took place that day.

31. (Human, Humane) treatment of animals is the chief purpose of the ASPCA.

32. The Green Mountains of New Hampshire provide an unusually (healthy, healthful) climate for those suffering from hay fever.

33. In an effort to keep people from trying to (immigrate, emigrate) from the country, the government made its constitution more liberal.

34. May I (imply, infer) from your remarks that you feel the whole matter is not worth while?

35. Thanks to many an (ingenious, ingenuous) person, our lives are far more comfortable today than ever before.

36. The test paper that he turned in was so (ineligible, illegible) that he failed in the examination.

37. The (latest, last) person to qualify before the field was closed felt himself extremely fortunate.

38. Despite the severe injury to his mouth, he was able to make himself (intelligent, intelligible) to the policeman.

39. (Laying, Lying) down on the job will not be tolerated in this company.

40. The (principle, principal) witness against the defendant did not show up.

41. They decided to (persecute, prosecute) the case when further evidence was uncovered.
42. "Please (pour, spill) the coffee, Jean," said Mother.
43. It was not found (practical, practicable) to put the plan into operation before the suitable personnel could be hired.
44. The judge instructed the jury to (precede, proceed) with the deliberations.
45. Our first and second choices are Edith and Joan (respectfully, respectively).
46. Please (sit, set) in those chairs in the front before filling those in the rear.
47. Because he had nothing to gain from either party's winning, the boy chosen to arbitrate was quite (uninterested, disinterested) in the case.
48. We liked that new documentary film so much we (stood, stayed) to see it twice.
49. Because of protests from the minority party, the (statue, statute) was revised before it was sent to the governor.
50. Please (rout, route) the traffic where there is the least congestion.
51. Mrs. Jones sent John to the store to buy some (stationary, stationery).

25 SPELLING

There are two kinds of people in this world:

1. *The perfect speller*

He's the despair and envy of his friends. He wins all the spelling bees. He never misspells a word. How does he do it? He has a *photographic memory*. He never forgets what he sees. It's a gift—but it's not impossible to cultivate it as you will see.

2. *The rest of us*

Some of us misspell words only occasionally. Others misspell words quite often. Many (too many!) of us throw up our hands and say "I never could spell, anyway."

This section is for the rest of us. Let's send the perfect speller home and talk about ourselves.

You don't have to spend the rest of your life being a poor speller. That's the most important thing to remember. If you don't spell well, don't think you have an incurable disease! No matter how poorly you spell, you can learn to spell better —and in a shorter time than you think.

Here's How

1. *Keep your eyes open.* Look at the word. See how it is constructed. Notice the parts that go to make it up. Try to get a mental picture of the word. About nine-tenths of spelling correctly is *seeing correctly*.

2. *Keep your ears open. Pronounce* the word correctly. Many words are misspelled because they are mispronounced. Take **library,** for example. It's often misspelled **libary** because so many people leave out the first r when they pronounce the word. Say library and you'll spell it library.

3. *Learn a few simple spelling rules.* We'll take these up in a few moments. Rules won't solve all your problems. But they are a great help.

4. *Keep a personal spelling list* of all the words you misspell. Write them out correctly at least three times. We all

misspell different words for different reasons. Make a note of why you made the error—and you won't make it again.

Take the Word Apart

Prefixes

How many s's in:
    di (?) appear
    di (?) olve
Did you guess? Or did you know? It's very simple if you take the words apart:

> disappear
> dissolve

Each of these words consists of two parts: The first part is *dis* which is called a *prefix*. A prefix is something you put *before* a word to change its original meaning. The second part consists of another word: appear, solve. So what we are doing here is *adding* a *prefix* and a word to get another word:

> dis + appear = disappear
> dis + solve = dissolve

Now let's try a few more:

> dis + similar = dissimilar
> dis + regard = disregard
> dis + possess = dispossess
> dis + service = disservice
> dis + appoint = disappoint

It's as simple as all that. Add the original word to the prefix and there you are. It's just a case of $1 + 1 = 2$.

The important thing to remember here is that we make the most errors when the prefix *ends* with the same letter with which the word *begins*.

Test Yourself
How many s's in:
    di (?) able
    di (?) armament
    di (?) ection
    di (?) atisfaction

There are other fairly common prefixes that you should know. They follow the same rule as dis.

mis

mis + step = misstep
mis + spell = misspell
mis + treat = mistreat
mis + place = misplace
mis + take = mistake
mis + shapen = misshapen

il

il + legal = illegal
il + legible = illegible
il + legitimate = illegitimate
il + licit = illicit
il + logical = illogical
il + literate = illiterate

un

un + natural = unnatural
un + necessary = unnecessary
un + nerve = unnerve
un + pleasant = unpleasant
un + real = unreal

im

im + mortal = immortal
im + mobile = immobile
im + moderate = immoderate
im + modest = immodest
im + moral = immoral
im + mature = immature

over

over + run = overrun
over + reach = overreach
over + take = overtake

under

under + take = undertake
under + rate = underrate

Now keep these few prefixes in mind and you'll have at least one magic charm to keep the spelling demon away from your door.

Suffixes

A suffix is like a prefix—but with this difference. The suffix is tacked on to the *end* of a word to change its meaning. The effect is the same, however. Something is *added*. If you know what is added and if you know the original word, you'll have no trouble.

ly

accidental + ly = accidentally
extreme + ly = extremely
actual + ly = actually
unusual + ly = unusually
incidental + ly = incidentally
sincere + ly = sincerely

Simple, isn't it? Now test yourself.
How many l's in:
helpfu (?) y

exceptiona (?) y
annua (?) y
financia (?) y
pure (?) y

ness
mean + ness = meanness
drunken + ness = drunkenness
wanton + ness = wantonness
clever + ness = cleverness

al
accident + al = accidental
vocation + al = vocational
occasion + al = occasional
function + al = functional
exception + al = exceptional

ment
wonder + ment = wonderment
entertain + ment = entertainment
arrange + ment = arrangement
improve + ment = improvement
achieve + ment = achievement

less
soul + less = soulless
heart + less = heartless
plan + less = planless
doubt + less = doubtless
taste + less = tasteless
fruit + less = fruitless

ful
success + ful = successful
doubt + ful = doubtful

est and er
kind + est, er = kindest, kinder
high + est, er = highest, higher
slight + est, er = slightest, slighter
sweet + est, er = sweetest, sweeter
soon + est, er = soonest, sooner

Note: When the word ends in e, just add st or r:
late = latest, later
handsome = handsomest, handsomer
humble = humblest, humbler

Note: When the word ends in y, change the y to i and add
est or er
kindly + est = kindliest, kindlier
likely + est = likeliest, likelier
happy + est = happiest, happier
snappy + est = snappiest, snappier

Silent Partners
The correct spelling of the following words depends entirely on how good your eye is. These words aren't spelled the way they sound. That's because they all contain *silent letters*. Keep your eye on them.

Silent b

climb	tomb
lamb	dumb
numb	plumb
crumb	thumb

Silent h

ghost	ghoul
ghastly	gherkin

Silent k

knack	knell
knave	knew
knead	knife
knapsack	knight
knee	knit
knob	knock
knot	know

Silent l

Spelled	Pronounced
almond	ah mond
alms	ahms
balm	bahm
calm	kahm
balk	bawk
palm	pahm

Silent t

Spelled	Pronounced
bristle	brissle
gristle	grissle
thistle	thissle
apostle	apossle
bustle	bussle
wrestle	ressle (silent w, too!)

Silent g

gnarled	gnash
gnat	gnaw
gnu	gnome

Silent p

Spelled	Pronounced
psalm	sahm
ptomaine	toe main
pneumatic	new matic

psychology	sy kol a gee
ptarmigan	tarmigan
pneumonia	new mown yuh
psychiatry	sy ky a tree

Silent w

wrap	wrath
wreath	wreck
wrench	wrest
wretch	wriggle
wrestle	wrinkle
wrist	write
writhe	wrong
wrought	wraith
playwright	

Silent s

Spelled	Pronounced
aisle	I'll
isle	I'll
island	eye land

The best thing to do with all of these silent fellows is to study them carefully. Fix in your mind's eye the silent letter and the rest is easy.

Doubling the Final Consonant

There was once a newspaper editor who hired a writer who couldn't spell—too well. For the most part, the errors this writer made were harmless. Those who noticed them were either amused or thought them unimportant.

But one morning the writer came to work and found on his desk a letter from his editor (correctly spelled) telling him that, as of this day, his services were no longer required. Attached to the discharge slip was a column written by our "original" speller in which the town's leading citizen was referred to as a "battle-scared veteran!"

Of course, this couldn't happen to you! Or could it? Think back over some of your recent letters.

Have you written	*When you should have written*
I am hopping to hear from you.	I am hoping to hear from you.
I am planing to come.	I am planning to come.

So you see that there is a very good reason for doubling the final consonant. If you don't, you very often find yourself saying something you don't mean. Hopping isn't hoping. Planing (which is what a carpenter does with a plane) isn't planning.

The Rule

Here's a rule that will help keep you out of this sort of trouble.

If a word has *one* syllable

and

If the word ends in a *consonant* (except **h** or **x**)

If the consonant has a *vowel* (**a, e, i, o, u**) before it, then

Double the final consonant before **ing, er, ed, est.**

Let's see how the rule works:

1. hop—one syllable—ends in consonant *p*; vowel *o* before consonant.
2. Therefore: hopped—consonant **p** is doubled before **ed**
   hopping—consonant **p** is doubled before **ing**
   hopper—consonant **p** is doubled before **er**

Try a few more:

bid	bidder	bidding
plan	planner	planning
star	starred	starring
step	stepped	stepping
sit	sitter	sitting
beg	beggar	begging
rob	robber	robbing
win	winner	winning
sad	sadder	saddest
hot	hotter	hottest
rub	rubber	rubbing
swim	swimmer	swimming

Words of More Than One Syllable

These are a little harder than words of one syllable—but not much. Follow carefully step by step and you'll see.

Take a word like admit. Notice a few important things about it:

1. It has *two* syllables—ad mit
2. It ends in a *single* consonant: **t.**
3. A vowel (**i**) comes *before* the final consonant.

4. When you pronounce the word, the accent falls on the *last* syllable: ad *mit'*.

What do we do when we want to add **ing, ed, er,** or **est** to words like these? We follow the same rule as for words of one syllable: Just (1) *double* the final consonant and (2) add the suffix: **ing, er, est, ed.**

Example:

admit   admitted   admitting

There are literally thousands of words that fall under this rule. So it's a good one to know.

Let's try a few and see:

defer	deferred	deferring	
regret	regretted	regretting	regrettable
control	controlled	controlling	controllable
begin		beginning	
prefer	preferred	preferring	
commit	committed	committing	
rebel	rebelled	rebelling	
compel	compelled	compelling	
occur	occurred	occurring	
excel	excelled	excelling	

Meet the Apostrophe (')

In speaking, we often run words together. It's a sort of natural and unconscious streamlining. These streamlined words are called *contractions*.

In writing these contractions, we insert an apostrophe (') where one or more letters have been left out. The trick is in knowing what has been omitted—and where.

Here's a list of the most common contractions. Note where the apostrophe has been inserted in the following words—and *why*.

aren't = are not	shouldn't = should not
can't = can not	there's = there is
couldn't = could not	weren't = were not
doesn't = does not	you've = you have
hadn't = had not	we've = we have
wasn't = was not	don't = do not
he's = he is	isn't = is not

you'll = you will
I'd = I would
let's = let us
hasn't = has not
haven't = have not
mustn't = must not

wouldn't = would not
won't = will not
he'd = he would
I've = I have
we'd = we would

The Terrible Trio—It's, You're, They're

These are the three most troublesome contractions in the language. They are misspelled and misused more frequently than any of the others. But if you approach them sensibly, they should present no problem at all. Just take them apart and look at them.

1. It's = it is. It never means anything else. If you're not sure whether you are using it correctly, try this sure-fire test:

> The cat lost it's tail.

That means: The cat lost *it is* tail. Does that make sense? Of course not. Then say what you mean:

> The cat lost its tail.

Its means the tail belongs to the cat.

> It's raining.

This means: *It is* raining. This makes sense.

2. You're = you are

> Is this you're cat?

That means: Is this *you are* cat? Of course you meant:

> Is this your cat?

The cat belongs to you.

> You're my cat = You are my cat.

That's better.

3. They're = they are

> They're not here = They are not here. (Right!)

Now you can't possibly confuse **they're** with:
there (place)—over there
their (possession)—their hats, their coats

Words Ending in "ceed," "cede," "sede"

The rule here is extremely simple.

1. Only *one* word ends in sede: supersede
2. Only *three* words end in **ceed**: exceed, proceed, succeed.
3. All the other words end in **cede**: precede, accede, intercede, etc.

So this whole problem boils itself down to just *four* words. Learn to spell them correctly and your troubles are over.

supersede	proceed
exceed	succeed

Quick Quiz

How sharp are you? How carefully have you read—and *looked*? Which of the following words are misspelled? See how high you can score. Don't look back until you've tried the test.

excede	preceed
succeed	recede
seceed	concede
procede	supercede
intersede	

How well did you do? Check your answers against the rule.

Is It "ei" or "ie"?

The rule here is:
When the sound is *ee*,
ei follows *c*;
ie follows all other letters.

ei after c

ceiling	deceive	receipt	conceive
receipt	receive	perceive	deceive

ie after other letters.

believe	chief	fiend
belief	pierce	relieve
relieve	sieve	reprieve
shriek	grief	mischief

But note these exceptions:

feign	reign	weigh	veil
freight	sleigh	weight	neighbor
heinous	their	vein	leisure
counterfeit	weird	forfeit	foreign
seize	height	neither	

This isn't a wholly satisfactory rule. But it's the best that we've been able to work out. You'll just have to remember that the **ei** and **ie** words are tricky. Learn all the exceptions and the rest should take care of themselves.

Dropping the Final e

When a word ends in e and we want to add **ing, able,** or any other suffix beginning with a vowel, we usually drop the **e.**

argue	arguing	arguable
come	coming	
love	loving	lovable
write	writing	
please	pleasing	pleasant
hope	hoping	
give	giving	
serve	serving	
store	storing	storage
grieve	grieving	grievance
fortune		fortunate
sense		sensible

Exceptions

1. Words that end in **ce** or **ge** *do not* drop the **e** before **able** and **ous.** This is done to keep the c and g sounds soft, like s and j, as they sound in the original word.

courage	courageous
outrage	outrageous
advantage	advantageous

notice	noticeable
charge	chargeable
enforce	enforceable
service	serviceable
trace	traceable
change	changeable
manage	manageable

2. Some words retain the final e in order to prevent mispronunciation and confusion of meaning.

hoe	hoeing
shoe	shoeing
toe	toeing
singe	singeing ⎫ Note what would happen here
dye	dyeing ⎰ if we dropped the final e.
hinge	hingeing

In the case of singe, this is what we might get if we dropped the final e:

I found her singing her hair. (A very neat trick!)

3. Mileage.
4. When we add a suffix beginning with a consonant, final e is usually retained.

sincere	sincerely
chaste	chastely
excite	excitement
hate	hateful
pale	paleness
love	lovely
live	lively
immediate	immediately
like	likely

But note carefully: Some words ending in silent e preceded by u drop the e when adding a suffix.

argue	argument
blue	bluish
due	duly
true	truly

Other Exceptions

whole	wholly
judge	judgment (preferred spelling)
acknowledge	acknowledgment (preferred spelling)

Final y

1. When a word ends in y and a *consonant* (r, s, l, etc.) comes *before* the y, change the y to i before all suffixes except ing.

Here's how the rule works:

Try ends in y
r, a consonant, comes before the y
Change the y to i = tri
Add suffix ed—tri + ed = tried
Exception: try + ing = trying (y not dropped, not changed)

Some Examples:

marry	happy	city	lonely	defy	pretty
married	happiest	cities	loneliness	defied	prettier

2. When a word ends in y and a *vowel* (a, e, i, etc.) comes before the y, the y usually does not change when you add a suffix:

Enjoy ends in y
A vowel o comes before y

enjoy + able ⎱ The y is not dropped or changed in any of
enjoy + ed   ⎰ these words when a suffix is added.

boy	boyish	play	played	lobby	lobbyist

Exceptions

The only words that don't follow these rules are:

say said	pay paid	slay slain
day daily	lay laid	

Say What You See

People misspell many words simply because they mispronounce them—and for no other reason.

Here's a list of words to keep your ear on! Take a good look at them. *Say what you see!* Don't add any syllables; don't subtract any syllables—and you'll have the spelling "down pat."

Say

accept   (ak sept)
arctic
asparagus   (no grass, no sparrows)
athletics   (only 3 syllables)
attacked
barbarous   (3 syllables)
candidate   (Watch the candi)
champion
chimney   (only 2 syllables)
close   (no t)
congratulations   (watch the first t)
cranberry   (no m)
disastrous   (only 3 syllables)
divide
divine
drawing   (no r in the middle)
escape   (no x)
February   (watch the first r)
government   (watch that first n)
hindrance   (only 2 syllables)
hundred
incidentally   (5 syllables)
introduce
laboratory   (watch the labor)

Say

law   (no r)
library   (watch the first r)
lightning   (only 2 syllables)
licorice   (lik'-o-ris)
modern   (er as in maker)
mischievous   (only 3 syllables)
once   (no t)
perform
perspiration
postponed   (watch the t)
prejudice
probably   (watch the second b)
pattern   (er like in maker)
protection
recognize   (watch the cog)
remembrance   (only 3 syllables)
secretary   (watch the first r)
saw   (no r)
sandwich   (no m)
surprise   (watch the first r)
temperament   (4 syllables)
temperature   (4 syllables)
tragedy
tremendous   (only 3 syllables—no j)
umbrella   (only 3 syllables)

A Basic Spelling List

As an educated person, you should be able to spell all the words on the following list correctly. Many are extremely simple. Others are somewhat more difficult. All of them are part of our everyday spoken and written language. There are no strange or "high-brow" words in this list. Take a few words each day and master them. Follow the suggestions on pages 260-61 and you'll be surprised at how quickly you'll improve your spelling. The rules in this chapter should prove helpful to you in getting over the "tough" spots in some of these words.

absence	carrying	dining	handling
accept	cemetery	disappear	handful
accidentally	certain	disappointed	handsome
accommodate	character	discipline	having
accustomed	chief	discussed	height
acquainted	chocolate	disease	hoping
across	choose	dissatisfied	hopping
address	chosen	divide	humorous
advice	cloth	division	hurrying
advise	clothes	doesn't	imagination
all right	coarse	easily	immediately
almost	coming	effect	incidentally
already	commission	eighth	independent
altogether	committee	eliminate	influential
always	community	embarrassed	instead
amateur	communication	equipped	intelligence
annual	completely	especially	intelligent
anxious	compliment	etc.	interested
appearance	concerned	excellent	interrupt
appreciate	confident	except	irresistible
approaching	conquer	exercise	knowledge
appropriate	conscience	exhausted	laboratory
argument	conscious	existence	ladies
arrangements	conscientious	expense	later
asked	consider	experience	latter
association	convenience	explanation	led
athletic	copies	extremely	length
author	course	evidently	library
awkward	courteous	familiar	lightning
balance	courtesy	fascinating	literature
beginning	criticism	February	livelihood
believe	customer	finally	loneliness
benefited	deceive	financial	loose
bicycle	decide	foreign	lose
brake	decision	forth	losing
break	describe	forty	loss
breath	description	fourth	maintenance
breathe	desert	freight	marriage
bureau	desirable	friend	mathematics
bulletin	despair	fundamental	meant
cafeteria	desperate	government	miniature
campaign	dessert	grammar	minimum
candidate	determine	grateful	mischievous
captain	didn't	guarantee	misspelled
careful	different	guardian	mortgage

movable
mysterious
naturally
necessarily
necessity

necessary
neither
nevertheless
nickel
niece

ninety
noticeable
occasion
occasionally
occur

occurred
occurrence
o'clock
omitted
opinion

opportunity
optimistic
organization
original
paid

parallel
parliament
particular
particularly
passed

past
pastime
perform
permanent
permissible

persistent
personally
persuade
physically
piece

planned
planning
pleasant
portrayed
possess

possible
possibility
practically
prairie
preceding

preference
preferred
prejudiced
preparation
presence

principal
principle
privilege
probably
procedure

prominent
pronunciation
propeller
prophecy
prophesied

psychology
quantity
quiet
quite
realize

really
receipt
receive
recognize
recommend

reference
referred
relieve
remembrance
repetition

representative
restaurant
rhythm
ridiculous
sacrifice

sandwich
scene
schedule
secretary
seize

sense
separate
sergeant
shining
shipped

siege
similar
sincerely
speech
stationery

stopped
stopping
straight
strength
studying

succeed
success
sufficient
superintendent
surprise

taking
tendency
their
there
they're

thorough
though
thought
through
too

tragedy
transferred
truly
twelfth
unnecessary

until
unusual
unusually
useful
using

valuable
vegetable
village
villain
weather

Wednesday
weird
whether
whose
woman

women
won't
writing
written
you're

Exercise 1. In each of the following groups, one word is mis-spelled. Find that word and spell it correctly in your notebook.

1. career, beginning, truely, judgment
2. successfull, illegal, carburetor, classic

3. misspell, government, believe, your's
4. occassional, disappear, asparagus, surprise
5. publicly, sincerly, pneumonia, courageous
6. dissolve, comming, supersede, villain
7. similar, coming, Britian, probably
8. writting, twelfth, livelihood, psychology
9. dissappoint, privilege, receive, succeed
10. unnecessary, accidentally, definately, achievement
11. hurrying, playwright, writing, freind
12. thier, sandwich, February, Wednesday
13. precede, incidently, argument, married
14. lonliness, buoys, situation, foxes
15. stationary, weird, mischievious, fascism
16. piece, seperate, women, disregard
17. disatisfaction, suggest, guarantee, attacking
18. unnatural, immortal, unecessary, unnerve
19. overtake, overeach, underrate, absolutely
20. commitee, usually, interested, literature
21. proceed, exceed, precede, supercede
22. receive, believe, sieze, foreign
23. knowledge, wholy, prejudice, describe
24. secretary, recognize, tragedy, congradulations
25. probably, cranberry, remembrance, disasterous

Exercise 2. Write the contraction for each of the following in your notebook.

1. here is	6. is not
2. cannot	7. Bill is
3. they are	8. I am
4. will not	9. who will
5. we have	10. you are

Exercise 3. Copy the following contractions, placing the apostrophe correctly in each.

1. wont	6. theyll
2. tis	7. therell
3. couldnt	8. shed
4. werent	9. youll
5. cant	10. shell

Exercise 4. Use the following pairs of words in sentences to show the distinctions in their meanings.

1. hoping hopping	4. stared starred
2. planing planning	5. scared scarred
3. they're their	6. biding bidding

7. wining
   winning
8. robed
   robbed
9. bare
   bear
10. cant
    can't
11. shed
    she'd
12. feat
    feet
13. coarse
    course

14. whose
    who's
15. its
    it's
16. your
    you're
17. wont
    won't
18. dying
    dyeing
19. singing
    singeing
20. weather
    whether

Exercise 5. Select the correct word from those in parentheses.

1. They're either (too, to, two) young or (too, to, two) old.
2. (Who's, Whose) that knocking at my door?
3. The old (lady's, ladies) were here last night.
4. Is this book mine or (yours, your's)?
5. Harry should have closed (your, you're) window.
6. (Your, You're) eyes don't glow like mine.
7. Don't laugh at my jokes (to, too, two) much.
8. John, (there, they're, their) suspecting things.
9. He (laid, layed) the book down on the desk.
10. There are (to, two, too) (secretary's, secretaries) in the office.
11. "(You're, Your) going to get (you're, your) nose punched," said Butch angrily.
12. "(Whose, Who's) going to get (whose, who's) nose punched?" replied Lafe in a threatening tone.
13. (You're, Your) right; (its, it's) not (you're, your) fault.
14. Don't forget to read (you're, your) instruction manual.
15. While (you're, your) in the store, buy me a pack of razor blades.
16. I'm beginning (to, too, two) see the light.
17. I'm (too, to, two) tired (too, to, two) see (too, to, two) movies and then go out dancing, (too, to, two).
18. I think (its, it's) (too, to, two) late now (too, to, two) return the tie.
19. We do not choose a book by (its, it's) cover.
20. His hair is so long that (its, it's) starting (too, to, two) climb upward, like a vine.
21. (It's, Its) only Jim from over the sea.
22. Victor always develops a headache when (there, they're) is work to be done.
23. When (there, their, they're) here, tell them the news.
24. If (you're, your) belt is (too, to, two) (lose, loose), you'd better (wear, where) suspenders.

25. He had no right (too, to, two) steal (they're, their, there) books.

Exercise 6. Some of the following words are misspelled. Correct the misspelled words in your notebook.

1. dissolve
2. dissappoint
3. dissable
4. mistep
5. ilegible
6. illiterate
7. unecessary
8. unerve
9. imortal
10. overrun
11. accidently
12. incidentally
13. unusualy
14. meaness
15. souless
16. admited
17. begining
18. regretted
19. prefered
20. commited
21. occured
22. exceed
23. procede
24. precede
25. supercede
26. intercede
27. freind
28. sieze
29. beleive
30. receive
31. hopeing
32. argueing
33. loveable
34. singeing
35. arguement
36. atheletics
37. barbarious
38. congradulations
39. cramberry
40. Febuary
41. mischievous
42. predjudice
43. tradgedy
44. probaly
45. rememberance
46. temperment
47. umberella

26 QUOTATION MARKS

Whenever, in your writing, you want to quote *exactly* what someone has said or written, you use *quotation marks* (" "). These quotation marks are put around the *exact* words of the speaker or writer to show where the quotation begins and ends.

> He said, "I won't be fooled this time."

or

> "I won't be fooled this time," he said.

This is called a *direct quotation*. The words within the quotation marks:

> "I won't be fooled this time"

are the speaker's or writer's own words. You have quoted him *directly* and *exactly*. You have added nothing, subtracted nothing.

You use quotation marks in this way whenever you are reporting something exactly as you have heard it or read it. It may be a bit of conversation, part of a speech you heard on the radio, or a paragraph or line from something you have read. But what is within the quotation marks must always be the *exact* words.

Indirect Quotations

Sometimes you don't remember the exact words you want to quote, but only the gist or general idea. For this kind of statement you don't use quotation marks because you aren't actually quoting anything:

> He said he wouldn't be fooled this time.

No quotation marks are used here because **he wouldn't be fooled this time** aren't his exact words. He did say something about not being fooled this time, but you aren't quoting the very words he used when he made the statement.

Where to Put Quotation Marks

There are a number of points to note about the correct use of quotation marks.

1. A comma separates the actual quotation from the **he said's, she said's**, etc.

"It's up to you," he said.

2. The comma and the period come *before* the quotation marks.

"It's up to you now," he said.
He said, "It's up to you now."

Remember it this way: *Comma-Quotes*
Period-Quotes.

3. The first word of a quotation is capitalized because it is the beginning of a sentence.

"You bet I'll be there," he said.

4. When a quotation ends with a ? or a ! do not use a comma. These punctuation marks serve instead of commas.

"Sit down!" he ordered.
"Is it you?" she asked.

5. When a quotation consists of more than one sentence, one set of quotation marks will do, at the *beginning* and at the *end* of the conversation. Don't use separate sets of quotation marks in a quotation consisting of a series of uninterrupted sentences.

Michael remarked, "I have tried over and over again to follow your advice. But I haven't noticed any improvement in my game. I'm not sure now whether I'm really following the advice you gave me. Something is wrong somewhere."

6. Where you are quoting a series of connected paragraphs, put quotation marks at the
  beginning of each paragraph
        but at
  the end of the *last* paragraph only—to show that the quotation ends there.

"There are times when men must stand up and face facts, and fight for the truth. If we do not now fight for what is right and decent, we shall have no one but ourselves to blame if our freedom is taken from us.   ←No quotation marks here. The quotation is not ended.

"By now we should have learned from recent history how men of ill-will work on the passions and prejudices of the common people. It is written large in the tragedy of modern Europe that the first step in paralyzing man's desire to seek truth and justice is to confuse and poison his mind."   ←Put quotation marks to show you are still quoting.

←Quotation marks at end of paragraph mean the end of the quotation.

7. When you are quoting or writing conversation, be sure to start a new paragraph for each speaker.

"Have you ever heard of this man before?" my mother asked.
"Never," I told her.
"Well, then, how is it that he seems to know so much about you?" my mother continued.
"I really don't know," I replied.

Note here that in writing you do not always use complete sentences since people do not always talk in complete sentences. Speech consists of streamlined sentences with many things left out because they are so clearly understood. So, instead of answering Mother:
"I never heard of the man before," you say, "Never!" and

there is no question in Mother's mind about what you mean. Just another example now to make this point clearer:

"How are you feeling today?" I asked Bill.

"In the pink," he answered. ("I feel in the pink of condition," is the complete answer. But in the pink is enough for you. You fill in the rest.)

"I suppose it's that new training schedule that makes you feel that way," I said.

"Of course," was Bill's enthusiastic answer. ("Of course it is that new training schedule that makes me feel that way.")

Broken Quotations

In all the quotations so far, the he said or she said has come before or after the quotation. That's one way of writing quotations or conversations. Very often, however, we *split* or *break* the quotation like this:

"You may go if you wish," my uncle said, "but I think it's a risky business."

Notice that my uncle said comes in the middle of the quotation. There are quotation marks around the two parts of the *whole* quotation—before and after my uncle said—to show that the quotation has been interrupted.

"You may go if you wish,"—"but I think it's a risky business."

Actually, the *whole* quotation is a single sentence.

"You may go if you wish but I think it's a risky business."

That's how it would look if we hadn't wedged my uncle said into the middle.

The following simple rules govern the placing of quotation marks in broken quotations:

8. Where the *first* part of the quotation ends, put a *comma* and *quotation marks*.

"You may go if you wish,"

Now watch what happens:

9. If the first part of the quotation is a complete sentence, this is what you do:

"You may go if you wish," my uncle said. (Period here.)

10. If the part of the quotation that *continues* is a complete sentence, do the following:

"You may go if you wish," my uncle said. "You know how I feel."

Start the continuing part with a *capital* because it is the beginning of a sentence.

The whole quotation (without my uncle said) consists of *two* sentences and looks like this:

You may go if you wish. (complete sentence) You know how I feel. (complete sentence)

11. If the first part of the quotation is *not* a complete sentence,

"Although I don't approve," my uncle said,

put a *comma* after said to show that this part is not a complete sentence.

The second part of the quotation which continues the same sentence is then written this way:

"Although I don't approve," my uncle said, "you may go if you wish."

The you is written with a small letter to show that it is part of the same sentence.

Whole quotation:

"Although I don't approve, you may go if you wish."

Exercise 1. Now do you have all these rules about quotation marks clear in your mind? Here's a test which will help you to see whether you can apply these rules. (Maybe you'd like to re-read the rules before you try your hand at the sentences.) A few of these sentences do not require any quotation marks because they are *indirect quotations*. Punctuate correctly the following:

1. Did anybody call while I was out John asked his mother.
2. Stop he shouted.
3. The principal said that school would be dismissed early.
4. Pick up that paper Jim said.

5. Jim said pick up that paper.
6. The clerk looked at me and remarked where is the form you you were supposed to bring with you? I can't sign this paper unless I have the form why are you so careless about these matters?
7. The dentist said that I ought to brush my teeth regularly.
8. The sign in the ice-cream parlor read in God we trust. All others pay cash.
9. Mr. Held said your salary will be thirty dollars a week.
10. Your salary will be thirty dollars a week Mr. Held said.
11. I don't know what makes you act this way John my mother said to me one morning. I suppose it's spring I told her. But you didn't act this way last spring she said. Well I'm getting older mother that may explain it I answered.
12. These are times that try men's souls is one of Thomas Paine's most famous lines.
13. The child is father to the man is a line from a poem by Wordsworth.
14. There is no more famous soliloquy than Hamlet's which begins to be or not to be that is the question.
15. If it rains said the coach we'll have to call the game off.
16. I don't care whether it rains or not the coach said we're going to play that game no matter what happens.
17. When I raise my hand said the ensign that will be your signal to start the test.
18. Do you mind I inquired if I stay a few minutes after the others have left.
19. Put up the storm windows my mother said the weather report says there's a hurricane headed this way.
20. The inside of a car the mechanic said pointing at the dismantled motor is an extremely complicated piece of machinery.
21. The duck-billed platypus is one of the queerest animals the lecturer remarked it is both bird and mammal it has hair on its body and lays eggs.
22. When you arrive at the station Janice wrote telephone me at home I will come and pick you up in the station wagon.
23. Come at once the telegram read you are needed.
24. Can't you come I asked even for a few minutes.

27 PLURALS AND POSSESSIVES

Forming the Plural

1. The plural of most nouns is formed by adding **s** to the singular:

boy	boys	girl	girls
hat	hats	tenement	tenements
tree	trees	age	ages
place	places	love	loves

2. Most nouns ending in **ch, s, sh, x,** and **z** add **es** to the singular to form the plural:

church	churches	kiss	kisses
brush	brushes	box	boxes
waltz	waltzes		

3. A few nouns add **en** to the singular to form the plural, or change the vowel:

ox	oxen	woman	women
man	men	mouse	mice
tooth	teeth	foot	feet
louse	lice		

4. a. Nouns ending in **y** preceded by a *consonant* change **y** to **i** and add **es:**

lady	ladies	enemy	enemies
study	studies	sky	skies
fly	flies	treaty	treaties

b. Nouns ending in **y** preceded by a *vowel* add **s:**

monkey	monkeys	turkey	turkeys
alley	alleys	key	keys
journey	journeys	attorney	attorneys
valley	valleys	boy	boys
play	plays		

5. Proper nouns form their plurals according to rules 1 and 2:

Alices, Johns, Joneses, Murphys, Pearsons, Maltzes

6. Many nouns ending in **f** and **fe** form plurals by (1) changing **f** or **fe** to **ves** or (2) by adding **s**.
These change **f** or **fe** to **ves**:

beef	beeves	loaf	loaves
calf	calves	self	selves
elf	elves	shelf	shelves
half	halves	thief	thieves
leaf	leaves	wife	wives
life	lives	wolf	wolves

These add **s**:

belief	beliefs	proof	proofs
chief	chiefs	reef	reefs
cliff	cliffs	roof	roofs
grief	griefs	serf	serfs
handkerchief	handkerchiefs		

7. Most nouns ending in **o** add **s** to form the plural:

auto	autos	piano	pianos
armadillo	armadillos	piccolo	piccolos
bronco	broncos	radio	radios
casino	casinos	solo	solos
contralto	contraltos	sombrero	sombreros
dynamo	dynamos	soprano	sopranos
Eskimo	Eskimos	tobacco	tobaccos

The following add **es**:

domino	dominoes	Negro	Negroes
hero	heroes	potato	potatoes
echo	echoes	tomato	tomatoes
embargo	embargoes	torpedo	torpedoes
mosquito	mosquitoes	veto	vetoes

These nouns form their plurals in either way:

bravo	bravos	bravoes
buffalo	buffalos	buffaloes

calico	calicos	calicoes
cargo	cargos	cargoes
flamingo	flamingos	flamingoes
grotto	grottos	grottoes
halo	halos	haloes
innuendo	innuendos	innuendoes
memento	mementos	mementoes
motto	mottos	mottoes
zero	zeros	zeroes

8. Plurals of letters, figures, signs, words, phrases, are formed by adding 's.

> There are two m's in **committee.**
> His 9's look like 7's.

9. In certain hyphenated words, only the principal or most important part of the word forms the plural:

editor-in-chief   editors-in-chief

The principal part of the word is **editor.** Therefore, in forming the plural of the word, only **editor** is pluralized: **editors.** Notice that the same holds true of the following:

Singular	*Plural*
court-martial	courts-martial
hanger-on	hangers-on
jack-in-the-box	jacks-in-the-box
knight-errant	knights-errant
maid-of-honor	maids-of-honor
man-of-war	men-of-war
mother-in-law	mothers-in-law
father-in-law	fathers-in-law
brother-in-law	brothers-in-law

10. The plural of **Mr.** is **Messrs.**

> The Messrs. Arnold and Jones are here.

11. The plural of **Miss** is **Misses.**

> We shall call on the Misses Grandgent and Wickersham.

12. The plural of **Master** is **Masters**.

The Masters Rorty are birds of a feather.

13. The plural of titles is formed in the regular manner.

Professor	Professors
Attorney	Attorneys
Judge	Judges

14. There is no plural for **Mrs.**

15. The following words are plural either in meaning or feeling, but they usually take a singular verb.

aeronautics	alms	civics	economics
ethics	mathematics	measles	molasses
mumps	news	phonetics	physics
politics	rickets	rabies	statistics
tactics	United States		

16. The following words are plural in meaning and form. They are very rarely used in the singular. They usually take plural verbs.

annals	links	billiards	clothes
goods	remains	pants	pliers
proceeds	suds	riches	scissors
shears	barracks	trousers	thanks
tweezers		belongings	

17. Some words are the same in the plural as they are in the singular.

cattle	sheep	deer	gross
salmon	trout	fish	grouse

Forming the Possessive

For the possessive form of *pronouns*, see page 230.

Nouns form the possessive case according to the following simple rules:

Singular Possessive: Add 's to the singular noun:

boy + 's = boy's   boy's bat

If the singular noun ends in s, then modern usage just adds the apostrophe:

H. G. Wells + ' = H. G. Wells'   H. G. Wells' books

(*Older usage:* H. G. Wells's books)
Plural Possessive: Add 's to the plural noun:

children + 's = children's   children's coats

If the plural noun ends in s, just add the apostrophe:

girls + ' = girls'   girls' galoshes

In general, it is preferable to show the possessive case of inanimate objects by means of the **of** phrase instead of 's:

the side of the house (not the house's side)
the cuff of my pants (not my pants' cuff)

Some exceptions:

thirty days' notice	for pity's sake	a day's travel
an hour's walk	a week's pay	a month's travel

Exercise 1. Change the singular subjects in the following sentences to the plural form and make the necessary changes in the predicates. In some sentences, where the predicate remains the same, just indicate the plural form of the subject. Indicate the words with only one form. *Example:* The *calves* snuggled close to the *cows* to keep warm.

1. The calf snuggled close to the cow to keep warm.
2. "Please buy a handkerchief," urged the Negro.
3. The thief escaped although efforts were made to catch him.
4. In late August, the mosquito becomes very annoying.
5. The Eskimo is a very hospitable person.
6. Last came the soprano who sang "Cara Nome."
7. Civics is a compulsory subject in most high schools.
8. There are two m's, two t's, two e's in the word committee.
9. The man-of-war has been made obsolete by the atom bomb.
10. The mother-in-law is the butt of many a radio joke.
11. The news about the United Nations is extremely encouraging.
12. Miss Jones came into the store to buy a hat.
13. Mr. Jones, her father, accompanied her.
14. The United States is the strongest industrial nation in the world.

15. A gross of pencils costs about $7.
16. The golf links were in excellent shape following the spring preparations.
17. The buffalo is extinct except for his appearance on nickels.
18. Is the tomato a fruit or a vegetable?
19. The roof of the house was shingled.
20. The hero of the afternoon was the pinch-hitter who drove in the winning runs.
21. The deer is a very friendly animal.
22. Mrs. Jones lives in the house next to mine.
23. Furnishing the power for the dam was a huge dynamo.
24. Molasses is supplied chiefly by the Caribbean countries.
25. The court-martial as a form of military justice is undergoing radical revision as a result of the experience of World War II.

Exercise 2. Write the plurals of the following words. Write the possessive form for both the singular and plural.

1. church	8. Mary	14. hero	20. country
2. Miss	9. calf	15. Negro	21. deer
3. tooth	10. leaf	16. soprano	22. gross
4. child	11. wolf	17. son-in-law	23. mathematics
5. lady	12. chief	18. life	24. father-in-law
6. secretary	13. roof	19. key	25. mosquito
7. monkey			

28 CAPITALIZATION

There's a reason for everything you do when you write. The use of capital letters (capitalization) is no exception.

Be sure you know and can apply the following rules and your writing will be clearer and easier to read.

1. Capitalize the *first word of every sentence*.

> Our country is still a land of opportunity.

The purpose of capitalization here is to tell the reader that a new thought is beginning. Of course, he may understand this without the capital letter. But by capitalizing the first word of the sentence, we make doubly sure that he will not miss it. For he will *see* it and *understand* it.

2. Capitalize the *first word of every line of poetry*.
3. Capitalize the *first word of a direct quotation*.

> He said, "There has never been a more exciting period in world history."

In the following, we use capital letters for only one reason. We want to show that we are talking about a *special* or *particular* person, thing, or group.

4. Capitalize names of *peoples, nations, races, tribes, religions,* and *languages*.

American	Mongolian	Protestant
Indian	Catholic	Shawnee
Negro	Jewish	South American

5. Capitalize the names of *particular organizations, buildings, schools, companies*.

Young Men's Christian Association	Youth Builders of America
Hotel Pennsylvania	Abraham Lincoln High School
Waldorf Astoria Hotel	Polyclinic Hospital
American Telephone and Telegraph Co.	Graybar Building

Note: The words **school, company, building, hospital, hotel,** etc., are not capitalized unless you are talking about *particular* ones. In the following sentences, they are not capitalized because you are just talking *in general* about these things:

> Mother was taken to the hospital this morning. (No particular hospital mentioned.)

but

> Mother was taken to the Polyclinic Hospital.
> High school prepares young people for life.

but

> I attended Abraham Lincoln High School.
> That's a very tall building.

but

> That tall building is the Graybar Building.

6. Capitalize the *days of the week* and the *months of the year.*

Monday	April
Wednesday	October

Note: Do not capitalize the names of the seasons—unless, of course, they are the first words in sentences.

summer	spring
winter	fall

> The spring rains came.
> The winter solstice is due soon.
> In the summer, beaches are crowded.
> Stores will soon be showing fall fashions.

7. Capitalize *holidays* and *holy days* generally.

Labor Day	Fourth of July
Armistice Day	Thanksgiving
Good Friday	Yom Kippur

8. Capitalize names of *cities, towns, countries, states, counties.*

| Baltimore | Hancock | Queens County |
| Virginia | Australia | |

9. Capitalize names of *streets* and *avenues, boulevards, squares, courts*, etc.

| Baldwin Street | Times Square | Trilby Court |
| Linden Boulevard | Hampton Avenue | |

10. Capitalize names of *rivers, lakes, seas, oceans, bays*. These words used alone are not capitalized.

Mississippi River	Sheepshead Bay
Yellowstone Park	Lake Huron
Red Sea	Pacific Ocean

11. Capitalize names of *parks*.

| Yellowstone Park | Central Park |

Note: Park used alone is not capitalized.

12. Capitalize *first* and *last* and *middle names* of people.

| George | Mary | Moses | John Henry Jackson |
| George Washington | | Andrew Jackson | |

13. Capitalize *first word* and *every important word* in *titles* of *books, plays, magazines, movies, stories, songs, poems*, etc. *Do not capitalize* such words as of, the, and, but, with, etc.

The Best Years of Our Lives	The Saturday Evening Post
"The Outcasts of Poker Flat"	Life with Father
"Red River Valley"	My Fight with a Lion

Note: Names of books, plays, magazines are generally underlined (or put in italics). Short stories, articles, poems, essays are usually put in quotation marks.

14. Capitalize names of important *historical events, historical periods, historical documents*.

Revolutionary War	Magna Charta
Middle Ages	Renaissance
Atlantic Charter	Potsdam Declaration

15. Capitalize *nouns* and *adjectives* that refer to the Deity.

God   Supreme Creator
Supreme Being   the Almighty
Trust thou in Him

16. Capitalize the name of the *Bible* or *parts of the Bible* and names of other sacred books.

Old Testament   New Testament
Scriptures   Koran
Book of Job   Book of Ruth

17. Capitalize **I,** and capitalize **O** or **Oh** when it comes at the beginning of a sentence.

When you and **I** were young, boys were allowed less freedom.
Oh! So it's you.

18. Capitalize words derived from proper names.

British   (Britain)   American   (America)
Virginian (Virginia)   Texan   (Texas)

19. Capitalize words showing a person's *title, rank, profession,* etc.; when these are used with a person's name.

Captain Mayo   Bishop Darcy
Dr. Smith   Mayor Foster
Professor Blanding   Officer Danforth
Chancellor Brown   Dean Kelly
Queen Elizabeth   King Gustav
President Truman   Senator Acheson

Note: When the title or rank or profession is used alone, *do not* capitalize the word because you are not referring to any person in particular.

When you speak of **doctor, lieutenant, senator, judge,** you do not capitalize these words because they are not attached to a specific name. When you *name* a person and give his title, then you capitalize his title. For example:

The judge threw the case out of court. (No judge named.)
The case was decided by Judge Hand.

20. Capitalize words showing *family relationship* when these are used with the name of the person involved.

Uncle Jim   Aunt Martha

a. Capitalize **Mother** and **Father**, **Grandmother**, **Grand**father when you are using **them** instead of names.

> May I go out, Mother?
> We stayed at home with Father.

21. Capitalize names of *planets, constellations, stars,* etc.

> Jupiter   Neptune
> Venus   Saturn

Note: Do not capitalize **earth, moon, sun** unless you are listing them with other astronomical names.

> Neptune and the Earth are both planets.
> In the solar system, the Sun and the Moon influence life on the Earth.

22. Capitalize points of the compass that refer to portions of a country or parts of the world.

> the Northwest   the North
> the South   the West
> Northerner   Southerner
> Westerner

Note: When you use these words to show direction, do not capitalize them.

> The boat was bearing due east.
> His house was two blocks west of Atkins Avenue.

23. Capitalize *abbreviations of titles and degrees, names* and *initials of persons.*

> Dr. J. C. Horn
> John Esme, M.A., Ph.D., LL.D.

Exercise 1. Supply the capital letters where needed in the following sentences. Cross out all unnecessary capital letters. Be sure you know the reason for capitalization. Refer to the rules if necessary. Underline and put in quotation marks wherever it is necessary.

1. peace treaties will soon be drafted.
2. The judge shouted, "order in the court room."
3. Most of us do not understand the American indian.

.. It isn't difficult at all to develop a taste for chinese food.

.. Meet me at the willard parker hotel.

6. Experiments in blood testing are being carried out at the wisconsin hospital.

7. The delegates will meet at the New York times building.

8. Thirty days hath September, april, june, and November.

9. We leave on monday.

10. During the Summer, we swim in Long Island Sound.

11. The first Monday in September is labor day.

12. Meet me in st. louis.

13. They moved to Carter street.

14. The climate at lake cayuga is delightful.

15. There are warm currents in the Indian oce..n.

16. This Fall we plan to visit hempstead park.

17. All americans revere george washington.

18. You'll enjoy that new picture, the plainsman.

19. I recommend that you read the forsyte saga by john galsworthy.

20. Have you heard gene autry sing?

21. The civil war was one of the turning points in American history.

22. These events took place during the middle ages.

23. The bible is one of the most important books in Western civilization.

24. The scandinavian people are generally blond and blue-eyed.

25. Did you visit general lewis at Fort Totten?

26. The delegation will call on mayor Ford sometime tomorrow.

27. You may come in, officer Smith.

28. When you arrive in courtley, call on uncle ned.

29. We are certain that there is no life on the planet, mars.

30. The northwest is one of the most romantic sections of our country.

31. The Hotel I like best is the Statler Hotel.

32. for whom the bell tolls is a novel by Ernest Hemingway.

33. My favorite section of the Bible is proverbs.

34. Walk three miles East and one mile South and you will come to the house.

35. Summer is my favorite season, although most people like Spring better.

36. Most of us want to be President when we are young.

37. The Doctor gave every patient equal attention.

38. The constellation familiarly known as the big dipper is known to astronomers as ursa major.

39. A famous radio program is based on the adventures of the Aldrich Family.

40. Edna Ferber has written a novel dealing with the northwest.

41. Read the short story the old demon in that magazine.

INDEX

Abbreviations, capitalization of, 295

About—around, 236

Abraham Lincoln: The War Years (Sandburg), quoted, 168-169

Accept—except, 236

Active voice, 152-154

Adapt—adopt, 237

Address, direct, 110

Adjectives, changing of, into nouns, 93; comparison of, 221-224; confusion of, with adverbs, 183, 224-226; defined, 220-221; saving words by use of, 90-93

Admission—admittance, 237

Adverbs, comparison of, 221-224; confusion of, with adjectives, 183, 224-226; defined, 221; two forms of, 226; use of, to save words, 92

Affect—effect, 237-238

Aggravate—annoy—irritate, 239

Agreement, of pronoun and antecedent, 213, 216-218; of verb and subject, 211-215

All together—altogether, 240

Allusion—delusion—illusion, 240

Almayer's Folly (Conrad), quoted, 169-170

Although and *though*, 81

Among—between, 240-241

Amount—number, 238-239

Anecdote, starting with, 73, 148

Antecedent, agreement of pronoun with, 213, 216-218

Apostrophe, 267-269

Appositives, 233

Apt—liable—likely, 242-243

Authors, information about, 28

Auxiliary verbs, 181, 204, 206

Background material, 35

Because and *since*, 81

Before and *after*, 81

Beginning, of business letter, 72; incident or anecdote at, 73; striking or startling, 74

Benchley, Robert, 162; quoted, 163

Benét, Stephen Vincent, 163; quoted, 164-165

Beside—besides, 241

Bet—beat, 241

Bible, capitalization of, 294

Books, how to find, 24; how to read, 24-25; as source of ideas, 23; capitalization of titles of, 293; underlining (italicizing) titles of; 293

Brandeis, Louis D., quoted, 170

Brevity, *see* Words, saving of

Bring—take, 241-242

Buildings, capitalizing names of, 291-292

Business letters, 70-72

Capital—capitol, 242

Capitalization, 291-295

Case, 229-234

Casual expressions, 69

"ceed," "cede," "sede," 269

Childish—childlike, 242

Children, talk of, 77-79

Cities and towns, capitalizing names of, 292-293

Clauses, 193-195; changing of, into phrases, 88-89; dependent (subordinate), 80-82, 194; incomplete, 233-234; independent (principal), 194; introductory, 109; order of, 82-83; relative, 80-82, 194; restrictive and non-restrictive, 111-112

Collective nouns, 214

Colon, 116

Comparative degree, 222-224

Comparison, of adjectives and adverbs, 221-224; care in use of, 101; and contrasts, 50-51; of ideas, 136-137

Comma, 108-112

Companies, capitalizing names of, 291

Compass points, capitalization of, in special cases, 295

Complement—compliment, 243-244

297